THE BOLSHEVIK TRADITION

THE BOLSHEVIK TRADITION

ROBERT H. MCNEAL is currently Chairman of the Department of History of the University of Massachusetts at Amherst. He received his Ph.D. from Columbia University. His books and essays on the history of the Communist Party of the Soviet Union include a biography of Lenin's wife, *Bride of the Revolution. Krupskaya and Lenin,* and a three-volume edition of Stalin's works from the years 1934–1953. He is also general editor of a four-volume work entitled *Resolutions and Decisions of the Communist Party of the Soviet Union.*

THE BOLSHEVIK TRADITION

LENIN
STALIN
KHRUSHCHEV
BREZHNEV

Second Edition

Robert H. McNeal

PRENTICE-HALL, INC.
Englewood Cliffs, New Jersey

Library of Congress Cataloging in Publication Data

McNEAL, ROBERT HATCH
   The Bolshevik tradition.

   (A Spectrum Book)
   First ed. published in 1963 under title: The
Bolshevik tradition: Lenin, Stalin, Khrushchev.
   Includes bibliographical references and index.
   1. Lenin, Vladimir Il'ich, 1870–1924.   2. Stalin,
Iosif, 1879–1953.   3. Khrushchev, Nikita Sergeevich,
1894–1971.   4. Brezhnev, Leonid Il'ich, 1906–
5. Russia—Politics and government—1917–   6. Com-
munism–Russia.   I. Title.
DK268.A1M3 1975   335.43′0947   74–20922
ISBN 0–13–079772–3
ISBN 0–13–079764–2 pbk.

© 1975 by PRENTICE-HALL, INC.
Englewood Cliffs, New Jersey

A SPECTRUM BOOK

10   9   8   7   6   5   4   3

Printed in the United States of America

PRENTICE-HALL INTERNATIONAL, INC. (*London*)
PRENTICE-HALL OF AUSTRALIA PTY. LTD. (*Sydney*)
PRENTICE-HALL OF CANADA, LTD. (*Toronto*)
PRENTICE-HALL OF INDIA PRIVATE LIMITED (*New Delhi*)
PRENTICE-HALL OF JAPAN, INC. (*Tokyo*)

CONTENTS

PREFACE

In the eleven years since the original publication of this book a good deal of additional writing about the history of the Communist Party of the Soviet Union has appeared. It has been one of the most actively researched fields of study in all of political science and history. This is particularly true of the early years of Russian Marxism, generally true of the pre-Stalin years of Soviet power, and significantly less true of the Stalin era. And, of course, there is a continuing stream of publication on more or less current Soviet affairs. In the light of this substantial increment to the library of materials on Russian Communism, I was obliged to ask myself if it was desirable to reissue, with only minor changes, the 1963 edition of this book. I concluded that it was desirable, because the work is not intended as a comprehensive text but rather as an extended argument concerning the problem of continuity and change in this movement. It seems to me that the large volume of new writing since 1963, for all its many merits, does not diminish the pertinence of the arguments advanced in this book. Questions of this sort are never "settled," and grounds for disagreement with my opinions were equally present in 1963 and at the present writing. All that I would claim for the interpretations in this book is that they represent a school of thought (not by any means my invention) that deserves a hearing as much, if not more, today as it did in 1963.

As for the increment of ten years to the history of Russian Communism since the fall of Khrushchev, I suggest that it fits very well into the older tradition. In the early period of the supposedly transitional Brezhnev-Kosygin administration, there was cause to wonder about the fate of authority in the Soviet political system. Would one man be able to establish substantial personal control? Was the supremacy of the party in the system in decline? For some time I suspected that my argument was too schematic and failed to take into account the forces for change in the Soviet Union. It now seems to me that these apprehensions were unnecessary, that the nature of the institution of the party is such that the role of individual leadership within the party, and of the party within the entire system, is fairly stable. The Brezhnev administration and its coming to full bloom has its share of peculiarities, but I was impressed, in trying to write the new chapters of this book, with how readily the main lines fell into place as an extension of the previous six decades of the Bolshevik tradition.

Robert H. McNeal

Leverett, Massachusetts

March, 1974

PREFACE TO THE FIRST EDITION

In 1952 the "All-Union Communist Party (of Bolsheviks)" changed its name to "Communist Party of the Soviet Union," just about half a century after the designation "Bolshevik" had come into use. Nonetheless, the term remains serviceable today as an alternative to "Russian Communist," partly because there is no equally handy label, partly because the claim of lineal descent from the first Bolshevik, Lenin, was never more ardently stressed than at present. Moreover, the name "Bolshevik" probably evokes a more vivid image in both friend and foe of the movement Lenin set on foot.

This is a book about the Bolsheviks, not about Communists or Marxists in general; it is an attempt to interpret the history of Bolshevism. It is not, however, a general history of the Bolshevik Party, much less of twentieth century Russia. Rather it traces the tradition or continuing theme of the party through the careers of three principal protagonists: Lenin, Stalin, and Khrushchev. The essay does not pretend to literal chronological balance; the twenty-three years of Stalin's personal ascendancy are treated as a comprehensible phase of the evolution of the Bolshevik tradition, as are the eight months of the Revolution of 1917. Such an approach has its limitations, but it follows from the Bolshevik view that their party is always characterized by a unique degree of unity and continuity. This approach is also consistent with an axiom of Bolshevism that the party has not usually acknowledged; the party depends upon the leadership of an individual dictator.

Although this essay makes considerable use of primary sources on the history of Bolshevism, it could not have been written without the substantial body of secondary scholarly works in this field, and it is a pleasure to acknowledge my debt to the authors of many of the works listed in the bibliography appended to this book.

It is a pleasure to thank my friend, Professor Warren Lerner, for reading the manuscript; its shortcomings, of course, remain mine.

I am happy to acknowledge the kind permission of Professor Dimitri von Mohrenschildt, editor of *The Russian Review,* to use the recollections of N. Valentinov as quoted in Chapter II of this book. This material first appeared in English in *The Russian Review,* July, 1954 (Vol. 13, no. 3) as an excerpt from Mr. Valentinov's book *Vstrechi s Leninym* (New York: Chekhov Publishing House, 1954).

THE BOLSHEVIK TRADITION

THE BOLSHEVIK TRADITION

PART ONE
LENIN

1

THE YOUNG "INTELLIGENT"

Vladimir Ilyich Ulyanov, later called Lenin, was born in April, 1870, in Simbirsk, a provincial capital on the eastern borderlands of European Russia. He was the second son of a respectable and successful school teacher and administrator, Ilya Nikolaevich Ulyanov, whose ascent from plebeian origins in remote Astrakhan shows that all careers were by no means closed to talent in tsarist Russia. Although he only lived to fifty-five, the senior Ulyanov's labors had brought him the post of Director of Primary Schools in the province and the bureaucratic grade of "Actual State Councillor." According to the "Table of Ranks" that Peter the Great had introduced, this dignity automatically made its bearer a member of the hereditary nobility. That is, Ilya Nikolaevich and his descendants became members of the most privileged class in Russia, the class that, until 1861, had possessed a monopoly on the right of owning serfs. In short, the future Lenin entered life under decidedly auspicious conditions, yet he devoted his life not to the pursuit of some legally sanctioned form of success, which surely could have been his, but to the seemingly impossible task of unseating one of the most powerful governments in the world.

The explanation of this seeming perversity lies not so much in Lenin's personality or family environment as in the temper of Russian society in the late nineteenth century, and especially that peculiar social formation known as the intelligentsia. Although this class had intimate associations with the intellectuals of Western European civilization and shared many attributes with them, it is perhaps better compared with intellectual elites of non-Western societies that have been influenced by European civilization (e.g., India, China, and—more

1

lately—Africa). In such countries there has arisen a class of people deeply influenced by European education and social ideals, who have come to revere such ideas as progress, freedom, nationalism, and material welfare, and have sought to pursue these goals in their own lands. But this typically has been a small minority of Europeanized persons in a sea of peasants and others who hold to the old ways and neither understand nor sympathize with these intellectuals and their strange notions. The result is likely to be extreme frustration for the intellectuals, who follow the Western democrats in idealizing the common man, but find themselves strangers in their own land, unable to fulfill their self-imposed mission of leading their countrymen to a more reasonable and happy life. One of the most common responses to this frustration is the development of a revolutionary spirit, an aggressive drive that may be directed against foreign domination, domestic traditionalism, or both. In many cases the revolutionary spirit of such an intelligentsia has been intensified when the existing government has refused to accept the intellectuals' vision, adding persecution to alienation.

In many ways, Russia has been the prototype of non-Western societies that have been deeply penetrated by European civilization and have given birth to a striving, frustrated intelligentsia. Such a social formation was visible in Russia among the educated aristocracy by the latter part of the eighteenth century. In its first generation the Russian intelligentsia was drawn predominantly from the landed nobility, the only group with the education and leisure to cultivate Western ideas. In this period the intelligentsia could be said to include both liberals and conservatives, but by mid-century the spread of education and the rise of the "liberal" professions brought about the appearance of an intellectual class that mixed people of noble and professional origin and even began to include former peasants. This new amalgam, in developing a social character quite its own, grew further apart from the established political and social order. Although there remained educated Russians of staunchly conservative outlook, the intelligentsia itself came to be nearly synonymous with "radical"—even its most moderate members aimed at the establishment of civil liberty and representative government. In a state that admitted no pluralism in political life, such opposition resulted either in emigration to various political sanctuaries in the West, or imprisonment and exile to Siberia. Although these experiences heightened the sense of futility that pervaded this group, neither obstacle could check its growth or alter its convictions. Exiled in Europe or America, the Russian *intelligent* (member of the intelligentsia) typically found a degree of disillusionment and a strengthened resolve to reform Russia. Although the prisons and Siberian wastes broke the health or spirit of some radical *intelligents,* not even the most severe repressions were effective discouragement; the milder treatment accorded many political prisoners served only to increase their moral determination and sense of *esprit.* An established practice of the intelligentsia was the formation of "circles," discussion groups that took the place of forbidden political organizations and publications. From the early decades of the nineteenth century the circles were the very life of many of the more devoted intellectuals. In fact, the educated youth was generally more attracted to the circles than to the universities that spawned many such groups. Despite the official censorship, which wavered in intensity, publication was also an important part of the tradition of the Russian intelligentsia. Indeed, the publication of influential books and articles was just about the nearest thing to concrete achievement that this frustrated class could show during the nineteenth century.

True, there had been several attempts at practical action. In 1825 a rudimentary political movement grew out of some discussion circles, and it attempted a *coup d'état* during the confusion that accompanied the succession to the throne of Nicholas I in December, 1825. Socially isolated and badly handled, the "Decembrist Revolution" failed dismally; the next significant practical steps did not come until after the serf emancipation of 1861 had disillusioned many *intelligents* with officially sponsored reform. This served to accentuate the question that plagued the intelligentsia: what must we do?

A rather vague but highly influential reply was proposed by N. G. Chernyshevsky, an archetypical radical intellectual of the time. Imprisoned in 1862 as the result of earlier writings, Chernyshevsky improved on the occasion by providing the model for the missionary *intelligent* in Russia in his novel, *What Is to Be Done? (Chto delat'?*—literally, "what to do?"). His fictitious hero, Rakhmetov, was a true puritan and potential martyr, although motivated by a scientific, secular faith rather than by religion. Even though it did not advocate a specific political program, the novel at least served to reenforce the zeal of the young intelligentsia to give themselves wholly to the cause of regeneration in Russia. This zeal soon found expression: the "movement to the people" and terrorism. The former reached its peak in 1873–1874, when substantial numbers of students attempted to bridge the gap between themselves and the peasant masses and pave the way for regeneration by going into the countryside to disseminate enlightened ideas. This naive adventure was frustrated by the apathy of the peasants and the effectiveness of the police. The grimmer expression of devotion was a series of attempts on the life of Tsar Alexander II, culminating in success in 1881. This event showed the intelligentsia to be capable of producing men and women as disciplined and dedicated as Rakhmetov, but the success of police countermeasures and the absence of public approval seemed to indicate that Chernyshevsky's model was not the whole answer.

During this period, an isolated emigrant intellectual, P. N. Tkachev, advanced a more precise conception of the mission of the intelligentsia: they must form the elite minority that alone could generate a revolution. Because of their unique mission, they "always have the right to call the people to an uprising." A seminal idea, perhaps, but there seemed to be no opportunity to test it for quite a few years.

Repressed and disoriented, the intelligentsia passed the decade of the eighties without appearing to move closer to the formulation of a definite program. But the nineties saw the rapid spread of a doctrine that seemed to many to provide an answer to their problem: Marxism. The first Marxist Russian group was essentially another intellectual circle—and an exiled one at that. This inconspicuous society, founded by G. V. Plekhanov in 1883, was called the "Liberation of Labor," taking its name from the small periodical it published. But this group was by no means solely responsible for the growing popularity of Marxism among the intelligentsia. *Capital* had been legally published in Russia, as had been the works of many earlier Western social philosophers. Although Marx certainly had not been thinking of Russia as a model when he wrote of capitalism and its revolutionary finale, his intellectual system was psychologically suited to the Russian intelligentsia: it was "scientifically" proven; it seemed philosophically coherent; it assured the regeneration of man. Perhaps it was especially appreciated by Russian radicals because it resembled their own contradictory attitude toward Western European civilization: approval of the ideals of freedom, equality, and material welfare, but rejection of the existing shortcomings. In any case, Marx was the most influential ideologist among the intelligentsia in the nineties, highly respected even by those who believed that his theories required modification in one way or another.

This background does much to explain why young Vladimir Ulyanov became a revolutionary instead of a professor, a lawyer, or a civil servant. In the last two decades of the nineteenth century it was not unusual for a highly educated and intelligent Russian youth to join the ranks of the intelligentsia; by the nineties it was quite likely that he would be a Marxist.

Against this background, the young Lenin may be perceived as a typical *intelligent*. Even in boyhood he had given indication of an extraordinarily keen mind, a trait that characterized the entire family. As his elder brother Alexander had done, he won the gold medal awarded to the best student in his secondary school, although Alexander was primarily devoted to the natural sciences while Vladimir was interested in the humanities. In the Ulyanov household native intelligence was

organized and disciplined by the firm hand of father Ilya, a schoolmaster to the core. Indeed, Edmund Wilson may well be right in suggest-
ing that Lenin followed his father, thinking and acting as a pedagogue
throughout his mature life, the headmaster of the Bolshevik Party.

No doubt the youth's iron will was tempered by the fate of his elder
brother and boyhood idol, Alexander. In March, 1887, only fourteen
months after the sudden death of his father, Alexander was arrested
as a leader of a group of students at St. Petersburg University who had
decided to "execute" Tsar Alexander III. The mild-mannered science
student had written the manifesto that was to announce the end of the
autocrat and had manufactured bombs for this purpose, although it
appears that their chemical effectiveness did not do credit to Alexander's talent as a scientist. Alexander faced his trial and death on the
gallows with a heroic tranquility which impressed even those who condemned him. His fate must have had a profound effect on his younger
brother, but Lenin never wrote or spoke at length about the event. Nor
did he speak of revenge, for it was part of the creed of a revolutionary
intelligent not to act out of personal motivation, but only on behalf of
some assumed objective necessity. This early effort to avoid personal
retribution probably contributed to Lenin's consistent rejection of individual terrorism as a revolutionary weapon. A later story that the
seventeen-year-old Lenin greeted the news of his brother's death with:
"We shall have to find a better path," is based on an unreliable source
and probably exaggerates the degree to which Lenin regarded the affair
as a mere trial of tactics.

Alexander's guilt provoked the state to regard Lenin as one likely to
become a dangerous subversive, hastening what would have been a
likely enough process even without official persecution. But the old
regime in Russia had not taken to heart Machiavelli's dictum about
caressing or annihilating dangerous men, and Lenin was sorely har-
assed without being effectively checked in his revolutionary development. He was admitted to the law faculty of Kazan University in 1887,
less than three months after Alexander was hanged, only to be expelled
four months later for participation in a minor student demonstration.
Like many another young *intelligent,* Lenin had his first taste of prison
as a student. A few days' arrest was enough to confirm his attitude toward the regime but not enough to interrupt seriously his education in
radicalism. He was required to spend most of the next year, 1888, on
the small rural estate inherited by his mother. Although Lenin was
refused readmission to the university in the fall of 1888, he was nonetheless permitted to move back to Kazan, where he joined a typical
radical circle and studied the writings of Marx. A second brush with
the authorities was accidentally avoided in 1889, for Lenin's mother
had persuaded him to come back to the estate to try his hand as a gen-

tleman-farmer. One summer revealed that he was miscast in this role, but it served to keep him out of prison when the police arrested the circle to which he had belonged. In the fall of 1889 Lenin, his mother, and his three younger brothers and sisters took up residence in the city of Samara. Refused permission to become an external, or self-taught, student of law, Lenin occupied himself with the study of Marxist and other social writings. He also made the acquaintance of some of the remaining members of the terrorist movement of the seventies. They were no longer active and could not compete in theoretical matters with Plekhanov, whose works Lenin was then reading, but they could impart a practical knowledge of the techniques of conspiratorial activity—the invisible ink, the smuggling of literature, and so on. These Lenin readily absorbed, confident that they would be useful sooner or later.

In 1890 the authorities gave in to the appeals of Lenin's mother and permitted him to become an external student of law. Lenin began his study in Samara that summer and by April, 1891, he went to St. Petersburg to take the final oral examinations in what was normally a three-year course. It was his first trip to a major city and the eager young radical from the provinces must have been tempted to seek out the more sophisticated Marxist circles of the capital. But with typical discipline Lenin stuck to the job that he had set out to do, passing some of the exams that spring and the rest in the fall—all with the highest possible grades. Evidently he stayed "clean" politically and avoided the radical circles. In early 1892 the government that had recently considered him too unreliable to study at the university granted him permission to practice law in Samara.

To any dynamic young *intelligent* of the period, the staid practice of law could scarcely seem an adequate aim in life, and Lenin drifted away from it in less than a year. His greater interest lay in the Marxist circle he joined in Samara, and especially in combatting the theories of the *narodnik* or "populist" socialists. According to this group, which included a substantial part of the revolutionary intelligentsia and reflected the principal tradition of Russian radicalism, the Russian peasant and his communal village represented the essence of egalitarian, socialist values; this native socialism could enable Russia to build the good society that the European socialists were seeking. A number of influential Russian radical writers of the eighties and nineties predicted that Russia could leap from the backward conditions of that era to socialism without passing through the purgatory of capitalism. Marx himself had acknowledged in 1881 that this might be so, for he was not certain that Russia conformed to the pattern of history that he had detected in Western Europe. But Lenin was more Marxist than Marx on this point, and rejected violently the suggestion that Russia could avoid capitalism any more than it could avoid the eventual overthrow of capitalism by the industrial working class.

Before he dropped his legal career entirely, the lure of St. Petersburg enticed Lenin to join a law firm there late in 1893. But in the first months of his residence in the capital he spent most of his time writing and arguing in the radical circles and making side trips to circles in Moscow and Nizhni-Novgorod. He established his reputation as a zealous defender of orthodox Marxism against the *narodnik* interpretation of socialism by circulating a crudely reproduced, illegal polemic entitled "What Are the 'Friends of the People' and How Do They Fight the Social Democrats?" By the end of 1894 it was clear that Lenin's revolutionary calling had asserted itself and was his sole concern.

As one might imagine, revolution is not a very lucrative vocation, and for the greater part of his adult life Lenin subsisted on a motley variety of financial sources: donations from his mother (who respected, although she did not share, her son's convictions), a modest literary income, a meager subsistence allowance from the tsar while under detention, and a scarcely larger salary from the party after about 1900.

In 1895 Lenin, like many another Russian intellectual before him, went to Western Europe. Swayed by the plea of ill health (Lenin did have a bout with pneumonia in the winter of 1895), the authorities granted the exit visa they had previously denied. The journey was an exemplary revolutionary's pilgrimage rather than a rest cure. Between May and September, 1895, Lenin managed to visit the principal emigrant Russian Marxists, including Plekhanov in Switzerland; Karl Marx's son-in-law in Paris; and the leading left-wing German socialist, Karl Kautsky, in Berlin. He just missed meeting the surviving founder of Marxism, for in Paris Engels was in his final illness at the very time Lenin visited that city.

Upon his return to St. Petersburg, Lenin and a handful of young radicals made the first serious effort to establish a Russian Marxist organization more ambitious than the usual circle. This was the "Union of Struggle for the Liberation of Labor," which attempted to unite all Marxist groups in the capital and bridge the gap between the revolutionary intelligentsia and the ordinary workers—the basic task that had frustrated most earlier revolutionary efforts. Lenin's closest associate was his future political opponent Y. O. Martov (born Tsederbaum), one of the few younger Marxists in Russia who could rival Lenin in doctrinal disputation. No sooner had a start been made than the police closed in and arrested Lenin, Martov, and most of the leaders of the movement in December, 1895.

This led to Lenin's first and last protracted experience as a political prisoner, an enforced withdrawal that proved to be the decisive period in the formulation of his answer to the question "What is to be done?"

For fourteen months Lenin was confined to a small cell in a St. Petersburg prison while his fate was decided. This was an administrative
rather than a judicial decision, for Russian law permitted the Minister
of the Interior to deal with subversives without recourse to the courts.
Lenin's extraordinary powers of discipline and concentration now
asserted themselves. He kept himself fit for future action by meticulously polishing his cell and performing calisthenics, such as fifty rever-
ential prostrations, before retiring for the night. Moreover, he began
his first book—*The Development of Capitalism in Russia.* The title
and the work were scholarly, partly because Lenin rightly believed that
this might make it acceptable to the Russian censors. It is probably the
only one of Lenin's works that would have commanded the attention
of scholars even if he had never become an important political figure;
it justifies the comment made by a noted Russian scholar in 1902 after
hearing Lenin lecture in Paris: "A perfect professor." For all its academic achievement, the book grew out of a stern political purpose: the
refutation of the *narodnik* socialists' belief that Russia could avoid
capitalism. Lenin hammered out his detailed economic arguments on
this point under the most peculiar conditions; he was a political prisoner, subject to police interrogation, yet he was also a "scholar," permitted to receive large quantities of research material from outside.
Lenin took advantage of this traffic in printed matter to carry on an
illicit political correspondence with Marxists outside the prison, using
invisible ink concocted in his cell from milk and lemon juice. The
manuscript was not quite finished in February, 1897, when the authorities determined that Lenin should spend three years in eastern Siberia.

Lenin spent eight days of freedom in St. Petersburg and Moscow, and
then set out for Siberia, traveling in relative comfort at his own expense—another lenient gesture by the government. After a pleasant
journey of two and a half months, he arrived at his ultimate destina-
tion: the hamlet of Shushenskoe. Supported by a modest but adequate
maintenance allowance from the government and living in a peasant
home under almost no surveillance, Lenin resumed his intellectual labors. In May, 1898, a year after his arrival, his situation was greatly
improved by the arrival of a comrade-wife-secretary-housekeeper, Na-
dezhda Konstantinovna Krupskaia. Such emancipated, earnest female
intelligents as Krupskaia played an important role in the revolutionary
movement after the middle decades of the nineteenth century—a larger
role, perhaps, than women played in the politics of any other country
at that time. Krupskaia had already been devoted to worker education
when she met Lenin at a radical circle in St. Petersburg in early 1894.
An ideal partnership—by the standards of the radical intelligentsia—
quickly grew up, and the two were deeply attached by the time of
Lenin's arrest. They sought to rise above the conventions of "bour-

geois" romanticism by rather prudishly regarding one another mainly as comrades, but although they probably had no intention of marrying legally, circumstances impelled them to this conventional conclusion. In 1896, some eight months after Lenin's arrest, the police picked up Krupskaia for her activities in the revolutionary circle, and after a long delay, during which Krupskaia was allowed to live at home most of the time, she was sentenced to three years' exile in Siberia. Whether on her own initiative or by prior agreement with Lenin, Krupskaia took this occasion to represent herself as Lenin's fiancée, which enabled her to make a compassionate appeal for sentence to Shushenskoe with him, rather than to another place that had been designated at first. This the police granted, providing that the engaged couple marry at once—which they did in July, 1898. Thus began a remarkably close political-marital collaboration that ended only with Lenin's death. There were never any children, however, a fact which later spared Stalin what might have been a touchy problem.

In Shushenskoe the young couple set up housekeeping with a servant girl and with Krupskaia's mother, who was no Marxist but accompanied her daughter to Siberia and followed her during the remaining years of her life, which ended in 1915. Although Lenin occasionally gave free legal advice to the peasants in the region, contrary to regulations on exiles, his real work was in Marxist scholarship. This was greatly facilitated by the assistance of P. B. Struve, a leading St. Petersburg Marxist editor, who sent Lenin most of the material needed to complete his study of capitalism in Russia, arranged for its publication in 1899, and assisted the finances of the exiles by obtaining for them a commission to translate from the English a book on trade unions by Sidney and Beatrice Webb. In 1898 Struve made another contribution to the Marxist cause in Russia. In March of that year in the city of Minsk, nine men and women, representing various Russian Marxist organizations, attempted to form a "Russian Social Democratic Labor Party," a name derived from contemporary European Marxist parties. Struve contributed a draft of a somewhat general manifesto, which the meeting adopted. But it accomplished little else, for the police soon arrested all but one delegate to this "congress." Lenin was, of course, confined to Siberia while this was taking place.

Although the organization of a national party was obviously not so simple a matter as this "First Congress" had conceived it to be, it became increasingly clear to Lenin by 1899 that this must be his main goal. To be sure, revolutionary organization began to occupy him in the year before his arrest, but it was only in the latter part of his Siberian retreat that the distinguishing characteristics of his ideas about such an organization began to assume a definite shape. Although aiming at the establishment of a party, Lenin saw as a necessary preliminary the development of an effective dogmatic underground news-paper. This was unusual, for Russian Marxists had enjoyed consider-able freedom from censorship in the past few years, for such of their works as had an academic flavor and did not openly call for revolution in Russia. Lenin himself had enjoyed the results of this official indul-gence, but he held that too much confidence in this "legal" Marxism was detrimental to the revolutionary spirit of the movement. Unlike many Russian Marxists, therefore, he gave highest priority to the estab-lishment of an illegal newspaper to be published abroad and smuggled over the border—a newspaper that would avoid academic considera-tions and devote itself single-mindedly to revolution. With the prolif-eration of various interpretations of Marxism in Russia and elsewhere, Lenin thought it most important to establish an organ that would campaign relentlessly for undiluted Marxist revolutionary "truth." Such a newspaper could separate the true believers from the heretics, expand their number, and knit them together throughout Russia. Lenin's insistence on the establishment of an ideological organ before the formation of the party is typical of his doctrinaire nature: first there must be substantial agreement on the truth; only on this basis can a working organization be established. One cannot assemble a lot of people who share only vague sympathies and antipathies and expect to mold from such diversity a useful party. "Before we can unite," Lenin wrote in an announcement of the new publication, "and in order to unite, we must first of all firmly and definitely draw the lines of demarcation between various groups. . . . We do not intend to use our publication as a repository of various views. On the contrary, we shall conduct it along the lines of a strictly defined tendency. This tendency can be defined by the word Marxism."

With this in mind, Lenin left Siberia in February, 1900, establishing Krupskaia in Ufa to complete the last year of her sentence. He left be-hind not only Krupskaia but also the habit of chess, which had given him—as it had so many other Russian intellectuals—much pleasure ever since boyhood. But Lenin's missionary zeal was so aroused that he determined to abstain from such a distraction. This was to be a symbol of his moral distinction among the revolutionary intelligentsia.

Shortly before Lenin's arrest Martov had written of him: "Ulyanov was not sure of himself nor of the role that history was to call on him to play." But in 1900 he went forth from his four-year withdrawal with what seems to have been a clear conception of his special mission and a matchless determination to succeed in it.

2

THE QUEST FOR A PARTY

The mature Lenin of almost thirty who emerged from Siberia was an *intelligent* who thought he knew "what is to be done." His answer reflected his roots in the traditions of the revolutionary intelligentsia, embodying the ascetic missionary spirit of Chernyshevsky's hero and Tkachev's confidence in an enlightened revolutionary elite. Such individuals, molded into a determined corps, were perceived by Lenin as the Russian vehicle of Marx's proletarian revolution against capitalism, and as the pathfinders to the promised society of complete freedom and abundance.

Although it is difficult to establish any man's ultimate priority in the realm of general ideas, Lenin was probably the first to conceive of the modern totalitarian party, the political instrument that in its Communist and non-Communist forms has played so large a role in the world since 1917—and, as George Orwell predicted in *1984,* could be the matrix for human society in the future.

The full measure of the originality of the Leninist type of party was certainly not clear to its founder in 1900. The mature form of the party and all of its logical consequences did not even come to light in Lenin's lifetime. But it is safe to say that the newly liberated Lenin understood the basic attributes of this party of a new type:

1. Absolute agreement on theoretical principles, especially on the necessity of the revolutionary overthrow of capitalism in Russia.
2. Absolute devotion and discipline on the part of party members; no compromise with dissenters, all of whom are ultimately enemies.
3. Long-term hostility to other political groups: even though they may be useful allies for temporary periods, they must be eliminated ultimately.
4. Firm leadership of the masses, who are incapable of fulfilling their socialist destiny if left to themselves.

With his release from Siberia, Lenin's whole life became bound with the quest for a party that would realize these principles. And it is one of the chief marvels of his career that he succeeded, at least in part, in achieving this goal by the time his one great revolutionary opportunity materialized. This required remarkably sustained will power and unquestioning confidence in his prophetic vision of the new party and the ultimate utopia. These were a source of strength in the long run, although it sometimes seemed that his dogmatism would succeed only in disintegrating the party and relegating him to the role of an isolated crank. Few, if any, prophets or politicians before him combined so searing a ruthlessness in practical tactics with so sublime a utopian objective. The Lenin who could advocate a simple appeal to the workers—"Kill them!"—in place of more elaborate theoretical propaganda could also assure Maxim Gorky, while watching some children, "These will live better than we. . . . Their lives will be less cruel."

Lenin the man was equally capable of humane charm and brutal animosity. He was a model of affectionate consideration toward his mother and wife, and a number of contemporaries bear witness to his unaffected and reciprocated love of children. His effectiveness as a party organizer was due in great part to the personal interest he showed in party members, giving new arrivals in exile a far warmer reception than did the aloof Plekhanov or the reserved Martov. Trotsky (Lev Davidovich Bronstein) recounts the simplicity and warmth with which he, whom Lenin had never met before, was welcomed in the small hours of the morning in London in October, 1902. Although these two were soon to quarrel, Lenin at first quite captivated Trotsky with his sincere interest in the young man's report on conditions in Russia, his generosity in taking time to give Trotsky a tour of London, and his unjealous efforts to advance the career of the young writer and orator.

But the humane and appealing Lenin coexisted—and not very peacefully—with a ruthless, dogmatic, and domineering Lenin, the slave of a consuming sense of duty before history. N. Valentinov recalls this ambiguity in his own relations with Lenin: "I discovered (in 1904) that much as I admired Lenin as a great man, much as I felt drawn to him and eager to follow him, his attitude towards some most important issues strongly repelled me." For example, Lenin would not even agree to read or discuss certain non-Marxist philosophical conceptions that attracted Valentinov and other important Russian socialists. "When you find a stinking heap in your path," said Lenin, "you don't have to dig your hands into it to know what it is, your nose will tell you it's dung and you'll pass it by." Soon after, Lenin began to insist that the simplest personal relations between Valentinov and some of Lenin's political opponents of the day, such as Martov, represented the vilest treason. When Valentinov protested against Lenin's violent abuse of fellow-socialists who disagreed with him, Lenin replied: "So you find it sickening that the tone within the party is less refined than that of a young ladies' finishing school? That's an old song, dear to those who would like to turn revolutionary fighters into milksops. God forbid that you offend Ivan Ivanovich by some rash word. . . . Kowtow to each other even when you disagree! Well, if we Social Democrats were to use only toothless, inoffensive words in our politics, propaganda, agitation, polemics, we should be no better off than those dreary pastors who preach futile sermons every Sunday. . . . All those who give up Marxism are my enemies, I refuse to shake hands with them, and I do not sit down at the same table with Philistines. . . . I break off the discussion and am going home. . . . It goes without saying that you will not stay in our organization, but even if you should, do not count on my cooperation in any way. . . ." Valentinov was not the only revolutionary Russian to discover this side of Lenin's character.

Lenin's personal affairs in the period between his return from Siberia in 1900 and his arrival in Petrograd in 1917 reflect clearly the intensity of his devotion to the goal. Except for a six-month interval during the revolutionary upheaval of 1905–1906, Lenin thrashed about in what Krupskaia once called "the dead sea of émigré life." * For a man of Lenin's remarkable vigor and moral determination, this was as severe a trial as prison. Even his iron discipline was sorely strained, and the pressures within him were reflected in his fitful wandering, continually moving his books, few bits of furniture, faithful wife, and resigned mother-in-law from one place to the next. Apart from many side trips and stopovers, the family moved from Munich to London to Geneva before the Revolution of 1905 permitted a brief return to Russia. Then came an unsettled series of residences in Finland, followed by temporary homes in Geneva, Paris and vicinity, Cracow and vicinity, Berne, and Zurich. Lenin's physical and nervous strength was often exhausted by the struggle, and it seems likely that only Krupskaia's ministrations saved him from complete collapse. Although anything but self-indulgent by nature, Lenin was induced to take fairly numerous vacations, including more or less extensive visits to the Swiss Alps (his favorite retreat), the Finnish lakes, Brittany, the Vendée, and Nice. On the whole, however, the Lenins lived with a frugality that was born of puritanism when the party was in funds and of necessity at other times. When reflected in the habit of traveling about various European cities by bicycle, this frugality came close to depriving the Bolsheviks of their leader, whose deep meditations caused him to collide with a capitalist trolley on one occasion and a car on another.

The natural and cultural charms of Western Europe were not wholly lost on Lenin (according to his secretary, he greatly enjoyed the Folies

---

* Lenin's residence in Finland in the latter half of 1906 and almost all of 1907 is treated here as emigration. Although Finland was part of the Russian Empire, the tsarist police respected its traditional autonomy while the spirit of revolution was abroad, and various Russian political factions sought refuge there. Next to Russia itself, Finland was by far the most acceptable location for Lenin, for it was close to St. Petersburg and not separated from Russia by an international border. Krupskaia refers to Lenin's Finnish residence appropriately as "emigration nearby."

Bergères), but nothing in his experience in emigration reduced his primary devotion to the cause of revolution in Russia. On the contrary, he shared with many other members of the radical intelligentsia a disillusionment with the West, and especially with the revolutionary movement there. Although he could admire individual socialist leaders and workers, he found the general temper of the German, Austrian, French, and English socialist parties lukewarm and self-satisfied. Krupskaia relates with disdain how they watched a German May Day demonstration—the workers headed peacefully for a beer garden. The conviction that the Western proletariat had temporarily deviated from its historic mission could only intensify Lenin's conviction that the oppressed of Russia, led by the new model party, could and must supply an example for the world.

Although Lenin never weakened in his intolerance of those who stood outside the Social Democratic Party nor of his opponents within the party, his tactics in seeking to impose his will on other Russian Social Democrats varied. There were four general tactical phases between his emergence from Siberia in 1900 and the Revolution of 1917: two (1900–1903 and 1906–1911) in which he attempted to impose his will upon other Social Democrats while collaborating with them in a common party, and two (1904–1905 and 1912–1916) in which he determined to break absolutely with those who would not accept his dictates.

From 1900 until 1903 Lenin tried to organize a party in collaboration with a number of leading Russian Marxists, but the fruits of their work—the Second Party Congress of 1903—revealed serious rifts between Lenin and other leaders. When Lenin failed to have his way with the party, he withdrew, and in 1904 he established an essentially separate Bolshevik organization. With the growth of revolutionary ferment in Russia in 1905, the trend toward common opposition to the regime obliged Lenin to accede somewhat to the spirit of proletarian unity, and by 1906 he ostensibly resumed collaborative work within a "unified" Russian Social Democratic Party. Despite continued quarrels and independent action on Lenin's part, he did not decisively break with the party as a whole until early in 1912, when he again established a separate Bolshevik Party, which claimed to be the only Social Democratic party of Russia. This second phase of stubborn separatism was reinforced by the advent of World War I, for although the war interfered drastically with the operation of the Bolshevik Party, it did not deflect Lenin and his disciples from their peculiar path.

This, then, was the pattern of Lenin's complex political career from 1900 to 1917. His first task was the establishment of the newspaper that was to lay down the true proletarian line and unite the local Social

Democratic groups in Russia. Together with Martov and A. N. Potresov, he laid the groundwork for the illegal Russian support of the paper. His headquarters were in Pskov, where he obtained a cover job with the statistical office of the obliging government that had just imprisoned him for sedition. The three young Russian Marxists then went abroad (legally, on their real passports) to arrange with the older generation of emigrant Marxists—headed by Plekhanov—for the editing and publication of the new organ, which was to be called *Iskra* (*The Spark*). Despite some difficulty with Plekhanov, who preened himself on his priority among Russian Marxists and obliged the younger men to award him two votes on the six-man editorial board, *Iskra* was born in December, 1900. In the next three years Lenin (who in 1901 had begun to publish under that pseudonym) and his colleagues were quite successful in propagandizing the Marxists back in Russia on behalf of organized, revolutionary Marxism, despite the difficulty in smuggling *Iskra* across the border. A small network of *Iskra* agents—not more than a dozen—worked to distribute the paper and to win members of the local Marxist circles away from heresy, especially "economism"—a school of Marxist thought that gained widespread adherence among Russian Marxists (including such notables as Lenin's former benefactor, Struve) at the beginning of the century. The "economists" generally held that the laws of economic development rendered proletarian political organization unnecessary, that economic struggle against employers should take precedence over political action against the state. While *Iskra* agents undermined economism in Russia, the editors of *Iskra* and especially the combative Lenin attacked the economists in exile, who were rather numerous and who published a rival newspaper, *Rabochee Delo* (*The Workers' Cause*). Meetings between the *Iskra* men and the economists took place in June and October, 1901, after which Lenin formalized the split between them and consolidated the *Iskra* Marxists by forming an "Emigrant League of Revolutionary Social Democrats" (the word "revolutionary" is critical, contrasting with "economist" Social Democrats).

Another step in this direction was the publication—in March, 1902 —of a booklet by Lenin, the title of which posed once again the classic question of the Russian intelligentsia: "What is to be done?" Lenin provided a more concrete answer to this question than his boyhood idol Chernyshevsky. Condemning the idea that the workers could spontaneously generate a revolution, Lenin forcefully demanded the formation of a disciplined party to lead the workers and emphasized the importance of establishing a newspaper that would integrate the local centers of such a party and attract the right kind of revolutionary members. The publication of "What Is to Be Done?" has long been regarded as a crucial step in the development of Bolshevism, but at the time of publication its dogmatic and authoritarian tone was not sufficiently appreciated to divide Lenin from his colleagues.

The Second Congress of the Russian Social Democratic Labor Party (and first important congress of the party) which met in Brussels and London in July and August, 1903, represented Lenin's principal effort to organize a party of his own design in collaboration with the other leaders of Russian Marxism. Lenin's disappointment when this proved impossible led him to the verge of nervous breakdown. Despite his professed contempt for parliamentary government, he had evidently hoped to use parliamentary tactics to establish his ideas under the guise of legitimacy. Working through the medium of an organizing committee (founded at a conference in November, 1902, in Pskov, an *Iskra* stronghold since Lenin's stay there two years earlier), Lenin loaded the congress with a four-to-one majority of presumably dependable *Iskra* delegates.

But it was not so easy to get the majority to approve his specific conception of a party. The voting revealed that the *Iskra* men, including such close colleagues of Lenin as Martov and the young Trotsky, did not accept Lenin's strictly elitist definition. Although backed by Plekhanov, Lenin lost by a vote of 28–23 when he opposed Martov's broader formula. At this moment it was Lenin's opponents who had the right to call themselves "bolsheviks"—the men of the majority (*bol'shinstvo*). But they lacked Lenin's instinct for power and the manipulation of symbols, and most of them were dragged to oblivion with the fatally modest label "mensheviks"—the men of the minority (*men'shinstvo*). The fateful switch from the status of "menshevik" to "bolshevik" was brought about by a parliamentary maneuver in which the Martov group, temporarily collaborating with the Lenin group, provoked the withdrawal of seven delegates who had previously provided the decisive votes in favor of Martov's motions. These were the representatives of the Russian-Jewish socialist Bund and the leading emigrant economist Marxist organization, both of which were affronted by the insistence of the *Iskra* supporters that their organizations submit to the control of the *Iskra* leaders. Shorn of these seven votes, Martov's supporters found themselves "mensheviks" in the voting on the membership of the three controlling bodies that were supposed to guide the new party: the Central Committee (three members, who were to operate inside Russia), the Central Organ (the editors of *Iskra*), and the highest body, the Party Council (five members, four of which were to be drawn from the other two bodies). Counting Plekhanov, who still sided with Lenin, the new "bolsheviks" gained a majority in each of these bodies, even though this required the exclusion of the three old *Iskra* editors, Potresov, V. Zasulich, and P. B. Akselrod, now opponents of Lenin, from the new Central Organ. The significance of Lenin's victory, as it later became evident, was not that he controlled the central party bodies (for Plekhanov soon abandoned him and the new bodies never really functioned as had been intended) but the symbolic value of the term "Bolshevik," which Lenin quickly adopted as his trademark, as if the rigged voting at the Second Party Congress proved that *his* was the main stream of Russian socialism from which a "minority" had deviated.

The failure of Lenin's effort to impose his will on the party without a schism became apparent in the fall of 1903. In October the Emigrant League of Revolutionary Social Democrats held a congress in Geneva which revealed that a substantial majority of former *Iskra* supporters in exile opposed Lenin. This persuaded Plekhanov to a reconciliation with the Mensheviks, three of whom he welcomed back to the editorial board. Lenin then resigned as editor, thus bringing to an end his influence over the party press and setting the stage for his next phase.

The keynote for the new effort was an article published in May, 1904, entitled "One Step Forward, Two Steps Back." In it Lenin wrote that the Menshevik "opportunists" have "disgraced our old *Iskra*," and he urged that a new congress be called to undo their work and establish a "real" party. Seemingly deserted by almost everyone at the beginning of 1904, by summer he had found a new corps of lieutenants which included such talented intellectuals as A. A. Bogdanov, A. V. Lunacharsky, and V. Bonch-Bruevich. In August, 1904, a group of twenty-two Leninists met in Geneva to demand a new congress, and in November Lenin established a purely Bolshevik "Bureau of the Committees of the Party Majority." These actions implied that Lenin would establish his own party if the Mensheviks did not agree to a new congress (which Lenin hoped to control, of course). Since the Party Council, headed by Plekhanov, did not yield, Lenin made good the threat by holding a "Third Party Congress" in London in April and May, 1905. The Mensheviks boycotted this conclave, and its existence signified that Lenin represented himself and his Bolsheviks as the only Russian Social Democratic Party. Although Lenin could not obtain a majority on all of his resolutions tending to excommunicate the Mensheviks, he was able to obtain approval for an elitist definition of a party member, the abolition of the Party Council, and the recognition of the new Bolshevik newspaper *Vperëd* (*Forward*—established in December, 1904) as the one authoritative organ of the party.

Lenin's effort to establish his ideal party without the collaboration of a substantial portion of the Russian Social Democrats made remarkable progress, despite his arrogance in defying Plekhanov, Martov, Trotsky, and almost all of the more distinguished socialist leaders of the day. But before a separate Bolshevik Party could be stabilized, the development of a revolutionary crisis in Russia obliged Lenin to revert to more conciliatory tactics.

An unpopular and unsuccessful war with Japan, which started in February, 1904, and ended in September, 1905, brought the tsarist government to the verge of collapse and provided oppositional political movements of all sorts with an unprecedented opportunity. The year 1905 opened with the shooting of numerous members of an unarmed demonstration in St. Petersburg ("Bloody Sunday," January 22*) and ended with street fighting in which the army suppressed the armed and barricaded workers of Moscow. Between these explosive turning points, the peasants organized a union and held two congresses to demand political and agrarian reform, various military and naval units mutinied, and the workers of St. Petersburg and Moscow conducted general strikes and established "soviets" (councils), which virtually ruled the two capitals for short periods in the latter part of 1905. Liberal political organizations now appeared beside the socialist parties (the Socialist Revolutionary or populist agrarian socialist party, and the Social Democratic Party) which had been formed in the past few years, but no party was responsible for the popular upheaval or able to control it. Finally, the government promised civil liberties and a measure of representative government (especially in the "October Manifesto" of 1905). Faced with the possibility of victory over the old autocracy, the various parties and factions set aside their differences. In October, 1905, the factory owners of St. Petersburg even paid the wages of the workers who were striking against the regime and the soviet was invited to establish its headquarters in the building of the artistocratic Imperial Free Economic Society.

The distinction between Bolsheviks and Mensheviks had not yet been fully established within Russia in the opening months of 1905, and in the developing crisis it became quite impossible for Lenin to maintain a separate party. In fact, his efforts to swim against the stream were partly responsible for Lenin's generally ineffectual record in the Revolution of 1905. To be sure, he talked and wrote like a practical man of action, calling for the arming of the workers, urging the study of street-fighting tactics, and even attempting to use the mutiny of the battleship *Potemkin* in June, 1905, as the basis for an amphibious operation to establish a revolutionary beachhead in Odessa. But Lenin showed little aptitude for the actual execution of military operations, and he was curiously slow in returning to revolutionary Russia. Although Trotsky returned as early as February and played a dramatic role as the last chairman of the St. Petersburg

* New Style, which is used throughout this book although it came into use in Russia only in 1918. Old Style dates are thirteen days earlier than New Style dates in the twentieth century.

soviet, Lenin lingered on outside Russia, continuing his factional poli-
ticking and writing various articles on revolutionary tactics that had
little impact on actual events. When he finally returned to Russia in
November, the peak of the revolution had passed. He dodged the police in St. Petersburg and Moscow, addressed various socialist groups,
and devoted his main efforts to editing a newspaper named *Novaia
Zhizn'* (*The New Life*). He was suspicious of the soviets, which were
extraparty organs, and he certainly did not lead the Moscow uprising
in December. The most that can be said of Lenin's role in 1905 is that
his booklet—"Two Tactics of Social Democracy in the Democratic
Revolution," published in Geneva in August, 1905—reenforced his
reputation as a determined revolutionary theoretician. While Lenin
joined other Russian Marxists in considering the 1905 Revolution a
bourgeois democratic one, he insisted that the proletariat, in alliance
with the majority of the peasantry, could and must establish a "revolutionary dictatorship of the proletariat and peasantry." While denying
that it was possible to establish socialism at once, he felt that there was
a chance for a government standing higher on the revolutionary scale
than mere "bourgeois democracy." Moreover, he hoped that a display
of revolutionary zeal in Russia might inspire the proletarians of the
West to arise. But Lenin could do almost nothing in 1905 to advance
the practical realization of this theory, which resembled ideas that
Trotsky put forward at about the same time.

By the end of 1905 Lenin had been obliged to resume his collaboration with the non-Bolshevik Russian Social Democrats, for many of the
local committees of Bolsheviks and Mensheviks had already reunited
without asking his permission. At the end of December the Bolsheviks
met separately in Tammerfors, Finland, but agreed to join with the
Mensheviks in a "unity" conference. This opened a six-year period in
which a façade of Social Democratic unity was maintained and was
accepted by Lenin despite his continued efforts to win control of the
whole party. In this period there were two party congresses (the fourth
in April–May, 1906, and the fifth in May–June, 1907), four party "conferences" (one in 1906, two in 1907, and one in 1909) and three sessions
of the Central Committee (1908, 1909, and 1910). Despite the disintegration of the pretense of unity, both Bolsheviks and Mensheviks participated in all of these meetings, neither group having the opportunity to decide matters in its favor. The main issues under discussion
were the question of participation in Russia's new representative body,
the Duma; the formulation of an agrarian program; and certain Bolshevik methods of raising funds. After much vacillation a majority at
the two party congresses finally approved of Social Democratic participation in elections for the Duma, which Lenin accepted as a tactical
device. His own agrarian program of "nationalization" of the land—

i.e., confiscation by the central authorities—was rejected in favor of the Menshevik program of "municipalization"—confiscation by local peasant bodies. And the Bolshevik fund-raising techniques, which included armed robbery, were repeatedly condemned, although this produced no contrition on Lenin's part.

In keeping with the tactic of working within a united Social Democratic Party, Lenin countenanced the existence of party publications that were not wholly Bolshevik, and in 1910 accepted a post on the editorial board of the principal organ of the "united" party, *The Social Democrat*. He also attempted to associate himself with two illustrious names in Russian socialism, Gorky and Plekhanov, the better to persuade the party to his views. He had met the great writer in 1905 and thereafter attempted by vigorous correspondence and occasional visits to win him to Bolshevism. But Gorky, while impressed by Lenin, remained undogmatic in matters of ideology and continued to lend his name and give his monies to both sides. Plekhanov was an ideologist to the core, but he proudly considered himself to be the one leader who could maintain the unity of the movement by remaining above the two chief factions. Trotsky, whose ego was inflated by his heroic role in 1905 and his escape from subsequent arrest, also attempted this feat and with as little success. Although Lenin was on hostile terms with Trotsky during this period, he found it desirable to form an intraparty bloc with Plekhanov in 1910 to give support to his attacks on the Mensheviks who still refused to accept his conception of the elitist party. The tactic of working from within a single party was applied in yet another way in the summer of 1911, when Lenin conducted a "school" near Paris at which he gave forty indoctrination lectures to a group of eighteen party members that included both Bolsheviks and Mensheviks.

Just as Lenin was willing to work within a Russian party that was not wholly Bolshevik, he also saw fit to participate in the Second International, the worldwide league of socialist parties, which at that time contained a majority that hardly met his standard of militancy. In 1907 Lenin attended the Seventh Congress of the International in Stuttgart and was elected to its presidium, and in 1910 he attended the Eighth Congress in Copenhagen, having participated in the work of the International Socialist Bureau in Brussels in the interval. In the International he attempted to make common cause with the leftist minorities in other socialist parties, but without any concrete results.

One factor that probably inclined Lenin toward working within the "united" party was the serious difficulties he experienced in maintaining his own faction. The postrevolutionary disillusionment and persecution caused a drastic decline in membership in Russia and reduced the Bolsheviks to only a half-dozen committees in all the Empire by

1909. This difficulty, which would have rendered futile any separatist Bolshevik movement, began to dissipate only in 1911. Another problem on Lenin's hands was the defection of several of his ablest lieutenants. Bogdanov and Lunacharsky, among others, were interested in an attempt to harmonize Marxism and idealist philosophy, and this led to a sharp controversy that reached its peak in 1909 when Lenin published a tedious polemical book entitled *Materialism and Empiriocriticism*. Another deviation from Lenin's line concerned the more practical question of participation in the Duma. A number of Bolsheviks, including Bogdanov and Lunacharsky, two of the mainstays of the period, had opposed participation in the Duma and now wanted to recall the Social Democratic deputies. Lenin insisted that the party would be best served if it could use the Duma as a tribune, and in June, 1909, Lunacharsky and Bogdanov were both formally expelled from the ranks of the Bolsheviks. This left Lenin momentarily weakened, but at the same time a new group of lieutenants was forming around him, including such future celebrities as G. E. Zinoviev, L. B. Kamenev, A. I. Rykov, and M. P. Tomsky.

By 1911 Lenin had ample evidence that he could not win the Mensheviks to Bolshevism, and at the same time the growing number of new disciples and the reviving revolutionary mood in Russia presented fresh inducements to form a separate Bolshevik Party. Only one Menshevik attended a "conference" of emigrant members of the Central Committee of the Party which Lenin organized in Paris in June, and this single Menshevik's departure was soon provoked. In October a purely Bolshevik "Russian Organizational Commission" met in Baku and Tiflis and called for a general party conference in Prague in January, 1912. Since the Bolsheviks were the only ones who recognized the legitimacy of the meeting, the Prague conference amounted to a reassertion of the claim, moribund since the end of 1905, that the Bolsheviks were the only Russian Social Democratic Workers' Party. A common Bolshevik-Menshevik Central Committee had existed for six years, but now the "party" conference selected a new seven-man Central Committee, which included Zinoviev, a police spy named R. V. Malinovsky, and Sergo Ordzhonikidze, a Georgian who had directed the "Russian Organizational Commission" which arranged (more precisely, rigged) the conference. Another Georgian, called Stalin, was one of two additional members whom Lenin at once co-opted into the committee. Lenin's new assistants were not as well known as his colleagues before 1903 or the Bolsheviks with whom he had broken in 1910. But the new circle was more devoted to Lenin, and a number of its members were destined to play crucial roles in the movement over the next generation. Lenin's reformed party marked its establishment by the publication in Russia of a new, purely Bolshevik newspaper,

Pravda (*The Truth*), which made its first appearance in April, 1912. Because of the penetration of police agents into the very core of the new Bolshevik Party, it was particularly difficult to carry out operations in the years 1912–1914. Despite the numerous arrests which ensued, new local organizations were established in Russia. Lenin, working from his advanced base in Austrian Poland, was able to keep close control over operations through emissaries sent into Russia and conferences with various party members who crossed the border for brief sessions with the leader.

In keeping with his defiant tactics toward the non-Bolsheviks, Lenin ceased his cooperative attitude toward the Second International, which lent a sympathetic ear to the protests of the Mensheviks against Lenin's unilateral action. When the leading German Social Democrat, Karl Kautsky, raised the "Russian question" (the Bolshevik-Menshevik quarrel) in 1913, Lenin heatedly denied that there was any question, and he personally boycotted a conference of the International Socialist Bureau that met in early 1914 to consider the dispute, sending representatives to restate his point. When the conference adopted a resolution favoring the unification of the Russian Social Democrats, the Bolshevik delegates walked out. Lenin refused to recognize the decision of the International.

The increasingly exclusive, separatist Bolshevik position was abruptly accentuated by the outbreak of World War I in the summer of 1914. Most European socialists—to the indignation of Lenin and a small minority of other European socialist leaders—supported their respective national war efforts. In Lenin's eyes the "opportunism" of Kautsky and the Second International was now revealed in its full scope, and as soon as he took up wartime residence in Switzerland (after a brief imprisonment in Austria as an enemy alien) he began a protracted polemic against the Second International and the "renegades" of European socialism. According to Lenin, the bankruptcy of prewar international socialism made it mandatory that the "true" socialists, such as the Bolsheviks, break away from their "renegade" colleagues and attempt to lead the proletariat in turning the "imperialist" war into a civil war. In the case of Russia, he held that defeat by the Germans would be a "lesser evil" than a tsarist victory. It was his hope that the strain of war would weaken the government of at least one of the powers and so provide an opportunity for a Bolshevik-type party to act. To his immense frustration it was more difficult than ever before to prepare the Russian proletariat for such a moment. Almost all the important Bolsheviks in Russia had been picked up by the police; communication by mail, much less by smuggled publications, was exceedingly unreliable; and Lenin was for the first time practically penniless.

In this depressing situation Lenin devoted himself partly to such active political life as was possible in the isolation of Switzerland. A number of important Russian Social Democrats were stranded there, including Plekhanov, Martov and two of Lenin's younger lieutenants, Zinoviev and N. I. Bukharin. This tense little community spent a good deal of time and energy addressing one another at meetings and writing heated credos in little-read émigré periodicals. Although Martov and a number of other Mensheviks shared many of Lenin's views on war and revolution and sought greater unity as the basis for effective opposition to the war, Lenin worked assiduously for a more decisive split in international socialism and called for the establishment of a new International. In September, 1915, he attempted to advance his position by organizing a small bloc of delegates who attended a conference of antiwar socialists at Zimmerwald, Switzerland. The "Zimmerwald Left" included Lenin; Zinoviev; a Polish-German Socialist named K. B. Radek, who now began a close involvement in Russian socialism; and a smattering of Western Europeans. The Zimmerwald Left called for a civil war to end the "imperialist" war, and repeated essentially the same line at another conference in Kienthal in April, 1916. These proclamations had little effect upon the bulk of European socialists (who were now "social chauvinists" in Lenin's eyes) and even less effect on the war in general.

Lenin found a measure of escape from the many frustrations of active politics by refining his basic theory. Between January and July, 1916, he wrote a small book entitled *Imperialism: The Highest Stage of Capitalism,* an economic treatise in which he attempted to show why the proletarian revolution had thus far been delayed in the advanced countries and how the backward colonial countries were an integral part of the capitalist order. Because he was attempting to write a book that would pass Russian censorship, Lenin did not state the implications that his theory of imperialism held for revolutionary strategy. But his writings over the period 1913–1916 indicate that Lenin was far advanced in a formulation of revolutionary Marxist tactics that would make use of nationalism and anticolonialism to add a new dimension to the struggle against capitalism. Just before the war began he had started to write intensively on the need to offer the right of self-determination to all countries in order to draw them to socialism. During the war he added special emphasis on the revolutionary potential of the economically backward countries on which imperialist capitalism depended to derive the high profits that enabled them to "corrupt certain sections of the working class." In 1916 he maintained that a successful proletarian revolution must include "movements of national liberation in the undeveloped, backward, and oppressed nations." While postwar events were to disappoint revolutionary Marxists with respect to the advanced Western countries, Lenin's conception of revolutionary tactics based on the colonial countries has come to form the theoretical foundation for some of the most successful advances of world Communism.

Although only the western borderlands of the Russian Empire had been penetrated by the Central Powers in 1916, the imperial regime was tottering, mainly because of economic dislocation and exceedingly inept political leadership. While Lenin had hoped for the collapse of imperial Russia under the strain of protracted war, he had not been able to influence the course of events. Although he continued writing about revolutionary tactics, he had made no specific plans for an upheaval in Russia. And it was only through the newspapers that he learned of the fall of the Romanovs in March, 1917.

3

THE CRUCIBLE OF REVOLUTION

In March, 1917, the political leadership of Russia passed from the hands of the Romanov dynasty into the hands of the intelligentsia. The downfall of the tsarist government, which the intelligentsia had for so many years struggled to bring about, was not the work of this social formation or any of the political parties that it had spawned. The Imperial government had obviously been on the verge of collapse for at least a year. In 1915 the tsar had unwisely taken over direct command of the army (although he never promoted himself above colonel, a rank that did more than justice to his military talent) and had left a large measure of domestic political authority in the hands of the Tsarina Alexandra, a hysterical advocate of autocratic government who was subject to the influence of Rasputin, the unsavory faith healer and counselor. On Rasputin's insistence, the abler Russian statesmen were set aside in favor of a disreputable coterie of ministers who did not compensate for their autocratic posture by even a trace of administrative ability. By the beginning of 1917 even the generals, the grand dukes, and the conservative politicians of the Duma were agreed that a radical reorganization of the supreme authority was necessary in the face of the German threat without and the increasing turbulence within. But the prospect of assuming responsibility for a palace revolution and forcibly imposed political reform overwhelmed these respectable "revolutionaries." Despite its sharply critical attitude and demands for the formation of a new ministry, Professor P. N. Miliukov's Constitutional Democratic Party was no better prepared for revolutionary action. A handful of conservatives finally roused themselves to the point of assassinating Rasputin in December, 1916, but no further action was taken.

The revolution that began in March was a spontaneous uprising of the masses of workers, soldiers, and ordinary citizens of Petrograd (as St. Petersburg was renamed in 1914). It was an uprising without a theory, without a party, without a central committee or a leader (contrary to Lenin's belief that the masses, left to themselves, were incapable of carrying off a revolution). Faced with swelling demonstrations in his capital and the defection of the troops sent to suppress them, Nicholas II abdicated on March 15 and formal sovereignty passed into the hands of the Provisional Government, really a committee of liberal Duma deputies.

The new government included a substantial mixture of statesmen—such as the Premier, Prince G. E. Lvov, and the Minister of War, A. I. Guchkov—who could not be described as radical intelligentsia, but it was immediately obvious that the dominant figure was the *intelligent* who served as Minister of Foreign Affairs, Miliukov. This eminent historian no longer seemed very radical, but his previous political career had consisted of an uncompromising campaign for complete political democracy, and his long connection with the revolutionary intelligentsia did much to make his rather conservative cabinet acceptable to the public for almost two months. Except for the right-wing generals, who made a belated and bungled attempt to take power in September, 1917, all the rivals and successors to the Miliukov leadership belonged to the revolutionary intelligentsia, who, after a century of frustration, now had their once chance in history to mold their country's fate.

It was an immense opportunity and an awesome challenge. One aspect of the challenge was the problem of passing from theory and criticism to practical decisions and public responsibility. Several factions of the intelligentsia entered the revolutionary arena with a burden of theory which helped to drag them down. Miliukov, for example, held that only a democratically elected constituent assembly could declare Russia a republic, even though it was obvious that monarchy was at the moment vastly unpopular and that any trace of association with it was a grave political liability. Many Socialist Revolutionaries and Social Democrats, including some Bolsheviks, were politically hampered by the theory that Russia could not progress from the "bourgeois" revolution of March, 1917, to a truly socialist state without passing through a considerable period of parliamentary democracy.*

Another broad problem that the revolution posed for the intelligentsia was the difficult task of controlling the masses. The intelligentsia, like the nobility of the old regime, was a small minority.† Unlike

---

* For the Marxist Social Democrats, the interval between the overthrow of tsardom and the establishment of socialism was to be the era of bourgeois liberalism or capitalism. For the Socialist Revolutionaries, guided mainly by Victor Chernov, who respected Marx but attempted to reinterpret his theory in the light of peculiar Russian conditions, this was to be an era of political liberalism without full-fledged capitalism.

† Although official statistics of the old regime do not enumerate the intelligentsia as such, data from 1914 show that only 1.4 percent of the population was employed by the civil service and the professions, two major categories in which members of the intelligentsia were to be found. Granting that a minority of the civil servants and professional people were members of the intelligentsia, and assuming that many of the intelligentsia were officially counted under other headings,

the old order, however, they could not depend on accustomed obedience from a large civil and military establishment. In 1917 the masses were in a fractious mood, drunk with the wine of liberty and sometimes with liquid spirits, which had been placed under prohibition in 1914 and were now "liberated" by thirsty mobs. The confrontation of the intelligentsia and the long-idealized "people," the peasant *narod* and the urban proletariat, was further complicated by the conscription of millions into the armed services, placing the weapons that might decide any political contest in the hands of soldiers and sailors who had recently discovered that they could ignore the authority of officers and government. The intelligentsia faced anew, though in more acute form, their long-standing problem of communicating successfully with the largely ignorant masses whom they hoped to lead to a better world.

In 1917 it was unthinkable that the masses would betray the hopes of the intelligentsia in favor of the autocracy, as had sometimes happened in the past. On the contrary, the crowds of workers and soldiers maintained a rather pretentious posture of constant vigilance against "counterrevolution" and gave their vigorous approval to all leaders who spoke in the name of the animistic deity called "Revolution." But the euphoria that followed the downfall of the tsar could not be expected to last indefinitely, and it was quite possible that none of the parties of the intelligentsia could actually control the masses, few of whom belonged to any party at all. The masses had spontaneously overthrown the tsarist government, and it was quite possible for them to do the same to any number of succeeding governments of the intelligentsia.

Three of the major parties representing the intelligentsia in the revolution, the Constitutional Democrats, the Mensheviks, and the Socialist Revolutionaries, faced the problem of controlling the masses through the kind of party organization prevalent in the parliamentary systems of the West. Assuming that majority support is the legitimizing force in a parliamentary democracy, they sought the membership of as many citizens as possible, and permitted democratic processes to operate within their parties, and freedom to exist within the party as well as within the state. The question of controlling the revolutionary masses was not, however, restricted to the parties as such, for the revolution of 1917—like that of 1905—gave birth to an extraparty organization that enjoyed greater popular authority than any of the parties. This was the Soviet of Workers' and Soldiers' Deputies, the makeshift parliament of the lower classes, which was formed in Petrograd even before the tsar's abdication and soon developed into a national net-

---

even a liberal estimate cannot count more than 1 percent of the population as intelligentsia.

work of similar bodies. This network culminated in the establishment of an All-Russian Congress of Soviets of Workers' and Soldiers' Deputies, which first met in June, 1917. The popular prestige of this institution, and especially the strategic location of the Petrograd Soviet, made it the vital link between the intelligentsia and the masses.

A third challenge facing the intelligentsia was the problem of their own internal relationships. Because of their limited numbers and strength in the face of a real foreign threat, the imagined threat of counterrevolution, and the difficulty of leading the masses, the various factions in the intelligentsia had powerful incentives to refrain temporarily from internecine strife. Thus the rather second-rank socialist intelligentsia leaders who were in Petrograd at the opening of the revolution agreed, in the name of the Petrograd Soviet, to recognize the legitimacy of Miliukov's "bourgeois" Provisional Government. N. N. Sukhanov, who played a major role in negotiating what amounted to a mutual nonaggression pact between the liberal and the socialist intelligentsia, later explained that he believed that the socialists were not yet strong enough to take power and therefore were obliged to avoid a frontal attack on the liberals for the time being. This was indeed a truce rather than a coalition, but in the spirit of revolutionary unity and with the permission of the Petrograd Soviet, Alexander Kerensky, a member of the Socialist Revolutionary Party and a vice-chairman of the Soviet, accepted the Ministry of Justice in the Lvov-Miliukov cabinet. This step toward coalition of liberals and socialists in the Provisional Government ran against the wishes of Sukhanov and other socialist leaders, who hoped to keep themselves and their parties free of the "bourgeois" liberals, awaiting the day when the workers would conduct an authentic proletarian revolution.

On the whole, the socialists themselves were guided by the tendency to set aside their differences in the face of the challenge of the revolution. The Mensheviks and the Socialist Revolutionaries jointly held a predominant position in the Petrograd Soviet at the time of its establishment, and they acted in alliance to a considerable degree thereafter, tacitly assuming that they would eventually establish a coalition government of socialists rather than one-party rule. From mid-March to mid-April the Bolsheviks, too, tended to cooperate with the other branches of the radical intelligentsia. Although a few minor figures in the party at first adopted a sharply antagonistic attitude toward the Provisional Government and the other socialists, the return from Siberia of Kamenev and Stalin brought a change of direction. For about a month preceding Lenin's return on April 16, the Bolsheviks refrained from hostility toward the Miliukov government and even began to make their way toward reunification with the Mensheviks.

But although the challenge of the revolutionary situation inspired a tendency toward temporary truce between the parties, the heated issues of the day—especially the war—tended to divide the intelligentsia. Although the liberals were at first agreed on remaining loyal to the Western allies, each of the three socialist parties was divided between a majority that favored continuation of the war—but only as a defense of the revolution—and a minority that favored immediate withdrawal. Although a tendency toward coalition blurred party lines, the parties themselves faced the problem of maintaining internal discipline. Like most of the important leaders of the socialist intelligentsia, Lenin was far from Petrograd at the outbreak of the revolution, and he was faced with the difficult practical problem of getting back to Russia before he could confront the opportunity and the challenge that the revolution posed. Switzerland was an island of neutrality surrounded by the Central Powers and the Entente. Both "imperialist" blocks had good reason not to permit the passage of a declared enemy, but the German government was more concerned with its short-run survival than with the long-term danger of socialist attack, and for some time before the outbreak of the Russian Revolution it had been keeping track of movements and leaders that might be expected to subvert the war effort of the enemy in the East.

Lenin realized that acceptance of German assistance could be a serious political liability in a Russia that was still permeated with a patriotic wartime spirit, but he was willing to run the risk to arrive at the scene. To minimize the taint of collaboration, he tried to appear aloof from the Germans and relied as much as possible on the services of Swiss socialists to negotiate his transit across German territory. The railroad car that carried Lenin's group was to enjoy extraterritoriality in Germany, and to avoid any taint of German money the passage of the returnees was to be paid for by the Swiss socialists. Thus, on April 9, Lenin, Zinoviev, Radek, Krupskaia, and about two dozen minor Bolsheviks and other Russian socialists whom Lenin took along as a hedge against criticism, departed Berne for Malmo, Sweden. In passing through this country Lenin lingered for a whole day in Stockholm, allegedly to establish a Bureau of the Central Committee there. Another reason for this delay in an otherwise impetuous trip could have been to arrange for the future transfer of German funds, intended to hinder the Russian war effort by helping the Bolsheviks.

On April 13 Lenin and his colleagues departed for Petrograd. Lenin's reception at the Finland station, about midnight on April 16, accurately reflected the spirit of the revolution in its early stage. Although Lenin's only publicized achievement in his forty-seven years had been to associate his name with the magic word "revolution," a large crowd, certainly not all party members, turned out to give him a hero's welcome. A military band played the *Marseillaise*, troops presented arms, spotlights played on triumphal arches in red and gold. If the ceremony, endlessly memorialized by Soviet writers and artists, had been staged by Bolsheviks, it nevertheless was possible only in the atmosphere of truce prevailing in the ranks of the radical intelligentsia. The official greeter in the waiting room formerly reserved for the tsar was the Menshevik N. S. Chkheidze, Chairman of the Petrograd Soviet, who publicly invited Lenin to set aside factional quarrels (as most socialists had done) and join in the common cause. Lenin disappointed him and most of the Bolsheviks, too. Before he had time to greet his colleagues properly, much less listen to their advice or become involved in the spirit of conciliation, Lenin set forth his uncompromising position. In a single, exhausting night Lenin gave impromptu expositions of his outlook—in the waiting room of the station, outside the station atop an armored car, at street corners along the route to Bolshevik headquarters, from a balcony outside that building, and at a supper reception given by the party. The main theme of Lenin's speeches was published on April 20 in the revived Bolshevik newspaper, *Pravda*, and is known in the scriptures of communism as "the April Theses." Three points formed their core: (a) the war is "an imperialist, predatory war" and "not the slightest concession to 'revolutionary defensism' is permissible"; (b) the soviets, to the exclusion of any Provisional Government, are the "only possible form of the revolutionary government," and the party must patiently explain to the masses that the soviets should not be left in the hands of the "petty bourgeois, opportunist" socialists who now dominate them; (c) all land should be "nationalized"—confiscated by the state, though subject to the management of local soviets for the present. To these ends the party should rededicate and reform itself by holding a new congress, by adopting a new, more revolutionary program and a new name ("Communist"), and by looking forward to the formation of a new International.

The April Theses revealed the main lines of Lenin's response to the challenge that the revolution posed for the radical intelligentsia. On the question of theory, he showed himself to be extremely flexible, despite his long devotion to neo-Marxist doctrine. An acute Menshevik *intelligent*, Sukhanov, who heard Lenin's first presentations of the April Theses, was properly struck by the absence of any reference to the Marxist philosophy of history. Lenin spoke of transferring power to the proletariat and poor peasantry without any attention, much less apologies, to the prevailing Marxist dogma that Russia could not approach socialism without passing through a protracted bourgeois-democratic era. It does not seem that Lenin was consciously cynical about theory when it proved inconvenient for the seizure of power; for him theory was "a guide to action," constantly informed by developing events.

"Theory is grey, my friend, but green is the eternal tree of life," he was soon to say in self-explanation, quoting Goethe. But he intended his theses to serve as dogma for the other party members and the masses, who evidently did not share his scientific or mystical intuition. In 1905, when victory had seemed possible, Lenin had jettisoned the conventional Marxist philosophy of history with its stately progression from feudalism through capitalism to socialism, and in 1917 he showed the same preoccupation with the tactics that might lead to victory rather than with long-term philosophical problems.

Lenin's April Theses pointed toward a solution of the problem of controlling the masses by means of leadership that only an elitist disciplined party could supply. The fall of tsardom had ended the police suppression that had badly disorganized the party in prior years, and even Lenin admitted that the Russia of the Provisional Government was the "freest country in the world." Not only political opposition and propaganda but even the formation of independent armed forces was now possible. One might have guessed that Lenin would have reconsidered his conception of the party as a small but militant minority, but in fact he adhered to his former insistence on a vanguard. In his opinion, the inability of the masses to find and follow a truly revolutionary socialist line was amply proven by their temporary acceptance of the "revolutionary defensist" leadership of the "petty bourgeois" socialists who had been elected to the leading posts in the Petrograd Soviet. Now, more than ever, Lenin defended the exclusiveness of the party; it must hold aloof from the mass trends and "patiently explain" the correct path to the lower classes.

The April Theses also formulated a general answer to another problem posed by the revolution: the tension between unity and factionalism within the radical intelligentsia. Lenin vigorously attacked any compromise with radical groups which did not accept his line; to the prevailing tendency toward coalition, which Chkheidze had described by way of a truce offer, Lenin replied with scornful hostility. In the Revolution of 1905 he had permitted himself to be drawn into the general spirit of a united front and this had led only to muddled "unification" of organization and the blurring of "truth" and "error." Rather than repeat this experience in 1917, he was willing to risk the hostility of all other radicals, even if some of his own followers objected strongly. And the April Theses at least implied a method for dealing with objections from the party ranks. In calling for a new party congress, Lenin indicated his confidence in his ability to impose his will on his cohorts by dint of prestige, personality, and forensic skill. His unabashed self-confidence in immediately attacking the generally ac-

cepted ideas of the moment was itself an excellent reflection of the
force of character that was always his main weapon against splits in the
party.

At first Lenin's uncompromising program had a mixed reception
within the Bolshevik ranks. The April Theses were welcomed by the
Bolshevik "Left," including the young V. M. Molotov (born Scriabin),
which had subscribed to similar views before Lenin returned; they
were accepted more or less automatically by a larger "Center," including Stalin, which had inclined toward compromise but did not think
of challenging the leader; and they were sharply opposed by the party
"Right," led by Kamenev, which insisted on continuing a conciliatory
line toward the other socialists. In only three weeks Lenin succeeded
in imposing his will upon most of the party. At the Seventh Party Conference, during the week beginning May 7, the three fundamental
points of the April Theses were accepted by overwhelming majorities
that proved Lenin's control over the party and foreshadowed the "da
votes" that became customary in Communist Russia. No delegates
voted against Lenin's resolutions on the war and the land; only three
voted against the resolution on the Provisional Government; a handful
abstained from voting on all these issues. Lenin could find no support
at all for his proposal to break with the Second International, but now
that he controlled the organizational weapon in Russia he could afford
to postpone this issue. To be sure, his troubles with dissenters were not
over, but he had succeeded in drawing the party to his policy without
incurring an open schism, and this in itself gave Lenin a marked advantage over the leaders of rival parties. Both Martov and the Socialist
Revolutionary Chernov were to spend the crucial months of 1917 bat-
tling unsuccessfully to unify their parties behind their leadership.
Lenin's reassertion of authority over his party on the basis of the April
Theses was his first major triumph of 1917 and a prerequisite to the
seizure of power.

Of course Lenin faced not only the necessity of setting himself at the
head of the party but also that of improving the effectiveness of the
organization. The Bolshevik Party of early 1917 was not a well drilled
army ready to take the offensive on command. At the beginning of the
year the party claimed 23,600 members, which was little enough but
probably an inflated claim at that. With no legal hindrance to recruitment, membership rose sharply in the next months; by the opening of
the party conference on May 7, 79,000 members were claimed; by
August, 200,000. This expansion had its difficulties as well as its advantages, for it was no easy thing to recruit comparatively large numbers
of real Bolsheviks—persons who both understood Lenin's line and were
wholly devoted to his leadership. No doubt many who did not meet

these requirements slipped into the party during those days, but it appears that the Bolsheviks kept a better semblance of control over their membership than did other parties. They continued to issue membership cards, supposedly only to qualified recruits (Lenin himself had received card number 600 from the party organization of a factory on the night he arrived); they maintained a secretariat in the ballerina Kshesinskaia's former palace (it was headed by a woman, E. D. Stasova, and an archloyal Leninist from the Central Committee, Ia. M. Sverdlov); and—most important—they had a small core of members (perhaps a few hundred) that had belonged to the party for some years, were accustomed to following the edicts of Lenin's Central Committee, and could provide a cadre of leaders for the expanding party membership.

The purpose of the party organization, as expounded by Lenin at the beginning of the century, was to guide the masses. And in the spring of 1917 Lenin set his followers to this task, concentrating on the workers and soldiers in the strategic center of the revolution: the Petrograd area. As a special means of reaching the workers, the Bolsheviks attempted with considerable success to gain control of the factory committees that had been set up in most plants in the capital early in the revolution. Through these committees the Bolsheviks could not only gain the workers' confidence, but could also hope to influence the voting for deputies in the soviets and—in time—to direct the formation of armed workers' groups. It was especially important to the Bolsheviks that they succeed in winning the factory committees, because the Mensheviks had a fairly firm hold on the trade unions.

In June the Central Committee established a Military Organization as a special medium for penetrating the armed forces. On June 29 a conference of the Military Organization, claiming to represent 26,000 party members—or perhaps a quarter of the total party membership—met in Petrograd and established as its goal the establishment of a party cell in every military unit from the company up. Massive propagandistic support for these efforts was marshalled; by August, forty-one periodicals—320,000 copies per day—were being published, the most important of which were the daily *Pravda* and a special edition for the troops of Petrograd, *Soldatskaia Pravda* (*The Soldiers' Truth*). All of this cost money, even at a time when the magic word "revolution" requisitioned buildings and a certain amount of volunteer labor. The income of the party from dues was insignificant; there was no longer any revenue from wealthy sympathizers, and armed "expropriations" could not be made without seriously affronting the prevailing revolutionary conscience. Where then did Lenin obtain the funds for this substantial campaign? Although Communist sources have always denied it, the most likely answer lies in the Imperial German government which, like other belligerent states, was willing to spend large sums on psychological or political warfare. The details regarding the size of the subsidy and the means of donation are not clear, but the German foreign minister, Richard von Kuhlmann, in a secret memo of December, 1917, stated: "It was not until the Bolsheviks had received from us a steady flow of funds through various channels and under different labels that they were in a position to be able to build up their main organ, *Pravda,* to conduct energetic propaganda and appreciably to extend the originally narrow basis of their party." In the atmosphere of wartime Russia it was understandably impolitic for Lenin to admit —even to most of his colleagues—the identity of his benefactor. By July, 1917, the Provisional Government, using fraudulent evidence, did charge him with treasonous relations with the enemy, and in the course of time more "documentation" was introduced to prove that he was a "German agent." The introduction of this charge and the unreliable evidence used to support it have obscured the basic point: the Imperial German government could not possibly have subverted Lenin from his self-imposed mission as a revolutionary, nor did it need to in order to gain a short-term advantage, if Lenin could hinder or end Russia's participation in the war. Nor did Lenin mind accepting aid from his "capitalist" enemies; for that matter, the Bolsheviks and Mensheviks had accepted a loan from the British soap magnate Joseph Fels in 1907. Secure in his Marxist faith, Lenin was willing to risk a temporary German victory.

Although the Bolsheviks may have possessed certain advantages over their rivals, their advances in 1917 depended to a considerable extent on the errors of their adversaries. The Constitutional Democratic leadership of the Provisional Government was in a weak position from the start, since it was derived from the undemocratic tsarist Duma and had unwisely allowed itself to become popularly associated with the principle of monarchy. Although these liberals had made a start toward greater popular prestige by officially establishing full civil liberty and democratizing the army, they soon fell victim to their nationalist war aims. On May 3, the publication of a note from Miliukov to the Allied Powers, affirming revolutionary Russia's adherence to the treaty commitments of the tsarist government, brought a storm of protest, which was only partly the work of the Bolsheviks. Alexander Kerensky, the one member of the government who was a member of the Petrograd Soviet and at least theoretically a socialist, utilized this crisis to advance the formation of a coalition of liberal leaders and socialists from the soviet. Provoking Miliukov and Guchkov to resign, Kerensky persuaded the Central Committee of the Petrograd Soviet to endorse a new cabinet composed of Constitutional Democrats, Mensheviks, and Socialist Revolutionaries. This was a momentous step for the socialist parties involved. By accepting coalition, they staked their future on the Provisional Government without securing much control over Kerensky, who became the dominant figure in it, first as Minister of War, later as Premier. At the same time the Menshevik and Socialist Revolutionary leaders who believed in coalition alienated substantial minorities in their own ranks, the "Menshevik-Internationalists" and "Left Socialist Revolutionaries." These factions, unlike Lenin's opponents within Bolshevism, refused to accept party discipline and increasingly sided with the Bolsheviks.

When the First All-Russian Congress of Soviets, composed of 777 voting delegates from soviets throughout the country, met in Petrograd on June 16, the labors of Lenin and the mistakes of his rivals had not yet reached fulfillment. The Mensheviks and Socialist Revolutionaries together had about 630 delegates, while Lenin's party counted but 105. But the assiduous Bolshevik concentration of effort on Petrograd showed impressive results. A massive demonstration, including armed troops, which the party planned to call out in support of their program, so frightened the Soviet leadership that they refused to permit it, and at the last minute Lenin reluctantly agreed to their wishes. In this incident—as in previous demonstrations against Miliukov—the ability of the radical intelligentsia to control the turbulent masses had been sorely tested, and in mid-July the plebeian hordes temporarily cast aside their self-appointed leaders.

Kerensky had only one real hope: to win a striking victory at the front before Lenin could exploit the growing unpopularity of the war for his own ends. On July 2 the Russian army attacked the Austro-Hungarian forces on the southern front and enjoyed temporary success against an adversary that was almost as disorganized and dispirited as themselves. But the advance soon turned to retreat, and the reaction of the Petrograd troops was explosive. Demanding that the soviets take power, armed military units, joined by workers, rioted against the Provisional Government for three days, July 16–18. The object of their hatred, Kerensky, having no armed forces on which to call, at first could do nothing to pacify the demonstrators. The Menshevik and Socialist Revolutionary leaders of the Soviet might have stilled the tumult by announcing the establishment of a Soviet government, but they were fatally bound to the idea of coalition by the theoretical dogma that the time for socialism could not come so soon. Chernov, the leader of the Socialist Revolutionaries who was Kerensky's Minister of Agriculture, was very nearly lynched by a group of sailors, one of whom summed up the frustration of the lower classes with the intelligentsia leaders when he shouted, "Take power when it's offered, you son-of-a-bitch!" Lenin, an intelligentsia leader himself, proved to be only slightly more competent in the face of the mob uprising. Oddly, he had not anticipated the reaction against Kerensky's bellicose gamble, and the uprising found him in Finland, recuperating from the nervous strain of the revolution. Returning to Petrograd on July 17, he faced a dilemma: if the Bolsheviks did not support the demonstrators, who were in effect rioting for Lenin's slogans, they might forfeit the degree of leadership thus far attained; but if they did support the demonstrations, they might find themselves in power prematurely, or might only succeed in pushing the Mensheviks and Socialist Revolutionaries into a more stable position as leaders of a Soviet government.

Lenin wavered. Speaking from a balcony at party headquarters on July 17, he encouraged the demonstrators in evasive terms, but later that night, at a meeting of the Central Committee, he supported a resolution to call off the demonstrations. This was probably the best tactic, for on the next day the Provisional Government was able to inflame some regiments with patriotic outrage by "revealing" that Lenin was a German agent and the demonstrations were a treasonous enterprise. By the end of the third day of the outburst, Kerensky had restored his tenuous authority. On the other hand, the affair revealed how far any of the intelligentsia leaders were from enjoying the secure support of the masses. The Bolsheviks in particular found their public prestige seriously threatened by the charges of treason and their inability to maintain their image as the vanguard of the revolutionary classes.

In the wake of the July Days Lenin's leadership suffered its gravest crisis of the revolution. On the advice of several of his lieutenants, he chose prudence before valor and on July 22 he fled the capital rather than face Kerensky's charges of treason, taking refuge in Finland as he had in the aftermath of the Revolution of 1905.* In hiding he was able to overcome this problem of distance to a considerable degree by correspondence, articles submitted to the party press and consultation with party leaders who came to see him. Lenin also took advantage of his enforced retreat to work on a substantial theoretical discussion of the postrevolutionary government, using notes that he had gathered in Switzerland. This work, *State and Revolution* (published in 1918), is a

---

* Lenin's decision to flee rather than face a trial is usually interpreted as a not unreasonable precaution against lynching at the hands of patriotic troops or a death sentence handed down by a rigged court. This may be, but it is also true that a trial might have provided Lenin with a superb rostrum from which to attack the insecure government, *if* he could have established his innocence. Perhaps Lenin decided to flee because he did not know just how much of the real evidence on his financial dealings with the Germans the government might be able to produce in court and preferred to avoid possible confrontation with charges that could not be refuted.

remarkable example of the utopian strain that runs through Lenin's life, sustaining him, one may surmise, in such bleak moments as the post-July interval of the Russian revolution. Lenin had often stressed the incompetence of the proletarian and peasant masses to care for their interests without the guidance of an elite party, an observation that the fickle behavior of the Petrograd masses in July seemed to justify. In *State and Revolution,* however, Lenin set forth a remarkably optimistic picture of the new, postrevolutionary society, in which the masses were to install a rule of equality and humanity quite spontaneously. The immediate sequel of the proletarian revolution was to be the "dictatorship of the proletariat"—but this was not depicted as the authoritarian rule of the Bolshevik Party. Instead Lenin predicted that the workers themselves could dispose of all bureaucracy, the police, and the army, and simultaneously purge the remnants of capitalism and establish true democracy. Placing immense implicit trust in the purifying and elevating force of the revolution, Lenin held that "no special apparatus of suppression"—only the "armed people"—was needed to enforce democracy, while the tasks of public administration could be carried on rather informally by "any literate person." This regime of the "armed workers," which is "no longer a state in the proper sense of the word," would soon be able to "wither away," said Lenin, leading to a fully communist society.

The impracticality of *State and Revolution* was revealed later, but it was harmless for Lenin in the summer of 1917. What did threaten his tactical position was his new attitude toward the soviets. From the April Theses to the July Days Lenin had maintained that the soviets were the proper vehicle for proletarian government and that the revolution should be conducted on their behalf. Even though the leadership of both the Petrograd Soviet and the First All-Union Congress of Soviets was mainly composed of "revolutionary defensists" of the Menshevik and Socialist Revolutionary parties, Lenin had supported soviet rule on the assumption that the masses could be persuaded to remove these "opportunists." The July Days showed that this could be done, for the popularity of the soviet leadership had certainly suffered. Nor had the soviets turned hopelessly right-wing. In the face of the mass uprising the soviet leaders, like the Bolsheviks, had merely tried to calm the storm rather than take power prematurely, and it was the Kerensky regime rather than the Soviet which had pressed the charges of treason (the Soviet opposed publication of the "incriminating" evidence and wanted an investigation committee of its own to investigate the charges). The soviets may have been somewhat humbled by their lack of authority in the affair, but they still had a better claim to legitimacy as a political organ of the lower classes than did any other body, including the Bolshevik Party. By withdrawing the slogan "All Power to the Soviets" between late July and mid-October, Lenin did not strike an effective blow at his enemies and threatened to deprive his party of the means by which it could seize and maintain power. This problem was the cause of some concern at the Sixth Party Congress, which met in Petrograd on August 8–16. In the absence of Lenin and some other leaders, it fell to Stalin to defend—rather lamely—the new line. All in all, it was a rather inconclusive congress, less important in the development of the party than the Sixth Conference of 1912 or the Seventh Conference of May, 1917.

Lenin's withdrawal of support for the soviets, which Communist historians have faithfully recorded as a stroke of sagacity, was probably a serious tactical blunder. Fortunately for Lenin and the party, this error was counterbalanced by an act of real statesmanship: the admission into the party of Trotsky, the man best suited to the task of winning the soviets for the Bolsheviks. Lenin's devotion to his cause and its transcendence of personal feelings were never so clearly revealed as in his acceptance of Trotsky as a near equal at the head of Bolshevism. It is easy enough to explain the partnership as a result of current revolutionary policy: both men were bitterly opposed to the war, the Provisional Government, and the conciliationist leadership of the soviets. But in human terms it is remarkable that Lenin accepted Trotsky, a younger man whom he had launched into the top ranks of the Social Democratic movement in 1902 only to be "betrayed" by his protégé after the Second Party Congress of 1903. In 1912 Trotsky had gained the foremost place among Lenin's enemies by attempting to undercut Lenin's party conference in Prague with a rival conference of his own in Vienna. It is true that the revolution immediately brought some measure of reconciliation. Trotsky had visited Lenin in May, almost as soon as the younger man returned from his wartime exile in America, and about a week later there were inconclusive negotiations concerning the entry into the party of Trotsky and a small band of followers, the "Interdistrict Committee." When Kerensky ordered Lenin's arrest in July, Trotsky asserted that he was just as opposed to the government as the Bolsheviks were and should therefore be arrested too (he was). While Lenin was in hiding and Trotsky in prison, the Interdistrict Committee and its leader were admitted to the Bolshevik Party at its Sixth Congress, which also elected Trotsky to the Central Committee. This in itself may be counted as a substantial show of magnanimity, but it was modest compared to what followed. On September 6 a Rightist general, Lavr Kornilov, started to move troops on Petrograd with the object of purging the Soviet and reorganizing the government on more authoritarian lines. Kornilov failed, owing to the demoralization of his troops and the noncooperation of the railroads, but he stirred up a grave crisis, during which Kerensky had to call for help from the soviets and all socialist parties. Now feeling too dependent on the Left to continue the prosecution of the accused of July, Kerensky released Trotsky, who directly proceeded to take the dominant role in the revolutionary movement.

Here was a test of Lenin's character. While he restlessly waited in hiding, Trotsky pressed forward in the limelight, ostensibly as a leader of the Soviet rather than the party. The workers' and soldiers' deputies were becoming increasingly dissatisfied with the Provisional Government, and Trotsky did not hesitate to accept election as Chairman of the Petrograd Soviet on October 6, replacing the Menshevik Chkheidze, even though Lenin had not yet restored the slogan "All Power to the Soviets!" * A smaller man than Lenin would have suspected possible treachery from a former disciple who had betrayed him once before and did not trouble himself even to correspond with his leader, much less visit him. For years before 1917 Trotsky had worked for the unification of Bolsheviks and Mensheviks, and with control over the Soviet he might well have been able to enforce a coalition within a Soviet regime following the overthrow of the Provisional Government. But if Lenin had such doubts about Trotsky's reliability, he swallowed them and increasingly supported his new partner, making no effort to curb or discipline his authority. When Trotsky protested against Bolshevik participation in a "Democratic Conference" convened by Kerensky on September 27, Lenin wrote, "Bravo, Comrade Trotsky," and on October 10, four days *after* Trotsky took the chair of the Soviet, Lenin responded by renewing the slogan, "All Power to the Soviets!" For all his partisan passion, Lenin was able to regard the situation with sufficient detachment to realize that both he and Trotsky stood for a Bolshevik revolution and that their partnership was essential to this enterprise.

In the month between his election as Chairman of the Petrograd Soviet and the Bolshevik *coup* of November 7, Trotsky accomplished the prodigious task of preparing the Soviet, psychologically and physically, to take power. The former he accomplished in large measure by his impassioned speeches, especially to jammed crowds at the Modern Circus, a large indoor amphitheatre. The physical preparation had already started during the Kornilov crisis, when Bolshevik-dominated factory committees formed paramilitary units called the "Red Guards." A further step was taken on October 22 when the Soviet established a "Military Revolutionary Committee," chaired by Trotsky and intended

* As early as September 25 Lenin expressed renewed confidence in the future of the soviets for proletarian self-government, but until October 10 he seems to have had grave doubts about the desirability of seizing power in the name of the soviets rather than the party itself.

to control the armed forces around Petrograd, a far more powerful weapon than the civilian irregulars. Trotsky hurled himself into this work with audacity and brilliance, even venturing unprotected into a hostile fortress to persuade its garrison to accept his committee's authority. By early October the Petrograd Soviet was so well prepared for revolution that it scarcely bothered to conceal its aims.

But Lenin still had a vital role to play. Trotsky could prepare a Soviet *coup d'état,* but this would not lead to the establishment of a Bolshevik regime unless the Central Committee of the party determined to exploit the opportunity. This Trotsky could not arrange, for he did not enjoy Lenin's prestige among the Bolshevik leaders. Indeed, it was all Lenin could do to persuade the Central Committee that the time had come to seize power, a much harder task than he had faced when imposing his April Theses on the party. No Bolshevik doubted that a proletarian regime should be installed at some time in the future, but the question of party tactics, especially timing, was highly controversial. Lenin believed that the party must seize power, by force and without dependence on any allies. He wanted to use the soviets as organs of administration after the *coup,* but he did not want to rely on them to make the revolution. Above all, Lenin insisted on the utmost haste, asserting that the Kerensky government was about to surrender Petrograd to the Germans or that a new attack from the Russian generals was imminent. His fears may have been exaggerated (perhaps deliberately, to frighten his dawdling associates), but it is probably true that the Bolsheviks could not afford to wait very long. The elections for the long-promised Constituent Assembly were finally set for November, 1917, and as events were to prove, the Bolsheviks would be a weak minority in such a body. If the Assembly succeeded in establishing a new government backed by the prestige of a universal election and perhaps supported by a number of army divisions, the Bolsheviks' future would be dim indeed. Moreover, it was possible that some non-Bolshevik government might make peace with the Germans after all. Kerensky was becoming disillusioned with the Allies, and by early 1918 (a year too late) even Miliukov made overtures to the Germans.

Kamenev and Zinoviev, two of Lenin's leading assistants, were the chief opponents of his plan. Their proposed tactic was much more solidly based on Marxist theory and at the same time demonstrated a fatal lack of the instinct for power, which may be considered a requisite for any true Bolshevik leader. They argued that the party should not run ahead of the spontaneous movement of the masses in Russia and the West. In Russia the Bolsheviks should await the Constituent Assembly, in which they could ally with the Left Socialist Revolutionaries to play a leading role. Soon the proletariat of Western Europe would arise, sounding the call for the proletarian party of Russia to take power.*

Lenin's first attempt to convince the Central Committee, two letters written on September 25 and 27, was an unprecedented fiasco. Not only did the committee fail to accept his proposal, they declined to reply and very nearly determined to burn the letters. Badly stung, Lenin moved from his retreat in Helsinki to Viborg, then near the Finnish border and not far from Petrograd, the better to press his campaign. In early October he wrote an article significantly entitled "Will the Bolsheviks Retain State Power?" and a stinging letter (October 12) to the Central Committee, threatening to resign and take his case directly to the rank and file of the party. Shaken, the committee on October 16 agreed that Lenin should come to Petrograd in disguise to participate in the resolution of the question of revolution. This he did, first moving secretly to the apartment of an obscure Bolshevik in an industrial section of Petrograd, and continuing all the while his barrage of written exhortations. The crucial meeting of the Central Committee was held on the night of October 23 in the apartment of the Menshevik Sukhanov, whose Bolshevik wife had arranged this unsurpassed act of political cuckoldry. After intense debate Lenin reasserted his authority over the party; by a vote of 10 to 2 (Kamenev and Zinoviev) it was resolved that the existing situation "places the armed uprising on the order of the day."

Lenin pressed forward in the next meeting of the Committee, on October 29, with the participation of a few representatives of the party military organization, the Petrograd city committee, and similar bodies. Sverdlov delivered a vital intelligence briefing on behalf of the Secretariat, which had gathered reports from the main districts of the capital that indicated the time was ripe for revolution. Similar briefings indicated that the Bolsheviks could take over the vital factories, military units, and communications centers. The decision to seize power was therefore reaffirmed, and although a precise date was not set, the meeting voted against Zinoviev's resolution to await the convocation of the All-Russian Congress on November 7. The immediate sequel of the meeting was a violent break between Lenin and his chief opponents within the party, Kamenev and Zinoviev. They had previously at-

---

* In theory Trotsky stood between the positions of Lenin and Kamenev-Zinoviev on the early seizure of power, but wanted to wait just a little while until the scheduled opening of the Second All-Russian Congress of Soviets. He was sure the Bolsheviks could win control of this body, thus considerably enhancing their claim to legitimacy. In practice this turned out to be a valid prophecy. Although Lenin at first argued against even this modest delay, he subsequently was quite satisfied with the actual resolution of the situation according to Trotsky's prediction.

tempted to persuade the rank and file of the party to their views in a letter that leaked out to a non-Bolshevik newspaper edited by Gorky, who was now at odds with Lenin. Lenin was infuriated at what he considered betrayal and demanded the expulsion of the sinners from the party. On November 2 the Central Committee, meeting without Lenin, compromised the issue by accepting Kamenev's resignation from the Committee and prohibiting further opposition.

The party and the Soviet were now primed for revolution. The exact timing of the uprising was dictated by Kerensky, who began a rather feeble effort to suppress the Bolsheviks on the morning of November 6. Trotsky, as chairman of the Military Revolutionary Committee, counterattacked by ordering military units to occupy the strategic centers, while the party press called for the overthrow of the Provisional Government. In the evening Lenin, still in disguise, arrived at the Smolny Institute, a former girls' school that now served as the headquarters of the Petrograd Soviet. That Lenin should come here, rather than to Bolshevik Party headquarters, to await the outcome of the issue is itself symbolic of his acceptance of Trotsky's insistence that the Bolsheviks must take power in the name of the Soviet, not openly on their own behalf. By the morning of November 7 (October 25 Old Style; hence "October Revolution") most of the city was in Soviet-Bolshevik hands and the Military Revolutionary Committee of the Soviet proclaimed the transfer of power to itself. Only two objectives remained by the night of November 7: the Winter Palace with its government garrison and the Second All-Russian Congress of Soviets, which convened at 10:45 p.m. Both fell quite easily, the Palace to Soviet military units, backed by a cruiser in the nearby Neva River, and the Congress to Trotsky's adept manipulation. Lenin had feared that the Bolsheviks could not hold a majority in this body, which would be a blow to his desire to establish a one-party regime. His fears at first seemed justified: of 650 delegates about 300 were Bolsheviks, and a working majority could be obtained only with the support of some 80 Left Socialist Revolutionaries. At first it seemed that this would lead to the establishment of a coalition government of all-socialist parties, but Trotsky outmaneuvered the non-Bolsheviks. (Lenin did not appear at the meeting.) The Mensheviks and most of the Socialist Revolutionaries refused to sanction the "conspiratorial" actions of the Bolshevik *coup,* but the Bolsheviks, aided by the Left Socialist Revolutionaries, defeated this move. Those who had supported the resolution walked out. This protest was doubly futile, for the city was in the hands of forces loyal to the Bolsheviks and the All-Russian Congress of Soviets was now in the hands of an overwhelming Bolshevik majority which has never relinquished its cunningly contrived advantage.

The October Revolution conformed to Lenin's conception of proletarian revolution. Unlike the March Revolution (or the mass upheavals of May and July), it was not a spontaneous upsurge of the proletariat but a *coup d'état* in which the "vanguard of the proletariat" had organized and directed elements of the lower classes. The party of Lenin's design had shown little ability to topple the tsarist government under normal conditions, and it is highly unlikely that it could have done better in a parliamentary democratic system. But in the crucible of revolution the party had proven its strength.

4

FAILURE IN TRIUMPH

Trotsky, in one of his most quoted anecdotes, recounts one of Lenin's first comments on the Bolshevik *coup:* "You know, from persecution and a life underground to come so suddenly to power . . . it makes one dizzy." Lenin, the *intelligent* who had spent most of his adult life in frustrating and often impecunious exile, now found himself the political leader of Russia. And the Bolshevik Party, whose previous experience involved only subversive activity, had to prove that it could exert authority and leadership over a sprawling empire of over 150 million.

For Lenin personally the transition to great eminence and responsibility was accomplished with remarkable ease, as if it were the most natural thing in the world. That lofty, almost unconscious self-confidence that he had displayed as an emigrant journalist and factional leader did not desert him in the period of great trial following the November Revolution (in contrast to some of his adversaries, and particularly Chernov, the leader of the Socialist Revolutionaries). In the words of I. N. Steinberg, a non-Bolshevik who saw a good deal of Lenin in the months immediately following his seizure of power, he "was usually simple, unaffected, an embodiment of poise and confidence." Even the two attempts on his life, one of which wounded him seriously, he seemed to take in stride as natural or even commonplace developments, although the assailant in one case (possibly in both) was a revolutionary socialist. Now famous, he continued to seem quite lacking in personal vanity, and he appeared to avoid encouraging the cultivation of a heroic myth. He politely reproached groups that sent him gifts and succeeded fairly well in preventing the party from deifying him; a proposed Lenin museum was rejected. The apparent genuineness of this modesty eventually was used by Lenin's heirs to reenforce the image of the almighty hero, and even in his lifetime—despite his efforts—the beginnings of a cult were apparent. Support for this tendency came from some of the party leaders, who made an occasion of his birthday in 1920 (but a modest one—the speeches in his honor were not carried in *Pravda*), and from local groups—although with how much inspiration from above it is hard to say. In November, 1922, for example, "the workers" of the Petrograd textile trust sent him a rug with a greeting that anticipated the era of Stalin: "Petrotextil wants you, our dear one, to feel not only a physical warmth from our modest present, but also the warmth of our workers' hearts in which we would envelop you. . . ."

Yet Lenin's way of life changed very little. He lived for four months in a room at Smolny, the headquarters of the Soviet government in Petrograd, and after a brief stay in a modest Moscow hotel made his home (with Krupskaia and his sister Mary) in a four-room apartment in the Kremlin. Except for brief holidays spent in the vicinity of Moscow, two official visits to Petrograd, and withdrawal to a nearby country house during his final illness, Lenin did not leave Moscow during his last six years. Unlike his imperial predecessors or his Communist heirs, he never maintained a country estate, much less a winter retreat in the Crimea. There were a few amenities, however, such as a Rolls Royce with chauffeur and meals served on plates bearing the two-headed eagle of the Romanovs, meticulously placed by a servant of the former tenants so that the eagle was opposite the diner. And Lenin took advantage of his lofty position to indulge himself in one luxury —a personal library of about ten thousand volumes. Despite his library, the pressure of work after the Revolution caused a decline in his scholarly activities. He did not undertake any book-length studies comparable to his major works before the Revolution, and he sent his *State and Revolution* to press unfinished. His journalistic activity, however, continued at a high pitch until his health gave way in 1922, and the production of these years—mostly written in his own hand—include several substantial brochures. Indeed, no other head of state in the century has been so active a working journalist and pamphleteer while in office.

By the beginning of the Civil War, many Communists both Trotsky and Stalin among them—affected semimilitary dress, including boots, military cap, and tunic without insignia (the tunic remained an unofficial party uniform until Stalin's death). But Lenin seems not to have sought such external symbols of revolutionary authority and persisted in dressing like a late nineteenth century *intelligent*, which is to say, like a somewhat rumpled bourgeois professor—black sack suit, vest, white collar, and black cravat. The proletariat was represented, as before the Revolution, only in his cloth cap. According to his secretary, he wore the same black overcoat from his return to Russia in 1917 until his death, even though the garment was somewhat the worse for bullet holes after the assassination attempt of August, 1918. His schoolmaster tendencies carried over in his leadership of the Council of People's Commissars: smoking was forbidden during meetings of the Council, and Lenin personally shushed his more talkative disciples.

Lenin in power does not seem to bear out Lord Acton's dictum that power corrupts and absolute power corrupts absolutely. He certainly proved himself capable of severity and ruthlessness in what he conceived to be the interests of his cause, but neither his use of the prison and firing squad nor his generally authoritarian regime should be attributed to intoxication with new-found power. Rather they are the practical application of his long-standing belief that the class enemy must be crushed without compunction, that all who oppose his party are class enemies, and that the workers require firm guidance and even coercion in their own interests. Yet Lenin did not reveal any sadistic lust for blood in his enforcement of stern dictatorship. His genuine horror upon learning of the murder of two arrested liberal ex-ministers was witnessed by his critic Steinberg, who brought him the news, and in most cases Lenin permitted his socialist rivals to emigrate or to remain in peace if they did not work actively against the Bolsheviks.* Within the party he relied entirely on nonviolent measures, even though the vigor of his opponents sometimes induced him to use harsh invective, threatened or actual expulsion from the party, or the threat of his own resignation. But all this was in keeping with his authoritarian method of leading the party in earlier years, and in general he seems to have used his great prestige to avoid recourse to force within the party, rather than as a tool to establish a reign of terror among Bolsheviks, as Stalin did later.

For Lenin and his party the first few months of power posed a severe test and probably form the most perilous period in the history of the Bolsheviks. Until November 7, 1917, they had been a party of subversive opposition with little to lose but their newspapers. After they passed the crisis of November, 1917, to March, 1918, they were the established regime with at least some kind of proven stability, however sorely their enemies beset them. But for the first five months it was uncertain that the new Soviet government would survive, and still less certain that the Bolsheviks and Lenin would survive at its helm. Lenin's successful transition of this difficult time constitutes the masterpiece of political maneuver in his career, an especially difficult achievement because his party was badly split during these months, depriving him of any substantial, dependable majority within the party leadership.

The basic problem was to achieve a minimum of public acceptance

---

* Lenin's complicity in the murder of the tsar, his entire family, and their small company is more complex and still unclear. It is not impossible that he really did approve in advance the massacre of July 16, 1918, but it is more likely that he favored the continued detention of the ex-monarch pending some sort of (class) war crimes trial, which would probably have resulted in death sentences for the tsar and tsarina. Lenin certainly showed little solicitude for this helpless family by leaving them in the hands of remote subordinates who were empowered to take any measures to avoid the capture of the family by anti-Bolshevik troops, but the actual massacre probably was not his intention, even though he never disavowed it after the event.

for Bolshevik rule through the Soviets. The *coup* of November 7 had taken power in the name of the Military Revolutionary Committee of the Petrograd Soviet, an act that certainly had the support of most of the populace and garrison of the capital and reflected a preference in most parts of the country for the rule of the Soviets instead of the Provisional Government. But most of the supporters of the *coup*, including some of Lenin's own lieutenants, conceived of the new revolutionary regime not as a purely Bolshevik affair, but as a coalition of the three main socialist parties—Socialist Revolutionary, Bolshevik, and Menshevik. Moreover, the Bolsheviks had made much of the need to convene the long-awaited Constituent Assembly, which was widely anticipated as the most democratic and only legitimate source of a new order. Even Lenin recognized in his decree on land that so basic an issue as the agrarian question could be settled finally only by the Constituent Assembly. Yet it was almost certain that the Bolsheviks alone would lack a majority in this body and that it would not provide a constitution acceptable to Lenin. Finally, there was the possibility that the Germans would advance with little resistance from the demoralized Russian army and put an end to the Revolution from without.* Thus the fledgling Bolshevik regime had to make itself acceptable to a large part of the populace if it was to retain exclusive control of the instruments of power.

Lenin met this challenge boldly, quickly improvising a program designed to win popular support at any cost. On the evening of November 8, less than twenty-four hours after the fall of the Winter Palace, Lenin appeared at the second meeting of the Second All-Russian Congress of Soviets, there to issue two decrees, the first on peace, the second on land. The chief Bolshevik slogan at the time, carried in a banner headline by *Pravda* on the day of the *coup* was "Peace —Land—Bread." The popularity of the slogan was undeniable, and Lenin realized that to create a public impression that the Bolshevik-Soviet government would fulfill this pledge was the supremely important objective of the moment, more important than past party policy or the actual application of the slogan in future years. Thus the Decree on Peace, a document of only a few hundred words, ten times repeated the key words "immediate" or "immediately" in calling for a "democratic peace" "without annexations." For the moment it mattered not that this might involve Lenin, contrary to his earlier affirmations, in making a separate and disadvantageous peace with the Central Powers. What was essential was to foster a popular association of the Bolshevik regime with the magic of "immediate peace," and in this he evi-

---

* It is now known that the Germans actually did not consider more than modest penetration of Great Russia itself, but it was impossible for the Bolsheviks or other Russians to be sure of this at the time.

dently succeeded to a marked degree. The Congress of Soviets, which was by no means a Bolshevik claque at this date, accepted the decree unanimously (or at least overwhelming popular disapproval squelched any who would dissent), and the vote was followed by a genuinely spontaneous outburst. According to the witness Sukhanov: "Long-drawn-out ovations alternated with singing the *Internationale*. Then Lenin was hailed again, hurrahs were shouted, caps flung into the air."

The same attempt to make an immediate impression marked Lenin's Decree on Land. Although the other socialist parties had advocated the confiscation of landowners' estates and private property, they had failed to implement this principle in 1917. Lenin's decree began: "Landed proprietorship is abolished immediately without compensation." To gain popular acceptance, Lenin not only made this immediate decision, but also sacrificed his long-term agrarian program. Until a few weeks before the November Revolution, Lenin had advocated the "nationalization" of all the land by the state. Now, however, he omitted any mention of nationalization, instead guaranteeing that the land of ordinary peasants and Cossacks would not be confiscated. More than that, he openly took over the whole of the current Socialist Revolutionary plan for the equal distribution of land by strictly local peasant organs. Lenin never believed in the long-term merits of this socialized version of a small-holder's paradise, and it fell to his successor to go the full measure in rescinding the promise to the peasants embodied in the decree of November 8, 1917. But for the moment Lenin was interested only in achieving the kind of popular impression that Sukhanov witnessed at the Congress of Soviets, which included many delegates of peasant origin: "Again the massed crowd applauded, jumped to their feet and threw their caps in the air. They firmly believed that they had now got the land that their fathers and grandfathers had yearned for."

The same tactical expedient underlay the "Declaration of Rights of the Peoples of Russia" (November 15) and the decree introducing "workers' control" of factories (November 27). The former guaranteed the right of all nationalities of the former Empire to secede, although Lenin certainly did not wish to encourage the disintegration of the multinational state, and the latter placed the management of industry in the hands of local bodies of workers, a scheme which was basically incompatible with Lenin's long-term desire for a centrally planned economy. But he rightly felt that his position was so insecure in November, 1917, that he must concede enough to popular demand to gain at least the acceptance, if not the active support, of the majority of the populace. Although the party had to spend the next fifteen years or more in revoking some of these concessions, Lenin was astute in recognizing that this price must be paid, and in a way it was not a high price, for the peasants were already taking land for themselves, the nationalities breaking loose from Russian control, and the workers taking over the factories. Since the Bolsheviks were as yet powerless to prevent these trends, they could at least turn them to their advantage by feigning support for what was popular, at the same time creating the impression that they were the one party that took the initiative.

It is indicative of Lenin's instinct for leadership that he proposed the decrees on peace and land to the Congress of Soviets before his position as head of the new government had been formally established. The last item on the agenda of the night of November 8 was the establishment of a "Council of People's Commissars," a title Trotsky devised to avoid using such bourgeois names as "cabinet" or "minister." The new body represented the Bolshevik capture of the soviets, for all of the commissars were Bolsheviks and Lenin was the chairman (premier, in bourgeois terms).

Although the establishment of one-party rule went off easily enough in the glow of enthusiasm following the decrees on peace and land (and the withdrawal of the Mensheviks and Right Socialist Revolutionaries the day before, of course), Lenin was still faced with the problem of avoiding a broad, genuine coalition of socialist parties. The drive toward coalition came not so much from the rival parties as from within the Bolshevik ranks and from the insistent leaders of the Union of Railroad Workers, who controlled the strategic arteries of the country. A notable group of Bolshevik leaders, including Kamenev, Zinoviev, Rykov and Lunacharsky, did not believe that the Bolsheviks could gain enough mass support to survive alone, and in the first month after the Revolution they almost succeeded in imposing a coalition on Lenin, or even in removing him from the new government. This latter, drastic step was a condition that the Right Socialist Revolutionaries and Mensheviks set for their entry into a coalition, and it is indicative of the precarious state of Lenin's personal leadership in the party at this time that almost half the Central Committee was willing to accept it. In the course of the heated conflict within the Bolshevik Central Committee in November, the advocates of coalition tried to enforce their views with both private and public declarations and by resigning their posts in the party and in the Council of People's Commissars. Lenin retaliated with invective (his opponents had "flinched in the face of the onslaught of the bourgeoisie . . ."; they had "acted like deserters"), with attempts to expel some from the party, and even with threats—perhaps unique in his career—of physical violence to his Bolshevik opponents ("If you want a split, go ahead . . . but we will go to the sailors"—that is, to the most violent, left-wing, armed group available). He managed to retain control of the party apparatus by a narrow margin and won back the heretics by a combination of bullying and compromise. The compromise was the acceptance of three Left Socialist Revolutionaries into the Council of People's Commissars, a step consummated on December 23, 1917. Although it silenced the most dangerous proponents of coalition, the railroad unionists in particular, this arrangement could hardly threaten Lenin's one-party rule, for the Bolsheviks retained an overwhelming majority in the Council.

Scarcely had this threat to Lenin's position subsided when another appeared: the meeting of the long-awaited Constituent Assembly in January, 1918. In view of the popular expectations for the Assembly, and because the Bolsheviks themselves had called for it to embarrass the Provisional Government, Lenin had permitted the elections to go off as planned on November 25–27. The result was ostensibly a major victory for the Socialist Revolutionaries, who polled 15.8 million votes out of 41.6 million cast, a plurality that gave them an absolute majority of delegates to the Assembly, 370 out of 707 in all. Lenin cared nothing for the principle of majority rule and was perfectly willing to disperse the Assembly by force, but he knew that others in the country respected this body and hoped that he might utilize this prestige by maneuvering some sort of majority vote for a "Declaration of the Rights of Toiling and Exploited Peoples." This document recognized the Soviets as the government of the land and confirmed the soviet decrees already in force. To pass it would be to abandon the Constituent Assembly, an unacceptable action to many delegates, but not so impossible an outcome at a time when discipline was lax in most parties and the Bolsheviks had been gaining support from Menshevik and Socialist Revolutionary defectors.

In fact, however, the Socialist Revolutionary majority, supported by other factions, held firm on January 18 when the Assembly was permitted to convene in Petrograd. Lenin's Declaration failed, and he was obliged to fall back on an alternative tactic: armed force. Early in the morning of the 19th a detachment of sailors insisted on adjournment for some rest, and armed force prevented the resumption of the session later in the day. The one body that could surpass the Congress of Soviets in democratic prestige had been shoved into oblivion. Lenin's easy success in this *coup* of January, 1918, silenced various advocates of more caution among the Bolsheviks just as effectively as the coup of November, 1917, had silenced similar dissenters.

Lenin signaled his victory by convening the Third All-Russian Congress of Soviets on January 23. With a safe majority of Bolsheviks and Left Socialist Revolutionaries the Declaration that the Assembly had rejected was passed, becoming a fundamental document of the new regime.

The climactic challenge of this precarious, formative period of Bolshevik power was the problem of ending the war with Germany. In this Lenin faced not only rival political parties and numerous dissident Bolsheviks, but also a formidable military machine that—had it wished to—might well have marched to Moscow in 1918. Up to the time he seized power, Lenin had specifically denied that he proposed to make a separate peace, for he realized that the irrational masses, despite their vigorous desire to end the war, were still too patriotic for a peace-at-any-price policy. In his "Decree on Peace" of November 8 he shrewdly refrained from specifically ruling out the possibility of a separate peace with the Central Powers, setting as his goal the negotiation of a "democratic" and general peace. Should this fail, said Lenin in reply to a questioner at the Congress of Soviets, he might consider carrying on a "revolutionary war" under some conditions but might find this impossible under other circumstances. It was thus possible for Lenin to maintain this equivocal position, which placated most of the populace and party members, until negotiations with the Central Powers were actually in progress. Following the signing of an armistice on December 2, the Soviet Government and Central Powers on December 22 opened negotiations in the German-occupied city of Brest-Litovsk, and the adamant position of the German negotiators soon brought Lenin up against the problem he had been evading: to make peace it would be necessary to accept German terms that would deprive Russia of a good part of her western borderlands. This not only would weaken the Russian state but also might arouse a popular uprising at home. On the other hand, it was quite doubtful that the Soviet government had any means of self-defense. The possibility of commanding substantial armed support and reforming the demoralized army in case of a German offensive was highly problematical—as were the intentions of the Germans, who still possessed the most powerful single army in the world. Trotsky, who was Lenin's Commissar of Foreign Affairs and served as chief negotiator at a number of the meetings at Brest-Litovsk, tried to evade the decision; after the Germans had proven intransigent he proposed the formula "no war, no peace," which aimed at ending hostilities on the basis of the *status quo* without signing a treaty. But Lenin, after studying a secret survey of opinion in the army as of late December, 1917, concluded that the soldiers would not fight. This left no alternative to peace on the German terms, however grave the risks that such a settlement might incur at home.

Thus on January 21 he began a campaign in the Central Committee to commit the party to a separate peace at any price. As on the eve of the November Revolution, Lenin found himself unable to enforce a vital decision upon the party he had established. At first his peace policy gained only fifteen votes out of sixty (in a meeting of the Central

Committee and other party leaders on January 21). He was opposed by one group led by Trotsky, supporting the "no war, no peace" formula, and another led by Bukharin, who insisted on carrying on a "revolutionary war," however suicidal, rather than compromise revolution through a deal with the class enemy. So incensed were they at Lenin's tactical expediency that both Bukharin and F. E. Dzerzhinsky (the head of the new Cheka or political police) considered his removal as leader, as did the Left Socialist Revolutionaries, who were still in alliance with the Bolsheviks. But none of the Bolsheviks who opposed Lenin could bring themselves to act decisively against him, and he remained the acknowledged leader even though he represented the minority on the most pressing issue of the day. Lenin had always insisted on the submission of the minority to the majority—except when he himself was part of the minority, and his opponents permitted him to get away with this. On February 18, Trotsky—perhaps swayed less by Lenin's arguments than by a renewed German offensive—gave in, and the Central Committee agreed to sue for peace on German terms. These turned out to be harsher than ever, and to persuade the committee to accept them Lenin had recourse to his ultimate, and highly undisciplined weapon—the threat to resign. Even so, he carried his point with only minority support: he could muster only seven votes for peace on German terms, while four opposed and four others, led by the still-evasive Trotsky, abstained.

Although he still represented a minority opinion in his own Central Committee, the directorate of a party that was itself a minority in the country at large, Lenin was quite willing to take responsibility for a peace that cost Russia about one-quarter of her prewar population and sown land and three-quarters of her coal and iron production. His self-confidence was such that the lack of a clear mandate from the party or the country did not deter him. And his judgment was vindicated politically if not legally. His opponents in the party fumed furiously for a few weeks, even publishing opposition newspapers in Petrograd and Moscow. But by the Seventh Party Congress on March 6–8, 1918, the force of Lenin's personality and logic had overwhelmed the opposition, and the peace was ratified by 30–12, with four abstentions. This victory was repeated on a larger scale at the Fourth All-Russian Congress of Soviets in the middle of the month. Despite Lenin's earlier fears, the masses—as the Socialist Revolutionaries soon discovered to their sorrow—accepted the peace. The Left Socialist Revolutionaries withdrew in protest from the coalition with the Bolsheviks, and in the summer attempted a campaign of violence against the peace, including the assassination of the German ambassador in Moscow and an attempt to seize that and several other cities. But the public did not respond and Lenin's security forces quite easily suppressed his recent allies.

By about April, 1918, the country was sinking economically, shorn of some of its most valuable regions and on the verge of civil war, for the right-wing anti-Bolsheviks were starting to organize for battle. But Lenin had successfully gained mass acquiescence to the rule of his party alone and had preserved his leadership and the unity of the party despite the most bitter internecine conflict. It was the crucial and most brilliant performance of his career.

From about June, 1918, through September, 1920, the fitful combustion of the Civil War preoccupied Lenin and cast him in a new role, that of national war-leader. During this period the Bolshevik-Soviet regime was beset from the four quarters of the compass, the most threatening anti-Bolshevik thrusts coming from Siberia in the summer of 1918 and again in the spring of 1919, from the Black and Baltic Seas in the fall of 1919, and from Poland in the summer of 1920. From these grave moments Lenin and his party emerged with a wider and more secure grip on the country than they had possessed before the Civil War, and in this sense Lenin was an obvious success in his new role. But he was really somewhat miscast, and it may be that his greatest military feat lay in permitting Trotsky to take the lead in the actual organization and direction of the armed forces. This Trotsky did brilliantly as Commissar of the new Red Army and Chairman of the Revolutionary Military Soviet, the special council of party leaders formed to direct the war effort. As in the preparation and execution of the *coup* of November, 1917, Lenin demonstrated his willingness to share glory and responsibility with this sometime foe. While Lenin remained in Moscow throughout the war, not even distinguishing himself as an inspirational wartime orator, Trotsky rushed from emergency to emergency in a special armored train, a typically dramatic vehicle that served at once as mobile supreme headquarters, propaganda center, and reserve combat force. On the question of how to organize a revolutionary proletarian army, Lenin yielded to Trotsky's judgment and accepted the principle of a conventionally organized, disciplined force, dependent for its tactical leadership on former tsarist officers. Lenin was astonished to learn in March, 1919, how many of these officers there were in the Red Army (an indication of Lenin's lack of contact with military affairs), but he supported his colleague and prevented the debates on this matter from splitting the party. Since the Central Committee of the Party retained ultimate authority on war policy, Lenin did play some role in forming military strategy, but he showed little talent in this field. Against Trotsky's wishes, he proposed to evacuate Petrograd before an enemy advance (Trotsky dissuaded him and the offensive failed); he supported an injudicious offensive along the Volga, which had to be withdrawn to save Moscow; and he chose to send the Red Army (despite its exhaustion) into Poland in an attempt to extend the revolution. This proved to be a costly failure because the Poles regarded the Red Army as Russian invaders and not—as Lenin had hoped—as revolutionary saviors.

Nevertheless Lenin played an essential part in the survival of the Bolshevik regime in the Civil War. No other leader had the prestige to hold the party together, and his will power was especially needed to enforce the severe and unpopular economic measures that were considered essential at the time. With characteristic boldness, Lenin enforced "War Communism," a makeshift series of decrees designed to squeeze the necessary food and industrial supplies out of the declining economy of Russia. Although he had long been an advocate of conciliatory relations with the peasantry (more so than most Russian Marxists) and had promised the peasants virtually free use of the land in his Decree of November 8, 1917, Lenin now risked alienating this majority sector of the Russian populace by enforcing a policy of compulsory food collections, which began in the summer of 1918. By the end of the war Lenin himself admitted that this policy had alienated the "overwhelming majority" of the peasants, but the cities and the Red Army had not starved and Lenin still had power. Such ruthless steps were not applied to the industrial proletariat, but the autonomy of the workers in running factories, promised in November, 1917, was sharply reduced, and a large part of the industrial economy was nationalized and directed in quite a disorderly and sometimes dictatorial way by a number of overlapping party and soviet organs.

As a "planned economy" war communism was a fiasco. Russian industrial production was almost liquidated by the end of 1920 and the allegiance of the proletariat was gravely weakened. But enough production had been squeezed out to win the war. As the external pressure relaxed in 1920, Lenin could reassign top priority to the proper organization of the "dictatorship of the proletariat."

Inside Soviet Russia this meant the transformation of the Bolshevik party from a revolutionary task force to an administrative apparatus, which required Lenin, who had previously been mainly a revolutionary theoretician and tactician, to devote his major energies to public administration. In this comparatively new field of endeavor Lenin acquitted himself brilliantly. Despite a number of false starts and the kind of bungling that accompanies the preliminary functioning of any huge administrative machine, the political institutions that emerged in Lenin's last active years have endured—in their main lines—to the present time and (most important to a Bolshevik) they have preserved tremendous power in the hands of the party and its leadership. Of course, the machine was not entirely Lenin's creation, and most of the economic planning apparatus was developed after his death, but he was the primary architect of the new edifice and personally decided a wide variety of questions, from the structure of the Soviet federation to the elevator service in the Kremlin. In all this he was well served by his talent for efficient, systematic work. His secretary recounts the severe but functional order with which he regulated committee meetings—allotting each speaker one five-minute and one three-minute opportunity—and his unflagging energy—she also recounts an unexceptional working day in which he presided at four major committee meetings, averaging about two hours each; read, wrote, or signed about forty documents; and had four formal interviews with visitors.

Before this regimen succeeded in undermining Lenin's health in 1922, the main lines of the Bolshevik-Soviet political system had been established. The party congress, inherited from the turn of the century, was retained as the highest expression, in theory, of the general will of the proletariat. It did meet annually in the postrevolutionary years of Lenin's life, but its size (687 delegates attended the Congress of 1922) and the authoritarian leadership of the party limited the practical competence of the body. The Central Committee continued to serve as a more active deliberative body and was often the scene of real debate, but it was too large (and probably too unruly from Lenin's point of view) to deal with the flow of current policy decisions and their execution. Thus in 1919 the Eighth Party Congress accepted Lenin's plan to establish three supplementary organs which were supposed to assist the Central Committee but soon came to be the chief centers of power. These were the Political Bureau (Politburo)* to make pressing political decisions, an Organizational Bureau (Orgburo) to allocate the personnel resources of the party, and a Secretariat to look after the administrative work of the Central Committee. Although there was no chairman among the five men who formed the initial Politburo, Lenin was the recognized leader in this body. Stalin, who was a member of the Politburo, became head of the Orgburo in April, 1920. The direction of the Secretariat was finally settled in April, 1922, when Lenin created the post of "general secretary," and awarded it to the ubiquitous Stalin. Under the Central Committee and its three main organs, a complex and swelling bureaucratic apparatus developed, greatly increasing the ability of the leadership to observe and direct the local activities of the party. Possibly the most crucial development in 1920–1922 occurred in the subdivisions of the Orgburo and Secretariat that dealt with the records and assignment of party members. The assignment of party personnel could no longer be handled informally, and if Lenin could not personally organize the record and assignment sys-

---

* The same name had been applied to a stillborn committee in 1917.

tem, especially its new card files on party members, he undoubtedly appreciated its importance. He also appreciated that the new system could assist his old ideal of party unity by keeping systematic account of the behavior of all Bolsheviks and by ensuring, as far as possible, that they enjoyed a degree of authority proportionate to their loyalty to him.

The transformation of the party on the lower levels was still more drastic. The membership of the party at the higher levels was composed mainly of experienced Bolsheviks or converts from other branches of socialism, but it was necessary for even an elitist party to broaden its membership in order to maintain itself in power. By March, 1921, the Bolshevik party membership reached almost 732,521, roughly a sixfold increase in three years and a 28-fold increase since March, 1917. Lenin recognized both the necessity and the pitfalls of quantitative growth in party membership; "We fear an excessive broadening of our party," he said in 1920, "for into a ruling party inevitably stream careerists and rogues who endeavor to latch on, and only deserve to be shot." Although Lenin did not have recourse to such violent measures, he did remain faithful to the Bolshevik tradition and doctrine that he had established: the concept of the elite vanguard. During the Civil War the party was first permitted to grow rapidly, then was drastically reduced by a reregistration of all members in mid-1919, then was deliberately increased again by an intensive recruiting drive during the autumn. A steady influx of members, spurred by idealism or opportunism, continued until the Tenth Party Congress of March, 1921, warned that "petty bourgeois elements" had entered the party and called for "a purging of the party of the non-Communist elements." Three months later the first purge of the Russian Communist Party began, and in the latter half of 1921 about one-fifth of the party membership was dismissed and recruitment was pretty well frozen. Only by 1923 did the membership of the party become temporarily stabilized at about half a million. Although willing enough to resort to the purge, Lenin hoped that selective recruitment would obviate this necessity, and the party statutes established in 1919 required that all party members must pass through a novitiate as "candidate members," a rule that was really enforced only after the Civil War (with the stipulation in 1922 that the probationary period of proletarian and peasant candidates could be shorter than others).

Expanded membership, however selective, required more complex organization of the rank and file, if the Leninist ideals of unity and discipline were to be maintained. The successive party statutes of 1919 and 1922 reflected the elaboration of the party hierarchy: five levels of command, including the central institutions, and a standard administrative system at each level.* This scheme not only introduced a formal system of subordination within the party but also attempted to insure that the party would permeate all the basic institutions of the country with the Communist spirit. Each factory, peasant village, army unit, school, or government department, was to have its own party cell. And in every nonparty meeting (of trade unions, soviets, co-ops, and the like) at which there were as many as three party members, these were required to form a "fraction" to provide organized Communist leadership within the meeting. In this lay the distinctive character of the twentieth century totalitarian state. Such a development had not been specifically prophesied in Lenin's writings and it was not to reach its climax until Stalin's time, but it was the founder of the Bolshevik party who laid the practical foundations for its new role as an omnipresent, omnipotent master.

The transformation of the party also included an effort to reformulate its program. At the Eighth Party Congress in 1919, the program of 1903—largely the product of Plekhanov's efforts—was replaced with one drafted by Lenin and approved by the Congress. The new program reflected the rise of the Bolsheviks from persecution to dictatorship and discussed the needs of Russia during the "transition to communism." It defended the Soviet form of government, called for a planned economy, introduced measures for education and public welfare, castigated the imperialists, and predicted world revolution. But it lacked any coherent or striking conception of the transition from chaos to communism, and it did not become a major Leninist gospel even though it was not replaced by a new program until 1961.

Lenin was probably more interested in insuring party supremacy in the state rather than in determining the particular form of state apparatus, for he did not participate directly in the commissions that drafted the constitutions of the Russian Socialist Federative Soviet Republic (RSFSR) in 1918 and of the larger Union of Soviet Socialist

---

* Over the years the labels and details in the party structure have been modified, but the main lines have remained approximately as follows: (a) the central or all-union level, including the Party Congress and the Central Committee of the USSR; (b) the level of the union republic with its own Congress and Central Committee (this level is omitted in the Russian Republic, the All-Union Congress and Central Committee serving in its stead); (c) the subrepublican level, usually designated as *oblast'*, which has a periodical conference and a standing committee; (d) the rural or urban subdivisions of the *oblast'* level, generally designated as *raion* and *gorod*, respectively, with a periodical conference and a standing committee; and (e) the "cell" or "primary party organization" in the factory, farm, school, military unit, and so on, headed by its "bureau." Each executive committee—from local bureau to Central Committee of the USSR—has its "secretary," who is in practice its responsible administrator.

Republics (USSR) in 1922–1924. After the October Revolution, however, he had no further doubts about the practicality of using the soviets as the principal medium through which the party would rule, and the new constitutions reflected the existing soviet institutions: the local soviets, the national Congress of Soviets, the Central Executive Committee of the Congress of Soviets, and the Council of People's Commissars. The main problem that the drafters faced was to make the constitutions acceptable to the diverse collection of nationalities controlled by the Communists. To assure such acceptance, Lenin cast aside his prerevolutionary rejection of federalism. Although he would not contemplate the federalization of his party, he was quite willing to drop his earlier, centralist objections to federalism for the state. He even insisted (over Stalin's objections) that there be a federation within a federation (the RSFSR within the USSR) to placate the national sensibilities of the larger non-Russian Soviet Republics.*

Another aspect of Bolshevik power was not reflected in the constitutional order. This was the growth of the police apparatus, which was nominally subject to the Council of People's Commissars, but actually was a coercive instrument in the hands of the party. Its first version, established on December 20, 1917, was called the Cheka (the contraction of the Russian for "Extraordinary Commission for Combating Counterrevolution and Sabotage"). Under the leadership of Felix Dzerzhinsky, a Pole by birth, it soon became adept at the techniques of the modern police state and showed its potentiality by establishing the first forced labor camps of the new regime and by executing 500 hostages in reprisal for the assassination of its Petrograd chief in 1918. In February, 1922, to symbolize the end of the civil war, Cheka was abolished —but its successor, the GPU (State Political Administration), was immediately organized under the Commissariat of Internal Affairs.

By 1921 Lenin had made considerable progress in imposing his new order on Russia, but not without provoking the last of his numerous intraparty quarrels and the first and only armed rebellion by a group close to the party—the sailors of the Baltic Fleet. At all times there were Bolsheviks who shared Lenin's zealous faith in the utopian goals of revolution but did not accept his concept of practical expediency in matters of organization and tactics. Some of those who objected to the development of authoritarian, bureaucratic rule within the party formed the "Group of Democratic Centralists" in 1919. Others who felt that the trade unions should be permitted to control industry and that the Communist leaders of the unions should be somewhat inde-

---

* In 1922 Stalin wished to incorporate the Belorussian, Ukrainian and Caucasian "independent" Soviet Republics directly into the existing Russian Federative Republic. Lenin successfully insisted that a new "Union Republic" be established to encompass the Russian Federative Republic *and* the others.

pendent of the central party leadership formed the "Workers' Opposition" in 1920. Neither group challenged the principle of Bolshevik rule in Russia, but both felt that the party could and should permit a degree of internal pluralism. In the latter months of 1920 and the winter of 1921 it appeared that Bolshevism and its founder might permit the development of an internal multiparty system; this tendency reached a high point in December, 1920, when the question of trade union autonomy was freely debated at a special convention of Bolsheviks in Moscow. Those who attended were not only free to express their opinions but were also invited to submit alternative programs. The monolithic unity of the party was doubly assailed: by the substance of the various demands for greater internal democratization and by the liberal procedure used to consider the demands.

Such a development was hardly Lenin's intention, and in the first weeks of 1921 he opened an intensive counteroffensive. Although the opposition groups were not united and lacked any first-rank Bolshevik leader to counterbalance Lenin's towering personal prestige, the Workers' Opposition was strong in the Moscow party organization and probably had substantial support among the rank and file of union members, a strategically sensitive sector of the populace. Moreover, Lenin's lieutenants were not firmly grouped behind him. Trotsky proposed the most centralist of all programs—the introduction of military discipline for the labor force—while various others wished to conciliate the opposition.

The solution, unexpectedly decisive to most Bolsheviks, came at the Tenth Party Congress in March, 1921. This meeting coincided with a major revolt ("mutiny," according to Communist historians) among the sailors of the Kronstadt naval base in the Baltic, the only armed rebellion by a group close to the party. The Kronstadt revolt was not precisely an intraparty upheaval (only a minority of the sailors and their leaders were party members) and they demanded not only an end to the dictatorial aspects of Bolshevik rule but also the abolition of the one-party monopoly. Nevertheless, the revolt shared the democratic, antibureaucratic goals of the Bolshevik opposition (although the latter certainly did not favor the revolt); there were numerous party members among the insurgents; and in earlier years the sailors had been a dependable Bolshevik shock-force. In short, Lenin was faced by a considerable opposition within the party, unarmed but not without popular support, and a simultaneous armed opposition whose democratic, revolutionary appeals were potentially more dangerous than any of the programs of the former political parties or White generals.

Lenin tackled the Kronstadt revolutionaries first. After the failure of a conciliation mission on March 1, the Soviet government demanded the surrender of the sailors' Provisional Revolutionary Committee. This being rejected, military operations were started a week later, and the somewhat uncertain morale of the government troops was bolstered by infusions of Communist military cadets, Cheka forces, and delegates to the party congress. Fortunately for Lenin the insurgents had unwisely made their break while the winter ice still permitted infantry assault on the island fortress; otherwise the stronghold founded by Peter the Great might have held out for many months, infecting the popular masses on the mainland with their example. On March 18, after over a week of bitter fighting, the fortress fell and an unrevealed number of the revolutionaries were executed without public trial.

The Tenth Party Congress met from March 8–16, almost exactly coincidentally with the fighting around Kronstadt, and Lenin relied on the atmosphere of emergency to suppress the intraparty opposition and to affirm the principle that Bolshevik power was to continue and even enhance the tradition of monolithic unity. On March 9 he stated: "We do not need opposition now, comrades," and on the last day of the conference he introduced a major resolution "On the Unity of the Party," which has endured ever since as a major bulwark against pluralism. Foreshadowing Stalin and Khrushchev, the resolution included a secret clause that authorized the Central Committee to expel from the party any members considered guilty of indiscipline. Although such a stricture was certainly in keeping with the spirit of Leninism, it was not published until after Lenin's death for fear of alarming the more democratically minded party members. With the passage of this resolution and a related one "On the Syndicalist and Anarchist Deviation in Our Party" (i.e., the Workers' Opposition) Lenin eliminated the last intraparty opposition of his lifetime.

Lenin's postrevolutionary transformation of the Bolshevik Party involved not only its internal role in the Soviet Union but also its ambitions in the entire world. The old party had been a minute conspiratorial nucleus in Russia and a comparatively minor component of the Socialist Second International. After 1917 Lenin aimed at making the Bolsheviks the ruling party in Russia and the very backbone of a transformed international proletarian movement, a Communist International. His ambitions in this direction began with his revulsion at the failure of the Second International to take a firm stand against the "imperialist" World War. His April Theses of 1917 referred to "a new International." The Bolshevik Revolution intensified Lenin's sense of worldwide mission, for Russia could now serve as a bastion for the new International, while the European proletarian revolution could and must succeed in order to save Russia from her capitalist enemies—he thought.

His objective, however, was not easily attained. At first his colleagues were unenthusiastic, and world war and civil war drastically impeded communication with the West. But Lenin persevered. When Karl Kautsky—the German Social Democrat who as much as any individual represented the leadership of the old International—published a pamphlet in August, 1918, attacking the dictatorial methods of the Soviet state, Lenin not only defended them but also attempted to clear the way for his own leadership in European Marxism. In "The Proletarian Revolution and the Renegade Kautsky," one of his major postrevolutionary writings, Lenin sought to establish, first, that Kautsky was guilty of "civilized belly-crawling and boot-licking before the bourgeoisie," and, second, that the main lines of the Bolshevik version of proletarian revolution and proletarian dictatorship were universally applicable.

Shortly after Lenin published his diatribe against Kautsky in November, 1918, the next step—the creation of a Bolshevized International—seemed feasible. He thought he saw in defeated Germany the beginnings of the expected proletarian revolution. The German equivalent of Bolsheviks, the "German Communist Party," had been formed —without Russian dictation—on December 30, 1918. A few days later Lenin and a few others determined to call a congress in Moscow for the formation of a Third International, and on January 24, 1919, he issued an appeal for delegates from socialist parties that opposed the Second International. The timing and composition of the First Congress of the Third International, which met in March, 1919, revealed that Lenin meant to apply the same self-confident and high-handed methods of organization that he had used in Russia. Except on Soviet territory there were as yet no substantial Communist parties to provide some sort of representative base for the new International, and in any case Russia was under blockade by the Western governments. The German Communist Party had been temporarily crushed after a premature uprising in January, 1919, and its leaders, Karl Liebknecht and Rosa Luxemburg, were killed. Moreover, the one German delegate who managed to reach Moscow had been instructed to oppose the immediate formation of a new International. But Lenin was characteristically unwilling to let democratic considerations obstruct his cause. Rather than wait for the formation of a body of genuine delegates, he gathered up about fifty Russians and foreigners living in Russia and five actual delegates from abroad. He then had himself elected chairman and on March 4 pushed through a resolution establishing this gathering as the First Congress of the Communist International (Comintern). The future of the body, which as yet existed only in Russia, was entrusted to an executive committee located in Moscow and headed by Zinoviev.

At the First Congress of the Comintern Lenin staked the Bolshevik claim to worldwide proletarian leadership, but it remained to transform aspiration into reality. The international revolution, on which Lenin counted heavily, could hardly be accomplished by a handful of unrepresentative Communists in Moscow. Events demonstrated that he was mistaken in his faith in imminent revolution, but his confidence that real Communist movements would materialize in foreign countries proved justified in the course of 1919 and 1920. The Bolshevik record of opposition to the World War and the luster of the word "soviet" made communism highly attractive to many Western socialists. The opportunities for Bolshevik recruitment were great, but the difficulties were equally imposing. Above all Lenin had to face a problem that remains unsolved in the Communist world today: how to retain Russian control of international communism, and yet encourage really vigorous national Communist movements, which sometimes prove obstreperous? In the infancy of the Comintern Lenin had to face the problem of discipline on both the left and right wings of European socialism. Some of the most promising militants seemed inclined to rush into revolution without coordinating their actions with Moscow. In April, 1920, Lenin reproached these comrades in what was to be the last substantial pamphlet of his career, "The Infantile Disease of 'Leftism' in Communism." The burden of his reproach was that foreign Communists should pay close attention to the Russian model, including the "iron discipline" of the Bolsheviks and their tactical flexibility. If the Left needed to grow up, the Right needed to be split, said Lenin. Some of the largest groups, such as the German Independent Social Democratic Party, were composed of both potential Communists and "renegades."

To win over the former and expel the latter, Lenin drew up a list of conditions for membership in the Comintern which he proposed at its Second Congress (the first that was based on real representation of foreign parties) in August, 1920. This list of conditions, which numbered twenty-one by the end of the Congress, insisted that all "reformists" be expelled from parties joining the Comintern, that an underground organization and "democratic centralism" be established in all cases, that the decisions of the Comintern Congresses and Executive Committee be binding on all member parties, and that the member parties signify their rebirth by changing their names: "Every party which wishes to join the Communist International must be called: Communist party of such and such a country (section of the Communist International)."

This was enough to produce the desired split in the principal Western socialist parties, and by the end of the year an international corps of disciplined Communist parties was emerging. From an organizational point of view this was a great success for Lenin. But it remained to be seen whether or not the alien direction from Moscow, which was implicit in this international version of Bolshevik organization, would interfere with the vitality and success of the foreign Communist parties.

In terms of power—its acquisition, organization, and maintenance— Lenin's career had been a remarkable success. The pragmatic politician in Lenin had much reason for satisfaction in 1922, the last year of his active life. But what of the other Lenin, the self-sacrificing, idealistic visionary who accepted ruthless measures only because he thought them necessary to reach Marx's promised land of justice, equality, abundance, and statelessness? While his health remained vigorous, Lenin seems to have been well pleased with the progress of his movement. To be sure, he recognized that Soviet Russia was still a long way from the Marxist goal, owing to her comparative economic backwardness and the impact of world war, revolution, and civil war. The general collapse of production and distribution had obliged him in 1921 to permit a resurgence of private enterprise in the form of the New Economic Policy (NEP). Although the major industries, finance, and international trade ("the commanding heights") remained in Soviet hands, NEP permitted free trade in agriculture (after the peasant had paid his tax in kind), in small-scale industry, and in distribution. Although a number of the purists in the party—especially in the ranks of the muffled opposition—considered this an excessive compromise, Lenin was not discouraged. His pragmatic character saw NEP as a necessary, temporary concession, and his visionary self took comfort in dreams of a planned economy and especially in massive electrification. "Communism" (the ideal society), said Lenin, "is Soviet power plus the electrification of the whole country." If his enthusiasm for electrification probably exceeded rational technical considerations, it had sound doctrinal and psychological motivations. Various Menshevik and foreign Marxist writers argued that Lenin's revolution was doomed because it had been premature in terms of Russian economic development. This problem could be dispelled and the promised land brought nearer by the vision of an electrically transformed country. According to Lenin even the most retarded sector of the economy—agriculture— could be electrified in about a decade. One photograph shows him examining an experimental electric plough, a Tom Swiftian attempt to revolutionize the peasant's life which remains impractical forty years later. Lenin accorded more deference to the State Commission for the Electrification of Russia (Goelro), established in February, 1920, than to several rival planning agencies that were attempting, with rather little success, to move toward a planned socialist system.

In foreign affairs Lenin was obliged to recognize that the European proletarian revolution was not imminent. After the failure of revolutions in Germany and Hungary in 1919 and the collapse of the Red

Army's attempt to carry the revolution into Poland in 1920, Lenin moderated his expectations, and at the Third Comintern Congress of June, 1921, he supported the policy of a "united front." This policy, which might be considered the foreign policy counterpart of NEP, consisted of cooperation with the members of non-Communist socialist parties and trade unions and, in some instances, even with their "renegade" leaders. While the practical Lenin accepted the necessity of delay in Europe, the visionary self took hope in the revolutionary potentialities of the East. The idea that "the West is digging its grave in the East" quite took Lenin's fancy after the revolutionary fiascos in Europe and received concrete recognition in a "Congress of Peoples of the East" in Baku (September, 1920) and again in a "Congress of Toilers of the East" in Moscow (January, 1922). Although a potent international tactic in the long run, the Soviet effort to foster the Asian revolution stumbled badly in its early years, enjoying just about as much success as the electric plough.

In May, 1922, Lenin underwent surgery to remove one of the two bullets lodged in him by the assassination attempt of 1918. While recuperating, he was seized by the first of the paralytic strokes that were to end his life in January, 1924. For almost a year after the first stroke he had intermittent use of his faculties but was unable to carry his accustomed burden of administrative work. Perhaps it was the enforced leisure to observe and reflect that brought Lenin to adopt a new and severely critical view of his life's work. He had succeeded in taking and securing power for his party, but were the Bolsheviks really on the road to the Communist goal? In the closing period of his life Lenin seems to have experienced grave doubts on this matter, which neither the Party Program of 1919, nor the hopes for Goelro, nor the prospect of an Asian revolution could assuage.

The aging and infirm Lenin seems to have begun to see some validity in that view of human nature which Christian theology knows as original sin. Is it possible for Man, with his basic frailties, to reach earthly perfection? The visionary Lenin, like Marx, had followed the most optimistic writers of the eighteenth century Enlightenment in giving a strong affirmative answer to this question. In late 1922 Lenin, although far from experiencing any personal religious revival, became deeply troubled by the thought that the human frailties of the Bolshevik dictatorship might prevent the realization of his vision. His illness —especially a second stroke that partially paralyzed him on December 16, 1922—prevented him from giving full expression to his anguished doubts, but their substance can be gleaned from his meager writings of December, 1922 and early 1923. These consist of some secretly dictated memoranda, including two that are usually called his "Testament" and its postscript, and his last newspaper articles. His critique of Bolshevism contains the germ of the idea advanced later by the exiled and partly disillusioned Trotsky and the still more disillusioned Yugoslav Communist, Milovan Djilas: that Bolshevism succeeded not in destroying all ruling classes but rather in supplanting the tsarist or bourgeois governing apparatus with a new, Bolshevik bureaucracy. Lenin suggested to Trotsky in early December, 1922, that the two form a "bloc against bureaucracy in general."

Lenin saw two related aspects to this problem: the separation of the party bureaucrats from the proletarian mass, and the personal failings of his possible heirs. On the first point Lenin showed little awareness of his own central role in fostering the rise of an authoritarian bureaucracy in Russia, nor did he succumb to complete pessimism concerning a cure. He reposed his faith in a series of proposals to draft some hundreds of real proletarians to the central organs of control, giving them the authority to check on the work of the party officials. These untutored workers, whom Lenin had once considered capable of achieving only "bourgeois trade-unionism" without party leadership, were now to become the conscience of the Revolution, taking lessons in Marxist theory in their spare time. They were even to be given all the papers of the Politburo in advance of the meetings of this privy council, so that the jaded party officials could get away with nothing. The article that summarized this fanciful escape from original sin so horrified the Politburo that one member even proposed that it be suppressed and a dummy issue of *Pravda* printed to pacify the old man. Actually, the article was published after some delay—but without practical consequences.

This effort to unite the governing apparatus and the masses reflected the second point in Lenin's anxiety: the impossibility of finding another, younger Lenin to carry on. In his "Testament" Lenin drew a remarkably acute sketch of the leading candidates and found them wanting. Trotsky was the ablest but suffered from excessive self-confidence and concern with "the purely administrative side of affairs." Stalin was next in ability and the most powerful, but incautious in his use of this power. Stalin held more leading offices than any other person, and he had reached this eminence because Lenin had fostered the growth of the governing apparatus and depended increasingly on Stalin to make it work. But Stalin and his apparatus, Lenin plainly believed, could not lead the way to the Communist goal. Here was a dilemma of ends and means that Lenin never resolved. On January 4, 1923, his anger at Stalin's dictatorial methods erupted in the postscript to his "Testament." Lenin wrote that Stalin was "too rude" and the comrades should "consider a means of removing Stalin" as General Secretary, replacing him with "another man . . . , more tolerant, more polite, more considerate of comrades, less capricious, etc." Torn between his pragmatism and his idealism, Lenin could not bring himself to fire his best administrator, a loyal supporter in all the major controversies since April, 1917. Instead, he feebly bequeathed to his heirs the difficult task of choosing his successor, even though he acknowledged that his lieutenants were weaker and less perceptive than himself.

In the weeks just before March 9, 1923, when a third stroke ended his political life, the old leader made one final effort to take action against Stalin. This was partly a personal matter, for Lenin belatedly learned that Stalin had rudely submitted Krupskaia to "vile invectives and threats" (Krupskaia's words) in December, 1922. Infuriated, the sick man asked Stalin for a retraction and apology unless he preferred "the severance of relations between us." The General Secretary made the apology. The incident was not made public, but it may have helped inspire Lenin to his last effort against Stalin—the preparation of a public, personal attack on Stalin to be delivered at the forthcoming Twelfth Party Congress. According to Lenin's secretaries, he was preparing a "bomb" of a speech against Stalin, focusing chiefly on Stalin's rough handling of minority nationalities, especially the Georgians. But after Lenin's paralytic stroke on March 9, the draft of this speech seems to have passed into Stalin's hands and may have been destroyed.* Between March, 1922, and his death on January 21, 1924, Lenin was almost completely deprived of the power of speech. Did he draw closer to his visionary Marxist faith and die in peaceful confidence that all would be well? Or did his recent doubts about the bureaucratized party pursue him to the end? If they did, fate arranged an especially ironic form of death, for although his illness rendered helpless the man who had done so much to influence history, it did not deprive him of his senses: he was able to realize that he had failed to stop Stalin. Lenin's wife and his faithful secretaries were powerless to prevent the embalming of his corpse for indefinite public display, a mawkish idea that surely would have revolted the austere founder of a party based on "scientific socialism." And no combination of persons in Russia was strong enough to prevent Stalin from claiming Lenin's legacy.

* On October 10, 1923, Lenin, unable to speak, summoned up enough vigor to return from his rest home near Moscow to his office in the Kremlin. There, according to one version, he tried at once to find some particular papers, failed to do so and appeared greatly disturbed. Quite possibly the missing papers were the notes for the final attack on Stalin, now safely in the hands of the General Secretary himself.

5

LENIN
AND THE BOLSHEVIK TRADITION

There is a temptation to minimize the stature of one who has been deified by almost two generations of unscrupulous propagandists, but the truth remains that Lenin is one of the most impressive figures in modern history. Although his creed denied historical free will to individual men, his life is a living negation of the theory of historical determinism. Surely the Communist regime that he established in Russia and its manifold consequences in the world at large owe far more to the personal qualities of Lenin than to the abstract conception of the dialectic. His achievement lies in the foundation of a party imbued with his own spirit of discipline and ruthlessness, and in the acquisition and maintenance of political authority by and for this party. His is the ominous achievement of pioneering the most striking new development in twentieth century political life: the party-dominated, totalitarian state. To be sure, the full flowering of this new creation came only after Lenin's death, and the parallel developments of the twenties and thirties—especially in Italy and Germany—were not simply imitations of Bolshevism. But the seeds of the Communist system were present in Lenin's writings as early as the turn of the century, and his experiment in totalitarianism preceded the others; his place as the theoretical and practical pioneer of totalitarianism is secure.

Lenin's historical role also concerns the problem of the radical intellectual class in societies undergoing modernization. Lenin's formation of the Bolshevik Party represented his answer to the question "What is to be done?"—and, in a sense, the Bolshevik victory in the revolutionary period represented the triumph of the radical intelligentsia over the traditional regime. Of course, the greater part of the radical intelligentsia were not Bolsheviks and many were later driven out of the country, but it is essentially true that the early Bolshevik regime was a dictatorship of revolutionary *intelligents* who were intent upon the rapid modernization of Russia and the ultimate realization of such Western ideas as equality, freedom, and material abundance for all. Lenin occasionally castigated the Russian intelligentsia as worthless talkers, but he himself lived and died as an *intelligent,* and most of his colleagues shared this peculiar social background. By taking power, these *intelligents* removed the restraints on modernization imposed by the old social hierarchy and tsarist government. In this sense Lenin changed the course of Russian history. But it now appears that this victory of the revolutionary intelligentsia contained the seeds of its own destruction. Few members of the old intelligentsia shared Lenin's practical political talent, and within a few years after his death the Bolshevik leadership had shifted from the old intelligentsia to another, less idealistic, less philosophical, and still more ruthless group which is associated with the name of Stalin and has been called the "quasi-intelligentsia." * In this sense, too, Lenin changed the course of Russian history—but not as he had intended.

Bolshevism, as Lenin sensed during his final illness, was drifting away from his ideal and his control even during his lifetime; a few years after his death Krupskaia is said to have remarked that—had he lived—he would have landed in jail. But the Communist Party of the Soviet Union remains in essence Lenin's party. It has remained devoted to at least one principle laid down by Lenin at the opening of the century: the conception of the party as a vanguard, an elite to provide the masses with the direction that they cannot find by themselves. A half-century after the revolution, the CPSU—and especially its leader —still constitute a narrow elite, maintained by its self-proclaimed vocation of leadership rather than popular election. Moreover, the party continues implicitly to recognize that this authoritarian order presupposes a supreme dictator-prophet, a point that Lenin expressed very effectively in practice, though not in theory.

Along with this tradition of the dictator and the elitist party, the Communist Party of the Soviet Union has retained Lenin's arrogant pretense of a monopoly on truth. It continues to maintain that those who reject the current party line are, *ipso facto,* class enemies. There has been no mellowing of that intensely dogmatic Leninist spirit that made no important distinction between Nicholas II, Woodrow Wilson, "the renegade Kautsky," Trotsky (from 1904 to 1917), and Zinoviev (when he opposed Lenin in 1917). Outside the party there can only be enemies; within, only true believers; as Lenin indicated in his resolution "On Party Unity" in 1921, there can be no loyal opposition. The "double-think" that follows from this dogmatism is another aspect of the Leninist tradition that is still operative in Bolshevism. In Lenin's time a "true" Bolshevik had to believe at one point that only class enemies would participate in Duma elections, and at another that only a heretic would *not* participate in them; that the Socialist Revolution-

* The label was suggested by Robert V. Daniels in "Intellectuals and the Russian Revolution," *The American Slavic and East European Review,* April, 1961. It seems to be the best available term to describe a distinction that has long been recognized in discussions of the evolution of Russian communism.

ary agrarian program was bourgeois and, later, that it was the "correct" program; that the federalization of the Russian Empire would be baneful and, later, that it was the one truly proletarian policy. In sum, one of the most durable traditions established by Lenin is the remarkable combination of unyielding dogmatism and opportunistic flexibility that makes communism so formidable an enemy. While adhering rigidly to a few basic premises—such as the elitist party, the division of the world into proletarians and capitalists, and the inevitable triumph of the proletarians—the party may otherwise make any compromise, concession, or maneuver whatsoever, exacting utter obedience from its members at every turn.

Finally, Lenin bequeathed to the Bolshevik tradition a superb heroic myth. This is embodied in the countless memorials to the founder—from the cheap print adorning remote village classrooms to the huge portrait displayed in Red Square on the anniversary of the Revolution. It is embodied in the scriptural literature of Leninism, including five editions of his "complete" works, an endless array of individual selections, anthologies, and commentaries. It is embodied in poetry, fiction, drama, scholarship, the city of "Leningrad," the numerous Lenin museums, and the names of innumerable streets and factories. And the myth is quite literally embodied in the outstanding tourist attraction in the USSR: the mausoleum in Red Square. Doubtless contrary to his wishes, he holds the endurance record for lying in state.

The mythological Lenin is all things to all men. To the party member he is, of course, the founder of Bolshevism. To the soldier he is the founder of the Red Army (so it is said). To the intellectual he is the brilliant and versatile scholar with an appreciation of all the arts and sciences. To the industrial worker he is the advocate of electrification and shorter working hours. To the peasant he is their champion against the landlords and the architect of a workers' *and peasants'* dictatorship. To the patriot he is an outstanding Russian who saved his country from foreign invasion and laid the basis for her present greatness. To the foreign Communist he is the founder of the Comintern. To the schoolchild he is the benevolent "uncle." To the youth he is the founder of the Komsomol (Communist Youth League). To the athlete he is the physical culturalist who conditioned himself with long walks and cold swims. To all he is the victor in the struggle against tsarism, capitalism, narodism, Menshevism, and intraparty factionalism.

This image contains a substantial measure of distortion, but the significance of a myth lies not in its truth but in its vitality. It is generally accepted by almost the entire Soviet populace, including the ignorant and suspicious peasant and the educated and skeptical intellectual. The party may suffer from substantial apathy and outright disaffection, but, shrewdly, it has built itself on this rock of Lenin's greatness. Stalin,

Khrushchev, Brezhnev, and whoever follows must draw their moral authority from this source; without it the party would lack both human appeal and a basis for its claim to invincibility and infallibility.

The historical Lenin was a political genius who founded a party, provided it with a body of dogma, maneuvered it into power, and transformed it into an effective dictatorship. With all his shortcomings he remains a major historical figure. But the mythological Lenin is beyond human talent and historical truth. For Communist believers he is the Savior.

PART TWO
STALIN

6

FROM COTTAGE TO KREMLIM

Few men in history began as obscurely as Stalin and rose to such worldly eminence. The most powerful, most worshipped, and most durable dictator of the twentieth century (yielding only to Hitler as the most feared and hated, and that by a small margin) was born of poor and ignorant peasant-artisan parents in a backward village of the Caucasus Mountains in 1879. Iosif Vissarionovich Dzhugashvili, the future Stalin, was handicapped not only by being the son of a poor peasant cobbler, but also by being Georgian. Georgia possessed an ancient, Orthodox Christian (but not Slavic) culture, and was quite capable of producing talented people. But it was a small, remote, and economically backward country, and no Georgian could aspire to world renown without assimilating himself to a larger and more prominent country, usually Russia, which had ruled Georgia since the beginning of the nineteenth century. This was no small difficulty, especially for a peasant from the mountains; Stalin was twenty-eight before he wrote anything for publication in the Russian language and thirty-three before he was able to transfer his career to the Great Russian centers. Slow as it was, his emergence from this remote borderland was made possible by the Russian Orthodox Church and the Russian Social Democratic Workers' Party, which—although diametrically opposed on many points—both strove for the russification of the peoples of the Empire.

Stalin owed his first step upward, his Russian Orthodox education, to his mother, Ekaterina Dzhugashvili (his father died when the boy was eleven), who was determined that her only living son would rise above her humble estate through the medium that was most accessible to peasants: the priesthood. Thus Stalin studied in ecclesiastical schools from 1888 until 1899, attending first the primary church school in his native village of Gori and then the seminary in Tiflis, the chief city of Georgia. Although Stalin's formal education ended before he had completed secondary school, it should not be concluded that Ekaterina's efforts to obtain an education for her son were a failure. Stalin not only learned Russian, an indispensable gain, but he had been exposed to a stiff curriculum that included a good deal more than divinity, for the centrally directed seminaries of Russia were at this time becoming very respectable ecclesiastical counterparts to the fine secondary schools of the Empire. And what the curriculum excluded in the way of social science, philosophy, and literature, the more adventurous students obtained on their own—despite the disciplinary precautions of the clerics in charge.

The details of Stalin's transition from Orthodox Christianity to orthodox Marxism are unclear, but it seems most likely that he was first attracted, when he was about sixteen, to the liberal Georgian nationalist movement, and then—through acquaintances within and outside of the seminary—to the nascent Social Democratic movement in Georgia. In any case he was expelled from the seminary in 1899, which is probably the same year that he joined the Georgian Social Democratic Organization. There was at this time neither an all-Russian Social Democratic Party nor a Bolshevik or Menshevik movement for the twenty-year-old seminarist to join.

For so young a man to devote himself entirely to so precarious a movement is a strong indication of profound conviction, and in this early conversion probably lie the seeds of Stalin's complete identification of himself with the party, which forms the psychological basis of his personal dictatorship in later years. However crudely he may have understood Marxist theory, the circumstances surrounding the beginning of his lifelong career in the Russian Marxist movement confirm the sincerity of his belief. Lacking even the modest private financial means that supported Lenin for many years, or the opportunity (or talent) to maintain himself by writing, as Trotsky often did, Stalin's first twelve years as a professional revolutionary were a severe test of his devotion, hardly the life for an opportunist. And in the years that elapsed between his entry into the movement in 1899 and the opening of the revolution of 1917, Stalin spent over half of his time, an aggregate of about nine years, in tsarist prisons or in exile. This record, which partly accounts for Stalin's comparatively slow upward progress in the party leadership, was not the result of inferior zeal or skill in eluding the police. Stalin has five escapes from exile to his credit, as compared to Lenin's one and Trotsky's two, and he became accustomed to living without a fixed name or address. His bad luck with the police was largely the result of his remaining in Russia instead of seeking the safety of emigration.

It has been alleged that Stalin was actually a police informer in these years, and there has been a considerable dispute concerning documentary evidence produced against Stalin. Without attempting to unravel this dispute, it may be said that it is incredible that the tsarist police would have kept Stalin under detention for so many years, had he really been their agent throughout this period. They might have arrested him occasionally to render reports and to mislead his colleagues in the party, but they would hardly have wanted to neutralize his effectiveness as a spy by detaining him for periods ranging from fifteen months to four years. Nor did they actually detain their real agents, such as the leading Bolshevik, Malinovsky, for such periods. It is not impossible that the police were at some time tricked into thinking that Stalin would serve them. Nothing in his moral character would have prevented him from informing on non-Leninists or possibly on his personal opponents in the party, thus serving his own ends *and* those of the police. But it is most unlikely that he was an authentic police spy. A Georgian Menshevik who knew Stalin in prison, and whose hopes and whole life were later dashed by Stalin, said: "I have every possible reason to hate Stalin, but even I cannot believe that he could have betrayed the movement to the police."

It was during Stalin's first period of incarceration (April, 1902, to January, 1904) that the Second Party Congress met and the split between Bolsheviks and Mensheviks occurred. Stalin's adherence to the Bolsheviks, like his adherence to the movement in general, occurred in circumstances that are now obscured by time and possible misrepresentation by Communist historians, but it is clear that by the end of 1904 at the latest he was a zealous Bolshevik and a fervent admirer of Lenin. Again, this was no opportunistic maneuver, for Stalin's native Georgia was from the first a stronghold of the Mensheviks, and in time it provided the all-Russian Menshevik movement with a number of its leading figures and world history with its sole example of a Menshevik Socialist Republic (1918–1921). Very likely Stalin—still something of an uncouth young peasant despite his training in the seminary—in 1903–1904 had already developed a sense of personal hostility to the Georgian Menshevik leaders, some of whom were well educated *intelligents* of the Russian type. If these leaders of Georgian socialism, who seem not to have taken Stalin into their midst in his first five years in the movement, were against Lenin, then Stalin was for him. Moreover, Lenin's writings, some of which presumably reached Stalin, probably appealed to the young Georgian by their emphasis on practical organization, discipline, and violence. Stalin's early years in socialism were given mostly to attempts to organize party cells, publications, demonstrations, and strikes, and his experience probably led him to appreciate such tracts as "What Is to Be Done?" and "One Step Forward, Two Steps Back." Bolshevism appealed to the ruthless character of this young socialist, and his attachment to the Bolshevik creed and organization was both natural and enduring.

Stalin did not attain much distinction as a Bolshevik until 1912. Although he had some success in his attempts to organize workers in Batum, Tiflis, and Baku, the Mensheviks continued to hold the upper hand in the Caucasus. Stalin was able to obtain a mandate to attend the Stockholm "Unity" Congress in 1906, but in the subsequent London Congress of 1907 his right to represent any Caucasian group was challenged with some success: he was permitted to attend, but was granted only a consultative vote. In these gatherings and at his one other appearance at a party meeting outside Georgia before 1912 (the Bolshevik conference in Tammerfors, Finland), he played a minor role and does not seem to have established any intimate connection with Lenin. As a political writer he attracted little attention. His compositions appeared only in exceedingly obscure newspapers in the Caucasus and many of them (including the longest single essay he ever wrote, "Anarchism or Socialism") were written in the Georgian language, which neither Lenin nor other leading Bolsheviks could read. His one extraordinary contribution to the party in these years was not considered very respectable and is shrouded in considerable obscurity. This was his supervision of the most notable of the Bolshevik attempts to raise funds by robbery—the theft by one Kamo of state funds in Tiflis in 1907. The technique was not really successful because the banknotes were too large to be safely used, and the Mensheviks succeeded in discrediting the whole operation in the eyes of many Russian socialists, so Stalin and his historians have refrained from illuminating his precise role in the episode.

But when Lenin ended his cooperation with the Mensheviks and at the Prague conference of 1912 proclaimed the Bolsheviks as the one legitimate workers' party in Russia, Lenin required a corps of experienced, devoted, and ruthless lieutenants. There were few indeed who could match Stalin's qualifications. Thus it was that Stalin was named to the reorganized Central Committee of nine (seven were elected at the Prague meeting, while Stalin and one other were co-opted by Lenin shortly afterward). Stalin was then in political exile in Vologda, to the north of Moscow, but was able to escape from his lax captors and proceed to St. Petersburg to take up his new assignment. This involved editing the new legal newspaper, *Pravda,* and directing the Bolshevik deputies to the Duma. This assignment—which comprised the two most responsible tasks for a Bolshevik inside Russia—was quite a promotion for a man whose previous career had been confined to Caucasia. Lenin's assessment of Stalin's performance in this difficult role evidently was mixed. The lieutenant did well in guiding an electoral campaign but seems to have lacked the desired rigidity in dealing with the Mensheviks (on this point Stalin may have been closer to current working-class opinion than was Lenin). There was no quarrel between leader and follower, but during the second of his two visits to Lenin's headquarters in Cracow in late 1912 and early 1913, Stalin was replaced as editor of *Pravda* and given a short leave to try his hand as a theoretical writer. In the course of about two months, spent mainly in Vienna, Stalin wrote a substantial article entitled "The National Question and Social Democracy" (later known as "Marxism and the National Question"), which constituted his debut as a theoretical writer for a leading publication. Although this did not establish him as a peer of the prolific and theoretically minded leaders of Russian socialism, it was successful enough to be reprinted as a booklet a year after its publication in a journal, and it gave Stalin some standing as a Bolshevik expert on the problem of nationalities, to which his long service in the Caucasus also entitled him.

He had scarcely returned to Russia in February, 1913, when he was arrested for the seventh time and sent deep into Siberia, where he remained until 1917, quite isolated from the searing issues that so split European socialism and agitated Lenin. After the overthrow of the tsarist government, he quickly returned to the capital, arriving there before Lenin and the other first-rank leaders of the socialist parties. The prevailing tendency was toward broad working-class unity, and Stalin joined the other Central Committee member then present, Kamenev, in the propagation of a moderate policy toward the Provisional Government, the rival socialist parties, and the World War. While "erroneous" from a Bolshevik point of view (and therefore concealed by Stalin in later years), this policy was almost inevitable: it took all of Lenin's prestige and persuasion to swing the party into line with his extreme views, which were not clearly stated in Russia until the leader's return in April. But Stalin was quick to associate himself with Lenin and was easily able to retain his place on the Central Committee when a new one was elected by the party conference of May, 1917. During the Sixth Party Congress, when Lenin was in hiding, Stalin's senior status was emphasized by his delivery of the report of the Central Committee, which the leader himself would have given in normal circumstances.

Stalin scarcely appears as a figure of critical historical importance in the crucial time before the November Revolution, but his services to the party—albeit unobtrusive—were very nearly indispensable. His primary assignment was the editing of *Pravda* (and its substitutes under other titles that were adopted to evade government closure), which was the Bolsheviks' leading and most regular organ of propaganda. Lenin's choice of Stalin for this post did not imply any journalistic flair (Stalin still had trouble with his Russian composition), rather, it indicated Lenin's determination to put one of the party's most important weapons in the hands of a tough and reliable Bolshevik. Stalin's duties on *Pravda*, editing the daily and writing for it regularly, were enough to occupy most of his time, and this probably explains his absence from the main scenes of operations during the seizure of power in November. Years later he would be satisfied only by accounts that placed him right beside Lenin. Trotsky and other writers were understandably disgusted by such fabrication and emphasized Stalin's absence from the drama of Smolny or the Winter Palace. In fact the future dictator probably spent most of his time during the critical period of the takeover carrying out his editorial assignment.* This was a task of prime importance although it lacked the heroics of Trotsky's role or the fictitious part later claimed by Stalin.

At the opening of the Bolshevik era Stalin stood behind Lenin and Trotsky but was no less powerful in the party hierarchy than any other man, even though Zinoviev, Kamenev, Bukharin, and a few others were more widely known. His authority was based not on any striking accomplishment or literary or oratorical talent, but on his practical administrative ability. This was demonstrated first in the Central Committee of the Party, then in the new Council of People's Commissars (where he held the portfolio of nationality affairs), and after that in a widening series of assignments. Only the brazen mendacity of Stalin's later version of the Civil War would deny Trotsky primacy among the Bolsheviks in that struggle for survival, but distaste for Stalin's lies should not obscure the fact he does deserve to rank second to Trotsky as a political organizer of Bolshevik military operations. His role was that of roving inspector and organizer, going first to the region of Tsaritsyn (later Stalingrad, now Volgograd), then to Viatka on the eastern front, then to the Petrograd region, then to the southern front,

---

* On February 14, 1919, *Pravda* carried a letter from Stalin refuting the claim of one Boris Shumiatsky that he had been the responsible editor of the main Bolshevik organ at the time of the October Revolution. Stalin asserted, almost certainly correctly, that G. Iu. Shumiatsky was only the "formal editor," while Stalin and Sokolnikov were actually in charge. The practice of selecting unimportant men to appear as editors of subversive newspapers was common in prerevolutionary Russia. When the government closed down a paper and arrested the nominal editor, the real editors would select another front man and change the name of the paper— which is exactly what was happening to the Bolshevik press (originally *Pravda*) in the fall of 1917. Stalin's refutation was not reprinted in his official *Works* years later because it was then unseemly to claim so modest a role as editor, and in collaboration with a Trotskyist at that.

and finally to the southwestern front, opposing with both General Wrangel and the Poles. His task was to coordinate military activities with party policy, returning frequently to Moscow to report to the central organs. This function was especially vital to Lenin and the central organs because Trotsky, performing prodigies of leadership on various fronts, was not always able to maintain close liaison with Moscow. Lenin's repeated selection of Stalin for such assignments presumably indicates that he performed them well, although not without coming into conflict with Trotsky on several occasions. Their enmity soon led to a polemical discussion of the Civil War and still renders it difficult to appraise accurately Stalin's impact on strategic decisions.

In any case, Stalin's political strategy within the governing apparatus of Russia during the years of Civil War was quite sound. Between trips to the fronts he managed to take part in a number of important activities, enhancing his status in the civil affairs of the party and laying the foundations for his later bid for supreme power. During 1918 he participated in the main debates in the Central Committee and played an active role in the formation of the Russian Soviet Socialist Federative Republic. His reliability as an administrator and supporter of Lenin's policies was richly rewarded in March, 1919, when he was named to the newly established Politburo—the new authority on over-all policy—and the Orgburo, or personnel directorate of the party. Stalin headed the Orgburo, which was to become a major component of his personal machine. Also in March, 1919, Stalin was given a second commissariat —that of State Control (renamed the Commissariat of Workers' and Peasants' Inspection in 1920), which was responsible for the investigation of the reliability and efficiency of the state apparatus, including local soviets. Finally, he was introduced to economic administration, first as chairman of the "Ukrainian Labor Army" (i.e., dictator in charge of reviving coal production in the Donbas area), and later as the head of a mission to the Caucasus to report on the condition of the Baku oil industry. All told, the Civil War years marked Stalin's emergence as the most versatile administrator among Lenin's lieutenants and as a possible heir to Lenin. If such a possibility had seemed remote to Stalin at the end of the Civil War, it very likely acquired greater plausibility during the next two years. Surely his assumption of the newly created title of "General Secretary" in April, 1922, whetted his ambition. This additional office, granted with Lenin's approval, made him sole head of the Secretariat of the Central Committee with substantial power over the practical workings of the Politburo, the Central Committee, and the party in general. Since Stalin was already a member of the Politburo and head of the Orgburo, his control of the Secretariat completed his potential capacity to manipulate all of the leading bodies of the party.

At the same time he remained the ranking expert on nationality affairs and played the leading role in the formation of the new, supposedly federal state, the Union of Soviet Socialist Republics. The USSR included not only the Great Russians and the comparatively minor nationalities of the Russian heartland (already organized as the Russian Soviet Federative Socialist Republic), but also the Ukrainian, White Russian, and Caucasian Soviet Republics. Regarded as an indication of his maturing power and confidence, the most important aspect of Stalin's role in the formation of the USSR was his policy toward his native Georgia. In this he revealed a growing willingness to follow his own policy independently of Lenin and even against Lenin's wishes. From May, 1918, until February, 1921, Georgia was a genuinely independent state, governed by able Georgian Mensheviks who had been forced off the Russian political stage. Lenin had no love for these socialists but evidently intended to avoid a blunt display of force against a government that had recently been under British protection, was widely respected by Western socialists, and represented a test of the Bolshevik slogan on the right of nations to self-determination. But Stalin concocted a Bolshevik government for Georgia and in February, 1921, established it as the sole authority there (contrary to Lenin, who wanted a coalition). In effect, Stalin was carrying out an independent foreign policy and disposing of Soviet armed forces on his own initiative. Of course, he had no idea of removing Lenin at this time; rather, he counted on winning Lenin's approval of the deed once it became apparent that no dangerous consequences—such as British intervention —would ensue. And he was right. During 1922, however, he rather overplayed his hand: not only did he insist on joining Georgia to the neighboring Soviet republics of Armenia and Azerbaijan, which was acceptable to Lenin, but he also applied physical coercion to some Georgian Communist opponents of this policy and provoked the resignation of the entire Georgian central committee. On learning of this use of force against loyal Communists and of its consequences, Lenin was incensed. Stalin's rough tactics in dealing with intraparty opposition and his "Great Russian chauvinism," as Lenin called it, were major factors in determining Lenin's anti-Stalin attitude at the end of 1922 and in early 1923, mentioned above. Stalin's new bids for independence in 1921–1922 might have cost him dearly, had not Lenin's illness prevented his intended critique of Stalin at the party congress of April, 1923.

It was, of course, Lenin's illness, beginning less than two months after Stalin became General Secretary, that forged the vital link in Stalin's fate. While Lenin remained active, his overwhelming personal prestige easily outweighed all the administrative offices that Stalin could accumulate. The removal of Lenin drastically altered the *de facto* constitution of Bolshevism by temporarily abolishing the unofficial but supreme position that Lenin occupied. Now the significance of the formal offices Stalin held ceased to be overshadowed, and Stalin could begin to play a decisive role in the history of the Bolshevik Party.

What was the character of this man, whose opportunity to become a historic figure was provided by the moral illness of the leader who had made him and who might well have unmade him if granted a few more months of health?

Stalin was a hard man to know. He was rarely loquacious and almost never wholly forthright. He wrote only a few published letters that could be regarded as personal and he was not the kind of person whom the usual Russian radical *intelligent* cared to recollect in memoirs. Trotsky, Krupskaia, Sukhanov, and others of their ilk seem to have regarded Stalin as a grey, uncouth nonentity. Lenin perceived the political talent which underlay this rough exterior, but in his "Testament" he seemed to agree that Stalin was culturally below the intelligentsia. Stalin spoke colorlessly and with a Georgian accent; he wrote awkward Russian, knew no Western European languages, read little, and never wore a cravat. His first marriage in Georgia had been to a simple peasant woman, evidently an Orthodox believer whom Stalin treated in the patriarchal manner that was customary in Georgia. It seems that she died in 1907. On one occasion he affronted Trotsky by finding coarse amusement in the amorous activities of Alexandra Kollontai, the Bolshevik apostle of free love. At this time Trotsky had left his first wife in Siberia and was living with his common-law, lifelong wife. But like most *intelligents,* he was something of a prude, and found Stalin's ribaldry unbecoming.

Stalin, then, was a member of the quasi-intelligentsia. He was not really a proletarian or peasant, for he had not toiled for a living since childhood. His formal education had stopped short of the university, and he had not compensated for this, as had Trotsky and numerous others, by intensive self-education and residence in Western European cultural centers. While the leading *intelligents* and many of lesser rank lived a rather Bohemian life in the West, Stalin chose to remain close to practical organizational matters in Russia and made no attempt to linger abroad on party business during his trips to Stockholm and London for party congresses. Perhaps there was more behind this devotion to the Russian underground than the call of duty to the proletariat. For all his vestigial Georgian manners, Stalin was highly russified in his political outlook and showed equally little admiration for the minority nationalities in the Russian Empire or for the Western European nations that most Marxists thought to be the leaders of world socialism. Lenin's charge that Stalin was guilty of "Great Russian chauvinism" is accurate, but it fails to take into account Stalin's apparent identification of communism and Russia. While most of the Bolshevik *intelligents*, Lenin included, looked to Germany to carry through the push started by Russia, Stalin told the Sixth Party Congress of 1917 that "the possibility is not excluded that Russia will be the country to lay the path to socialism." Quite apart from this theory, Stalin displayed a streak of nationalism that verged on xenophobia and set him apart from the cosmopolitan intelligentsia.

While the *intelligents* utilized their enforced leisure in prisons and places of exile to read, write, and debate, Stalin made very little use of his nine years of detention. Although he was able to smuggle out short articles on local affairs from his prison cell in Baku in 1908, he never wrote a single theoretical work while under detention—even though much of it was passed under fairly lenient conditions of enforced residence in small villages rather than in prison. But this deviation from the pattern of the radical intelligentsia should not be interpreted as a want of devotion to the cause. Stalin's Bolshevik convictions quite possibly stemmed not merely from hatred for the established order, as Trotsky later charged, but also from a none-too-precise faith in the future utopia (as the title of his longest work, "Anarchism or Socialism?" implied). In any case it is clear that Stalin was at least as dogmatic as Lenin, with no compunctions concerning the use of authoritarianism or political expediency to achieve the Communist goal. He alone among Lenin's lieutenants was not disturbed by the more severe tactics to which Lenin resorted in 1917–1922, such as the crushing of the rival socialist parties, the Treaty of Brest-Litovsk, and the fate of "intraparty democracy" and trade-union autonomy.

Despite this rigid interpretation of Lenin's precepts about the nature of the class struggle, Bolshevism, and heresy, Stalin did not appear to be a ferocious combatant in the domestic strife of the party. He generally played the moderate, lagging well behind his party allies and enemies alike in intraparty polemics, and even continuing to display affability toward Trotsky after the decisive struggle had begun. This moderation was not the result of natural mildness but the manifestation of what his foes came to consider his paramount characteristic: ambitious cunning. The evaluation is just, for he was vain, shrewd, and certainly deceptive. He rightly saw that his cause would best prosper if he appeared to be the man who divided the Bolsheviks least, while Trotsky, Zinoviev, Kamenev, Bukharin, and the rest slashed at one another's jugulars. But neither is "cunning" a sufficient answer: Stalin's dissimulation also revealed depthless resources of strategic patience and self-control—qualities which were to serve him well in the years following the death of Lenin.

7

PRESERVING THE MONOLITH

The exceptional unity of the Bolshevik Party was to a great extent Lenin's personal achievement. He had founded the party, and his personal prestige held it together, despite the varying perspectives and rivalries in the membership. Since this degree of unity was so much a personal—and in a sense unnatural—achievement, it would scarcely have been surprising if the fissures in the party had grown wide after Lenin's death. In his "Testament" Lenin himself had expressed concern that the problem of succession might lead to splitting within the party, and it seemed at times during the years following his death that more than one variety of Bolshevism would establish itself. The very respect for Lenin's memory that his heirs professed seemed to work against the Leninist principle of concentrated authority. His lieutenants acted on the proclaimed principle that no individual—only a collective group—could fill Lenin's position at the head of the movement, and as all political experience indicates, nothing is more likely to inflame rivalries than dictatorship by committee.

Sooner or later the Bolshevik tradition required the establishment of a new dictator. At least as early as Lenin's death in January, 1924, Stalin seems to have made this his goal. He appeared at the funeral not only as a mourner but almost as one prepared to canonize a saint—and thereby assert his own pontifical powers. Stalin's recommendation that Lenin be embalmed and laid out in a permanent national shrine fitted in well with his highly publicized, almost liturgical eulogy, for both the plan for a mausoleum under the walls of the Kremlin and the eulogy sanctified the Leninist myth and implied Stalin's close connection with the hero. Among other alleged behests of Lenin, Stalin stressed the crucial issue of maintaining party unity, without which his own administrative offices might prove impotent in the coming struggle: "Departing from us, Comrade Lenin enjoined us to guard the unity of our party as the apple of our eye. We vow to you, Comrade Lenin, that this behest, too, we shall fulfill with honor!"

But Stalin could not move rapidly to transform himself into another Lenin. As early as 1922 he held all of the important party offices that he ever occupied, but he lacked the moral authority and the organized following to assert his apostolic claims until about six years after Lenin's death. To move too quickly might provoke the other leaders to unite in support of Lenin's testamentary proposal that Stalin be ousted as General Secretary. Later, there was also the danger that a real schism in the party might be opened, setting the Stalinist Bolsheviks against the "Bolshevik-Leninists," as some of Stalin's opponents came to call themselves. And the introduction of anything resembling a two-party system or genuinely representative government would have had incalculable effects on the fate of Stalin and Bolshevism. It is true that Stalin had fairly good control over the political police (then the OGPU) by about the mid-twenties, but he dared not enforce unity by sheer police terror. Such a step, taken prematurely, would have been likely to galvanize all his enemies into united opposition. Nor could Stalin afford to risk his position by supporting radical policies, especially on domestic matters. To foster the impression that he was the true apostle of Lenin, and neither "left" nor "right," he was obliged to straddle the fence as much as possible, postponing major policy decisions until he had won the struggle for power.

Perhaps the most celebrated of Stalin's maneuvers to maintain party unity was his maintenance of alliances with other major leaders. Fortunately for him, there was at first very little suspicion that he was capable of establishing a personal dictatorship; that ambition was more often attributed to Trotsky, a military hero and, some implied, a potential Bonaparte. At the same time a combination of personal enmities and policy differences among the other leaders presented Stalin with the opportunity to arrange advantageous alliances—first with Zinoviev and Kamenev, later with Bukharin, Rykov, and Tomsky. Thus an appearance of collective leadership could be maintained to overawe his opponents.

Of course, no combination of maneuvers, nor even the most impassioned references to the mythology of Leninist monolithism, could prevent some oppositional activity on the part of his frustrated rivals. This modest degree of schism could, however, be turned to good advantage, for rivals could not be effectively defeated until they were removed from the party, and the only adequate pretext that Stalin dared offer in the twenties was the sin of factionalism, a violation of the edict of the Tenth Party Congress of 1921. In a way, Stalin used light cases of the "disease" of factionalism to immunize the party against an ailment that would have been mortal in its more severe forms.

The removal of rivals from political life implied their replacement with more suitable associates. Thus the recruitment of dependent, dependable henchmen became another crucial aspect of Stalin's strategy. In this he depended in large measure upon the wide powers of patronage that Lenin had unwittingly granted him by installing him in the Secretariat and Orgburo. But even this ability to promote, demote, and transfer could not assure Stalin to a band of followers. In effect he was obliged to "sell" himself to a substantial number of Bolsheviks, and this effort accounts for his unusually active role as a writer and public speaker in the years 1924–1929, during which his volume of published verbiage almost equalled the combined output of all the other years of his life. Although few of the Bolshevik intelligentsia could comprehend the appeal of so seemingly crude and dull a man, Stalin was an effective persuader to many of the new, less intellectual members of the party, especially those who flocked in during the recruiting drives dedicated to Lenin's memory in 1924 and 1925. Through this pious device Stalin added over 600,000 new members to the party, largely men and women of proletarian and peasant background, who had little natural affinity for the *intelligents* who were Stalin's chief rivals. To many, Stalin probably succeeded in conveying a sense of solidity, common sense, utter devotion to Lenin, and confidence in specifically Russian communism. The new corps of Stalinist party leaders—Molotov, V. V. Kuibyshev, Ordzhonikidze, Kirov, Kaganovich, Voroshilov, M. I. Kalinin, A. I. Mikoyan, and others—were no doubt attracted by the increasing momentum of Stalin's popularity, but it is not to be assumed that they supported him simply because he had furthered their careers. As late as 1928, at least two of Stalin's supposed followers—Kalinin and Voroshilov—dared to threaten Stalin's entire campaign by siding with the opposition on a point of economic policy, and Stalin had to persuade them to his view by some combination of personal charm, flattery, promises, threats (probably not physical), and economic arguments. In the crucial years of struggle to build up his following, Stalin relied far more on persuasion than on coercion. His success in this technique should not be overshadowed by his later reputation for shortening by a head even the most mildly recalcitrant follower.

The crucial problem of party unity underwent four major crises in the years between Lenin's death and Stalin's final assumption of dictatorial power. The first crisis, in 1923–1924, was the possible split between the majority, represented by Zinoviev, Kamenev, and Stalin, and the opposition, headed by Trotsky. The second crisis, of 1925–1926, pitted the party, represented by Stalin, Bukharin, and others, against an opposition headed by Zinoviev. In 1926–1927 the third challenge to unity saw the same official party leadership and a united opposition that included both Trotsky and Zinoviev. Finally, in 1928–1929 the threat to Stalin and the official party was mainly from an opposition headed by Bukharin.

The Twelfth Party Congress of 1923, the first one since the Revolution that was not directed by Lenin, marks the beginning of this era of crisis. The reservoir of prestige that Trotsky had accumulated during the Revolution and Civil War naturally endowed him with the strongest claim to the succession, and at the same time arrayed more opponents against him than against any other candidate. On the highest level, anti-Trotsky sentiment was manifested as early as April, 1923, by the formation of an unofficial triumvirate which consisted of three of the six active, full-fledged members of the Politburo: Zinoviev (who was the most obvious alternative to Trotsky), Kamenev, and Stalin. Stalin was willing to join Kamenev and Zinoviev to prevent Trotsky from taking effective action in the highest party council, but he evidently regarded the coalition as a temporary union of expediency. On the eve of the Party Congress of 1923, Stalin even proposed that Trotsky, rather than Zinoviev, deliver the main report of the Central Committee in place of Lenin. While Stalin's offer may well have been intended to lure Trotsky into a display of personal ambition, it was certainly not likely to have pleased Zinoviev, who wanted the prestige of making the report. After Trotsky declined Stalin's proposal, Zinoviev volunteered for the task and was in fact assigned it. If Stalin had done little to help his fellow-triumvir assume Lenin's mantle at the Congress, Zinoviev reciprocated in the late summer of 1923 by attempting to reduce Stalin's authority in the Secretariat, his stronghold. Probably in August, Zinoviev melodramatically convened a small gathering, including Bukharin and Voroshilov, in a cave in the Caucasian resort of Kislovodsk and there—with neither of the other two triumvirs present—proposed that control of the Secretariat be vested in a collective leadership of several leading Bolsheviks. Zinoviev had correctly recognized the instrument of power that was destined to destroy him, but he guilelessly informed Stalin of the proposed reform before adequately organizing support for it. This was enough to antagonize Stalin without crippling him, and the General Secretary disarmed Zinoviev's supporters by offering to resign, then arranging a less costly compromise by which a few Bolshevik leaders were made nominal members of the Orgburo.

With Zinoviev entertaining his ambitions openly, and Stalin doing the same privately, the triumvirate was doomed, but it survived long enough to quash Trotsky's belated effort to take the initiative in the closing months of 1923. At this time the NEP was having temporary difficulties. Strikes and unemployment plagued the cities, and the peasants, faced with low, fixed grain prices, were not delivering enough of their produce. Moreover, the first real revolution to be ordered directly by the Comintern failed dismally in Germany in October, 1923. At the very time that Trotsky and others felt the need to subject party policy to a critical review, the head of the police, Dzerzhinsky, proposed that all party members should be obliged to inform on any suspected factional tendencies, thus pretty well precluding substantial opposition or criticism. Trotsky protested against this in a secret letter, which was followed by a "Declaration of Forty-Six" Bolsheviks who were closely associated with him, and finally by his critical article, "The New Course." Although Trotsky and his associates disclaimed any desire to introduce factionalism into the party, their basic demand for pluralism or democracy (some called themselves the "For Democratism" group) could not but erode the monolith of Bolshevism. The Trotsky opposition established a local stronghold in Moscow, especially among Bolshevik university students, and even maintained its own separate bureau there. In view of Trotsky's prestige and potential power as Commissar of Defense, the danger to the Zinoviev-Kamenev-Stalin leadership was real. The triumvirate had either to silence their critics or to admit a degree of pluralism into Bolshevism that could only mark the end of totalitarian unity. They had no trouble in making their choice: in December, 1923, the triumvirate publicly charged the Trotsky opposition with heretical factionalism and privately prepared a rigged party conference, the thirteenth, for January, 1924.

At this gathering the first post-Lenin crisis of Bolshevik unity was passed. The meager representation of the opposition listened helplessly while Stalin enumerated Trotsky's "six errors," and the conference adopted a resolution condemning their "un-Bolshevik view on the significance of party discipline." They could not muster the votes to compel the introduction of some form of pluralism and would not call the bluff of the triumvirate by proclaiming themselves as the "true" followers of Lenin. Instead of attempting to call on the Red Army, his last resource in the event of open split, Trotsky went off for a curative trip to the Caucasus and so found himself far from Moscow when Lenin died on January 21. Even if Stalin misled Trotsky concerning the date of the funeral, as Trotsky later claimed, the absence of Lenin's most illustrious co-revolutionary among the eulogists was a grievous error which tended to give credence to Stalin's allegations that Trotsky was not a very reliable Bolshevik.

The epilogue to this affair occurred in the fall of 1924 and ended with the temporary elimination of Trotsky (on his own) as a serious threat. On the occasion of the seventh anniversary of the Bolshevik Revolution, Trotsky published an essay entitled "Lessons of October," which served as the preface to an anthology of his writings of 1917. In it he called attention to the un-Leninist behavior of Kamenev and Zinoviev on the eve of the Bolshevik Revolution and suggested that this kind of Communist leadership had been responsible for the failure of the revolution in Germany in October, 1923. This time the threat to the party was less acute, partly because Trotsky himself was vulnerable to charges of anti-Leninism in the period 1904–1916 and partly because there was no semblance of an organized grouping behind him. He was quite effectively counterattacked in speeches and articles by the triumvirs and in January, 1925, removed from the post of Commissar of Defense, the ultimate weapon that he had never used.* The first danger of a division in Bolshevism had passed, but the very meeting of the Central Committee that stripped Trotsky of his military authority marked the faint beginnings of the next crisis: the Stalin-Zinoviev duel. Zinoviev, who did not share Stalin's gift for tactical patience, wanted to expel Trotsky from the party at once—a step that might well have driven Trotsky to organize a competing party. Stalin, as the apostle of moderation, successfully resisted Zinoviev's effort to finish off his principal rival.

At about this time Stalin also began to develop differences with Zinoviev (as well as with Kamenev and Trotsky) in the realms of theory and economic policy. While Lenin lived, Stalin had played only a limited role in the high level theoretical discussions within the party. But after the demise of the chief dogmatist, Stalin began to promote himself as the prime interpreter of Leninist theory. His effectiveness was all the greater among the mass of new and less sophisticated party members because he presented himself as a simple apostle of Lenin, too modest to be an original theoretician in his own right, as were Trotsky, Zinoviev, and Bukharin, among others. In this spirit Stalin delivered a series of lectures at the Sverdlov University in Moscow in April–May, 1924, entitled "The Foundations of Leninism" and dedicated to the "Lenin enrollment," that is, the new recruits among whom Stalin sought to establish his leadership. In this didactic work he presented what came to be the official Bolshevik apologia for the coming of a "proletarian" revolution in a country which had not achieved the high level of capitalism that Marx had predicated as the basis for the dialectical upheaval. Stressing Lenin's theory that the most advanced stage of capitalism was the worldwide development of imperialism, Stalin argued that Russia, although not very advanced economically, was the country in which all of the "contradictions" of world capitalism were most highly concentrated. This justified the Bolshevik revolution and moved toward the dogma of "socialism in one country," set forth in December, 1924. This catchphrase meant that Soviet Russia not only could make a proletarian revolution before the more advanced Western countries, but also could proceed successfully to establish a socialist society without waiting for the West. It might be quite a while, he argued, before revolution would come in the West, owing to Lenin's "law of the uneven development of capitalism," which Stalin interpreted to mean that revolution comes in successive waves rather than all at once. Thus, in May, 1925, he acknowledged "a temporary stabili-

---

*Trotsky apparently offered his resignation from this post in a letter of January 25, 1925, to the Central Committee. Whether he really expected to be taken up on this proposal or was driven to make it by threats of expulsion, it was quite acceptable to the triumvirate.

zation of capitalism," "a lull" in the revolution in Europe, a temporary stage of "peaceful coexistence" between capitalism and communism.

This theoretical outlook challenged the assumptions that almost all Bolsheviks had held in 1917 and that Trotsky and Zinoviev still held in the twenties. In reality the issue was somewhat unreal, for none of the oppositionists advocated a headlong sacrifice of Russian socialism in the cause of world revolution, and Stalin insisted that he too was eager for the next wave of upheavals. But the doctrinal issue was well designed to embarrass Trotsky and Zinoviev, for neither of them would accept the idea that socialism could be achieved in Russia alone. In this they may have been closer to Lenin's beliefs than Stalin was, but they were made vulnerable to charges that they lacked faith in the Russian Revolution and even that they resembled the "liquidators" before World War I who had despaired of revolution and wished to disband the party.

The economic issue that began to separate Stalin and Zinoviev in early 1925 was the question of the peasant. All agreed that the NEP and its temporary respite for the independent farmer were necessary, but some were willing to go much further than others in making concessions to the more prosperous peasants, who bore the opprobrious label of *kulaks* ("fists"). In the Politburo, Zinoviev, Kamenev, and their archfoe Trotsky were inclined toward a policy of narrowly limited free enterprise on the countryside, while Bukharin (who became a full member of the Politburo in June, 1924), Rykov, and Tomsky supported broad concessions to the prosperous peasants on the grounds that this was beneficial to the entire economy. As early as March, 1925, Stalin moved toward the latter group (conventionally given the rather arbitrary label of the "Right"), not so much as to commit his career but just enough to precipitate the crystallization of a new majority alignment in the Politburo: Stalin, Bukharin, Rykov, and Tomsky.*

Thus it was that the second crisis of party unity developed in 1925: a respectable minority headed by Zinoviev opposed the official party leadership headed by Stalin and supported by Bukharin and others. Despite the somewhat erratic quality of Zinoviev's leadership, his assets were not to be underrated. In addition to his minority membership in the Politburo and Central Committee, he was also president of the Comintern and of the hallowed Petrograd (renamed Leningrad) Soviet. With a lieutenant in charge of the party organization in the region, Zinoviev had relatively autonomous control over a major regional division of the party—including its important newspaper, *Leningradskaia Pravda*. Moreover, Krupskaia, who was respected for her own ac-

---

* From June, 1924, until January, 1926, the full members of the Politburo were Stalin, Bukharin, Rykov, Tomsky, Trotsky, Kamenev, and Zinoviev.

complishments as well as for her association with Lenin, favored Zinoviev in 1925 and in September joined him, Kamenev, and Sokolnikov in signing a "Declaration of the Four," which criticized the official leadership.

It was very likely respect for Zinoviev's power that led Stalin twice to postpone the Fourteenth Party Congress, which should have met early in 1925 but convened only in December. By then, Stalin had successfully outmaneuvered Zinoviev on several points. In the Comintern, hitherto considered to be Zinoviev's private preserve, Stalin succeeded in disgracing the Zinovievites in the German party, the most important in Europe. On the domestic front Zinoviev was goaded into publishing a polemical work in which he denied the doctrine that socialism could be achieved in one country, thus leaving himself vulnerable to the charge that he still lacked confidence in the Russian Revolution. His associate in charge of the Leningrad party organization, R. A. Zalutsky, went further in invective against the Stalin-Bukharin leadership and provided them with a pretext for his removal in October, 1925.

With this careful preparation Stalin could face the party congress in December with the knowledge that he could count on about a nine-to-one majority among the delegates. But he could not enforce total unity in the Bolshevik tradition, nor stop Zinoviev from delivering an officially permitted minority report, backed by Kamenev. Despite his majority, Stalin evidently feared that his rivals' speeches might influence some of the audience or the public and increase the danger of a real split. To minimize this danger Stalin had his more reliable delegates submit the opposition speakers to a severe heckling, which understandably reached its climax when Kamenev declared: "I have arrived at the conviction that Comrade Stalin cannot fulfill the role of unifier of the Bolshevik staff." The stenographic record thereupon indicates:

> *Voices from the audience:* "Untrue!" "Nonsense!" "So that's what it is!" . . . "Stalin! Stalin!" *Delegates stand and cheer Comrade Stalin. Stormy applause.* . . .

Stalin appeared as an exemplar of modesty and moderation, supporting the principle of collective leadership and charging that the opposition wanted to disrupt the party by "chopping off heads." The charge of indiscipline—factionalism—levied against the opposition magically discredited the oppositionists and paralyzed their will, since none wanted to accept the logical corollary of their position and bring about a split in Bolshevism.

The Congress enlarged both the Central Committee and the Central Control Commission (to 106 and 163, respectively), which permitted Stalin's Secretariat to place more "reliable" Bolsheviks in these bodies.

Both bodies were important throughout the twenties, but the significance of their expansion in December, 1925, can be appreciated only through the realization that a new device—the joint meeting of the Central Committee and Central Control Commission—came near to supplanting the party congress in 1926–1929.* The new Central Committee further exploited Stalin's victory at the congress by shuffling the membership of the Politburo in January, 1926; Kamenev was dropped to candidate member, while three new full members who were aligned with Stalin were added: Molotov, Voroshilov, and Kalinin. Although Stalin still had to count on the voluntary support of Bukharin, Rykov, and Tomsky in the Politburo, the new lineup was the first in which there were men on whom Stalin could count as followers rather than allies.

The culminating blow to the Zinoviev threat to party unity was the capture of his Leningrad bastion. At the end of December, 1925, the Zinovievite editors of *Leningradskaia Pravda* were replaced, ending this nascent pluralism in political journalism. Early in January, 1926, a persuasion squad of Stalinists, headed by loyal Molotov, invaded Leningrad and in about two weeks managed to address 652 groups of party members, persuading almost all of the rank and file to support the official party line and leadership. Kirov, one of the energetic young Stalinists who were now appearing at the second highest level in the hierarchy, succeeded Zinoviev as the Bolshevik leader in Petrograd, while various opposition leaders were assigned to remote posts. Stalin prudently celebrated his victory by publishing another discourse on theory, again appearing as a loyal disciple rather than an intellectual pioneer. This was the weighty essay entitled "On Questions of Leninism" which was soon reprinted in a still weightier anthology of didactic works, *Problems of Leninism*; the book, from that time until Stalin's death, served as the basic reference work on Stalinism.

The third crisis of party unity began soon after the debacle of the Zinoviev opposition in early 1926 and lasted until the end of 1927. Although the leadership of the new opposition consisted of individuals who had already lost one round, the movement was a serious threat to totalitarian unity, partly because it combined several major talents and partly because its leaders were desperate enough now to engage in more serious factional activity. The basis of the new opposition was the rapprochement of erstwhile archenemies, the Zinoviev-Kamenev team and Trotsky, which has suggested the label "united opposition."

---

*Although the party statutes called for annual congresses in this period, only one was held between 1925 and 1930, while seven joint sessions of the Central Committee and Control Commission met in the same period and handed down decisions of basic importance. Two party conferences—gatherings smaller than a congress—were also convened in the period indicated.

In April, 1926, the three agreed that their main adversary was Stalin, and Kamenev told Trotsky, "It is enough for you and Zinoviev to appear on the same platform and the party will find its true Central Committee." While exaggerated, there was enough truth in this to cause concern to Stalin. The three had great prestige, augmented by the support of Krupskaia; they retained a foothold in the Politburo; Zinoviev headed the Comintern; and at last it seemed that they might be ready to fight to the finish. Moreover, their critique of the existing leadership, formulated in a "Declaration of Thirteen" (July, 1926), might prove persuasive to many Bolsheviks if the official leadership faltered or suffered serious tactical setbacks. The declaration stressed the allegedly unproletarian growth of bureaucratic rule in the party, the equally unproletarian lag in industrial growth, the soft policy toward the richer peasants, and the need to support a more militantly revolutionary line in the Comintern. Although the declaration disclaimed any factionalist intentions, the united opposition sought to propagate its ideas through an underground network of local groups, meeting in secret and linked by a clandestine system of messengers. Some of its lesser adherents explicitly proposed that the united opposition establish itself as a separate organization.

Stalin reacted quickly to this threatened split. In July a joint session of the Central Committee and Central Control Commission severely condemned indiscipline and removed Zinoviev from the Politburo, to which five rising lieutenants of Stalin were now named as candidate members. An important supporter of Zinoviev—M. M. Lashevich—was selected for exemplary punishment: removal from the Central Committee with a warning that he might have been expelled from the party altogether.

But the united opposition neither confessed misdeeds nor refrained from a campaign for support among the local party organizations. Only at the beginning of October, 1926, the opposition leaders lost their nerve and drew back from the campaign. In part this withdrawal seems to have stemmed from their lack of success in persuading the workers, although they had succeeded in organizing one major demonstration at a Moscow factory. But the greater cause for hesitancy was very likely their own reverence for the ikon of Bolshevik unity, which Stalin continually held before them. As Krupskaia explained, following her defection from the opposition at the end of October, there was fear that the militancy of the opposition might lead the workers to question the rightness of Bolshevik rule.

Stalin exploited the opportunity with consummate skill. Since he too realized that the new tactics of the opposition were leading toward a two-party system, he feigned moderation and offered a kind of amnesty if the opposition would publicly renounce its "factional" campaign and promise to observe party discipline. In return, he promised the opposition the right to expound its views in party meetings, including congresses ("the opposition had this right as a matter of course"), and said that "the Central Committee has no desire to expel people from the party." The leaders of the united opposition accepted this proposal in a declaration published in *Pravda* on October 16. Having thus disarmed his adversaries, Stalin almost at once lashed out in a series of theses for the Fifteenth Party Conference, and when that body convened (October–November, 1926) Stalin labeled the opposition "a social democratic deviation in our party." Since Lenin had discarded the name "social democratic" in 1917, calling it a "soiled shirt" because the European social democratic parties supported the "imperialist" war, Stalin's allusion almost implied treason. The undeceived opposition leaders could not seriously threaten the Stalin-Bukharin leadership within the framework of the party conference, which was so well arranged that they had not a single vote. And since they desisted from further underground activity they could only attempt to embarrass Stalin with a rigorous critique of his doctrine of socialism in one country, the economic policy of the regime, and the bureaucratism that was stifling criticism. Trotsky and Kamenev did succeed in striking close to home by pointing out that Marx, Engels, and Lenin did not believe in the possibility of socialism in one country. Stalin, who normally depended heavily on scriptural authority, neatly shifted his ground and argued that "Marxism is not a dogma but a guide to action," that if Engels were alive he would say, "To the devil with all old formulas! Long live the victorious revolution in the USSR!" And if Lenin had plainly said that the victory of socialism in one country is impossible, said Stalin, he must have meant merely that the "complete" victory is impossible.

However transparent this evasion, it did not cost Stalin votes at the conference. His resolution condemning "the social democratic deviation in our party" was unanimously passed, paving the way for new punitive measures. Trotsky and Kamenev were at last removed from the Politburo and Bukharin replaced Zinoviev as president of the Comintern. Stalin is reported to have said that the Comintern "represents nothing" and "exists only because of our support." Nevertheless, he could not afford entirely to ignore its prestige as the supposed vehicle of the world proletarian movement, and in 1926 he started to make a serious effort to advance his stature as an international Communist. In a series of speeches to the Presidium of the Executive Committee of the Comintern and in interviews with foreign Communist delegations, he called attention to his eminence in this area, all the while arranging the removal of foreign Communists who favored the united opposition.

This proved to be a shrewd precaution when the opposition revived its efforts in April, 1927, devoting heavy emphasis to the fiasco of Bolshevik policy in China. Lenin had hoped for colonial revolutionary movements against imperialism, despite the backward, unproletarian social order of colonial countries. He believed that Communists should support colonial upheavals even when they were dominated by nationalists, and out of this tactical doctrine had developed a reluctant coalition of the fledgling Chinese Communist Party and the Nationalist (Kuomintang) Party. Aided by various Soviet military and political advisors and headed by Chiang Kai-shek, the Kuomintang in July, 1926, began a fairly successful military drive to unify the nation, and the Russian tactics seemed justified. But in April, 1927, only a few months after the apparent defeat of the united opposition in Russia, Chiang occupied Shanghai and turned on the Communists there, massacring some thousands of the workers and their Communist leaders. The disaster for the Communists was especially acute because they had been armed and organized but had followed strict orders from Moscow not to resist Chiang's occupation of Shanghai. Nor did the Stalin-Bukharin leadership break off their support for the Kuomintang immediately after the massacre.

The Chinese fiasco rekindled the determination of the opposition, which in May, 1927, issued yet another manifesto, "The Declaration of the Eighty-Four" (actually signed by three hundred Bolsheviks in the course of a few weeks). "For any Marxist," said the Declaration, "it is indisputable that the incorrect line in China . . . is not accidental." The explanation, it alleged, lay in the policy of the Stalin regime: "the false, petty-bourgeois 'theory of socialism in one country,' which has nothing in common with Marxism and Leninism." Trotsky now tried a new tactic and carried his complaint to the Executive Committee of the Comintern, of which he was still a member. Had not Stalin taken care to cultivate foreign Communists who were susceptible to his own views and to expel those who were not, Trotsky's appeal might have been favorably received by a significant portion of the Comintern leadership. But Stalin's preparations were thorough, and the Executive Committee not only remained untouched by Trotsky's speech but in September even called him to account for "indiscipline" and expelled him from its ranks.

Within the Bolshevik Party itself, Stalin was still unable to dispatch the opposition so easily. The idea of expelling former Bolshevik heroes was as yet unfamiliar and apparently frightened some of Stalin's associates in the Politburo. The fiasco in China probably had shaken Bukharin's poise (he had been the chief spokesman for the policy), and the rupture of diplomatic relations with Britain in May, 1927, produced a war scare that probably unsettled the nerves of more than a few of Stalin's colleagues. From June through August Stalin attempted to have Zinoviev and Trotsky expelled from the Central Committee of the Party (Kamenev had been temporarily packed off as ambassador to Italy), but even Stalin's most assiduously prepared instrument, the joint session of the Central Committee and the Central Control Commission, failed to carry through a resolution to this effect. In the months of September, October, and November, 1927, the united opposition made its final desperate effort, again attempting to take their case to the rank-and-file Bolsheviks, and even to hold public demonstrations. For this campaign they carefully worked out a new declaration ("Platform") and planned to have it printed and circulated among local Party groups as a kind of petition. And at the joint meeting of the Central Committee and the Central Control Commission in October, Trotsky was to bring into action the weapon that might yet have a crucial effect: Lenin's Testament.

Stalin had shrewdly avoided risking a premature attempt to finish off the leading oppositionists, but now he could afford to wait no longer. The opposition now understood that he meant to end their political and even biological existence, and they were never more likely to break off from the party, even if it meant going underground. Stalin ruthlessly suppressed each enemy thrust and by the end of 1927 had completely scattered their forces. The publication of the "Platform" was forbidden, and when this edict was violated, a clandestine opposition printing squad was arrested and its leader imprisoned. The public demonstrations, which reached their peak on November 7, the tenth anniversary of the Bolshevik Revolution, were forcibly broken. And in the October meeting of the Central Committee-Central Control Commission, Stalin once again evaded the question of Lenin's Testament. According to Stalin the deceased leader only considered him "rude," while his opponents were judged politically untrustworthy. This was a *tour de force* of thought control, perhaps the first fully developed emergence of intellectual Stalinism. Not only did Stalin's followers cheer his patent distortion of Lenin's words, but they did so with the knowledge that Stalin dared not release the document to the party at large.*

Now he could successfully insist that Trotsky, Kamenev, and Zinoviev had violated not only the Tenth Party Congress prohibition of factions but also their own pledges not to form factions, and on October 23 they were expelled from the Central Committee. The suppression of the attempted demonstrations of November 7 convinced Stalin

---

* Although the Testament was discussed and acknowledged to be authentic at limited party gatherings in 1925 and 1927, it was denounced when published abroad in 1925–1926. When Khrushchev published it for the first time in the USSR in 1956, it did indeed undermine Stalin's reputation.

they were now sufficiently discredited and they were expelled from the party itself on November 14.

Since December, 1925, Stalin had avoided the risk of holding a Fifteenth Party Congress, and in 1927 had several times postponed the date. By December, 1927, however, the united opposition was crushed and the Congress convened. The delegates were regaled not only by the speeches of Stalin, Bukharin, and others among the victors, but by an abject confession of error and plea for readmission by Zinoviev and Kamenev—another milestone in the development of Stalinism. In his reply Stalin could at last discard the cloak of moderation and clemency:

> Kamenev's speech appealing for readmission to the party was the most lying, hypocritical, fraudulent and scoundrelly of all the opposition speeches delivered here. . . . the opposition works underground to split the party, to organize a second party, to undermine party unity. . . . Is it not time to stop this criminal, swindling game?

In December several thousand oppositionist party members were expelled or obliged to sign recantations, and in January, 1928, Trotsky was placed in enforced residence in Alma Ata, near the Chinese border. The third and most dangerous crisis in party unity had been weathered.

The fourth and final crisis, which pitted Stalin against the Bukharin-Rykov-Tomsky leadership, is inextricably bound up with the question of economic development. In this phase the danger to Bolshevik monolithism did not lie so much in the effectiveness of the opposition leaders themselves as in the hazards of the new economic line that Stalin undertook in 1928–1929. By committing himself to a radical departure from the path indicated by the NEP, Stalin seemed likely to alarm a number of his presumed followers and to face the un-Bolshevik prospect of a fairly open debate—at least within the party—on an important aspect of policy. At stake was Stalin's personal supremacy, and also the principle that major decisions emanate from the leader's infallible wisdom, not from the consensus of the party or the public.

To be sure, certain shortcomings of the NEP were becoming increasingly obvious. Partly because of the regime's limitations on the development of private enterprise and free cooperatives in agriculture, partly because of the high price of industrial goods and artificially low price of farm products, less and less grain was being delivered to the cities (one third less in January, 1928, than in January, 1927). This, together with the serious shortage of capital, posed a major obstacle to industrial growth. Nothing in Stalin's public statements on economic policy prior to 1928 indicated that he was the man to attempt a radical solution to the problem. He had opposed the solution offered by Trotsky and Zinoviev (in its most theoretically sophisticated form, by Trotsky's follower I. A. Preobrazhensky) which involved greater pressure on the peasant, aiming at the "primitive socialist accumulation of capital" which would enable Soviet industry to advance rapidly. This, retorted Stalin, Bukharin, Rykov, and Tomsky, would endanger the coalition of the peasantry and proletariat on which Lenin had founded the Bolshevik regime. They too favored the central planning of industrial growth and the collectivization of agriculture but, as Stalin told the Party Congress of December, 1927, only under conditions of balance between industry and agriculture, with "the gradual unification of individual peasant farms into general, collective farms." Because such a path to "socialism in one country" seemed to most Bolsheviks safer than any other that was compatible with their socialist economic assumptions, the Fifteenth Party Congress unanimously accepted a Five-Year Plan.

Despite his previous conduct, which had apparently justified his enemies' charges of unprincipled self-aggrandizement, Stalin did have convictions, however crude or totalitarian. And as he demonstrated in the course of the First Five-Year Plan, he was willing to risk his career in the attempt to achieve his conception of Marxian-Leninist goals. In retrospect it appears most likely that Stalin had for some time dreamed of a gigantically industrialized, completely collectivized, totally disciplined utopia, but saw no sense in making a major push until power was securely in his hands. In 1928 he even embraced Trotsky's rapid-development industrial program, which he had ridiculed as recently as April, 1926, when he compared a proposal for a gigantic hydroelectric dam on the Dnieper to the decision of a peasant to buy a gramophone when he needs a plow. His reversal was probably less than honest, but his actions seem very much in keeping with the precedent established by Lenin in 1917 when he abandoned his previous agrarian program and admittedly stole the Socialist Revolutionary program because it was what Bolshevism (and Lenin's own career) needed at that moment.

In early 1928 Stalin understandably became alarmed by the grain deficit and undertook an extensive series of speeches on the economic dilemma, increasingly emphasizing the need to break the power of the *kulaks* (loosely defined to mean almost any uncooperative peasant) and to increase the tempo of industrialization. Here he met real resistance. As Stalin later admitted, orders to take a tougher line with the *kulaks* were opposed by many party functionaries from the local organizations up through the Central Committee, and numerous local peasant uprisings were reported. In the Politburo itself not only Bukharin, Rykov, and Tomsky, but even Voroshilov and Kalinin opposed him,

while Rudzutak and Kuibyshev hedged. Among the full members only
the loyal Molotov supported Stalin. Since no legal mechanism for the
expression of party (much less public) opinion existed, the actual alignment of forces will never really be known. It was clear, however, that
Stalin faced a grave dilemma: whether to retreat from his economic
policy and perhaps endanger the long-term survival of Bolshevism, or
to press ahead and risk a split in the party.

His handling of the crisis demonstrated well his mastery of maneuver, deception, and persuasion. By July, 1928, he had induced his er-
rant followers in the Politburo to fall in line. "Voroshilov and Kalinin
funked at the last minute. Stalin has some special hold on them," com-
plained Bukharin, who now turned to Kamenev for support. Marshal-
ling his supporters, Stalin skillfully maneuvered to play down the controversy, thus impeding the formation of clear-cut battle lines in the
party. In October, 1928, he castigated the "Right Danger" in the party,
but named no names—and his opponents, much to their disadvantage,
refrained from an open challenge. In November, incensed by new and
greatly increased goals for industrial production, the three opposition
leaders threatened resignation, but, in Stalin's later words, "all disagreements were smoothed over in one way or another." Despite further threats of resignation and the composition of a "Right" opposition "Platform," Stalin did not begin a real counterassault until April,
1929, when he enlightened the Central Committee-Central Commission concerning "The Right Deviation in the CPSU (B)" and "the factionalism of Bukharin's group." At about this time it appears that
Rykov was at least partially separated from his former allies, possibly
by promises of moderation in policy and personal honors. Then began
the slow but systematic removal of important oppositionists from their
offices. Although the three leaders submitted a humiliating confession
of error in November, 1929, it was only by the end of 1930 that all had
been shorn of their important offices, including membership in the
Politburo, the presidency of the Comintern (Bukharin), of the Council
of the Trade Unions (Tomsky), and of the Council of People's Commissars (Lenin's former post, transferred from Rykov to Molotov in
1930). By December 21, 1929, Stalin could congratulate himself on having crushed the last serious threat to Bolshevik unity and was honored
by *Pravda* with the following banner headline—a ponderous birthday
message:

> To the true continuator of the cause of Marx and Lenin, to the staunch
> fighter for the purity of Marxism-Leninism, for the steel-like* unity of the

---

* "Stal'noi"—a complimentary pun on Iosif Dzhugashvili's famous pseudonym,
which he no doubt intended for such associations.

ranks of the All-Union Communist Party (of Bolsheviks) and the Communist International, for international proletarian revolution; to the organizer and leader of the socialist industrialization and collectivization of the Soviet land; to the old *Pravda*-ist; to Comrade Joseph Vissarionovich Stalin from *Pravda*—militant Bolshevik greetings.

8

THE AGE OF STALIN
The Myth and the Machine

With the conclusion of the competition for power and of the danger of pluralism within Bolshevism, a new era in the history of the party began: the age of Stalin. For almost a generation this enigmatic Communist from the borderlands of Asia held sway over the Soviet Union (and, in his last years, over much of Europe as well), probably exercising more nearly total authority over more human beings than any other man in history. Stalin's Communist sycophants, his posthumous Communist denigrators, and observers in the non-Communist world implicitly agree that his impact upon the development of Bolshevism was tremendous. How could so seemingly drab and limited a man leave so profound an imprint on the course of human affairs? Unless one accepts the Marxist articles of faith and can agree with Trotsky that "the dialectics of history hooked onto him and raised him up," one must be prepared to accept the paradox that this seemingly petty man—whose outstanding characteristics in the first fifty years of his life were cunning patience and tactical caution—possessed a genius, however perverted, for the immense.

The apparent abruptness of the transformation of Stalin's character might be explained as the symptom of incipient madness, which is implied in Khrushchev's portrait of Stalin and in the more capricious acts of violence that he is known to have instigated. But Stalin, even if psychotic, retained a great capacity for leadership and rational calculation, as is affirmed by a variety of sober witnesses from the West. Churchill, for example, was clearly convinced during World War II that he was dealing with an able leader who was certainly capable of great political rationality. The major policies of Stalin may not have emanated from a normal mind, but they certainly cannot be passed off as mere lunacy.*

---

* Other Bolshevik leaders may have been mentally or emotionally disturbed. Lenin repeatedly suffered nervous breakdowns and had to take rest cures in the country. Trotsky suffered from a "cryptogenic fever" that may well have been psychosomatic (Bernard Wolfe, an American who knew Trotsky in exile, has suggested that he was severely disturbed, to the point of wishing for his own death, by guilt feelings dating from the Kronstadt revolt). As for Khrushchev, would any really bal-

It may be more helpful to suggest that Stalin's behavior when he finally assumed power was the attempt of a single-minded fanatic to realize a grandiose vision. This was not the dream of a radical *intelligent,* striving to achieve in Russia the ideal of human freedom that had been absorbed from the Western traditions of liberalism and socialism. Granting that Lenin's approach to the ultimate goal was deeply imbued with centralism and authority, he nevertheless shared something with the Western tradition of human freedom in matters of ultimate objectives and moral justification. The same cannot be said of Stalin, who came to Bolshevism with only the scantiest background in Western political idealism. He passed his formative years in Lenin's movement but not in close association with westernized *intelligents,* and it seems likely that he became imbued with the unlimited authoritarian spirit of Bolshevism, untempered by any vestigial liberal ideals. The only goal that he could comprehend after more than twenty-five years in the party was the realization in total form of the discipline that Lenin preached for party members—or, as G. T. Robinson has described it, the construction of a "perfect prison from which the prisoners no longer wish to escape."

A somewhat cryptic expression of this world view is found in a frequently quoted statement of Stalin to the Sixteenth Party Congress in 1930:

> We stand for the withering away of the state. At the same time we stand for the strengthening of the dictatorship of the proletariat, which represents the most powerful and mighty authority of all forms of the state which have existed up to the present day.

Stalin's explanation that this contradiction "reflects Marxian dialectics" has often been dismissed as nonsense. But it may also reflect, however awkwardly, the truly totalitarian belief that the state can become nothing only by becoming everything, by engulfing individual identity to the point at which the state is no longer distinguishable from mankind.

As Stalin was presumably aware, the approach to his utopia demanded terrible human costs, including the terrorization of the party. Trotsky, Zinoviev, Bukharin, and Kamenev were no doubt willing to use terror as a technique in the struggle to achieve the Communist dream, but they were not disposed to the use of such unlimited terror, nor to the incorporation of terror into the Communist dream itself. While these rivals, with their residual scruples and their comparatively

---

anced person indulge in such infantile exhibitionism as the famous shoe-banging incident at the UN? Yet the history of Bolshevism cannot be dismissed simply as a protracted mental illness.

liberal vision of the goal, retained any semblance of authority in the party, Stalin had to suppress his grandiose dreams of a totalitarian utopia. Only when he had rendered impotent the last of the opposition groups could he apply his organizing genius and unflinching will power to the immense projects, both constructive and destructive, which will always be associated with the name of Stalin.

In practice, if not in theory, the Bolshevik tradition had stressed the necessity of a strong leader during the "construction of socialism." After 1929 Stalin not only raised the position of the leader from hero to deity but evidently sought to make the worship of the dictator a part of the Communist goal itself. This appears to be the implication of the progressive intensification of the Stalin cult with every year of advance toward what was to be the highest stage of human development. The city of Tsaritsyn was renamed Stalingrad as early as 1925, and Stalin's fiftieth birthday four years later was celebrated with such noisy pomp that it is often considered to have marked the birth of the Stalin cult. But the cult grew throughout the rest of Stalin's life, proportionate to the alleged advance toward Communism and in close association with the goal. When a new Soviet constitution was adopted in 1936, supposedly signifying arrival at the "socialist" phase on the path to Communism, it was called the "Stalin Constitution." In 1950 five gigantic, much-publicized construction projects that were supposed to accelerate significantly the economic approach to utopia were known as the "Great Stalin Constructions of Communism." At about the same time the role of the leader in the oncoming earthly paradise was implied in the slogan "Stalin will change the climate of Russia," which accompanied an immense (though not very successful) project for the development of shelter-belts on the steppes. And in general there is no doubt that the sheer volume of articles, books, speeches, posters, films, plays, and other demonstrations in praise of Stalin increased with each year of "progress" toward the ultimate goal. There was never any suggestion that the leader and his cult would wither away under utopian conditions; communism would simply give the workers and peasants more leisure in which to sing his praises, one would gather.

The propagation of this idolatry suggests that Stalin himself recognized the great disparity between his unimposing personality and the immensity of his program. Quite apart from the Communist theory of historical determinism, he may have sensed that the logic of mass psychology required the myth of a superhuman leader to implement a gigantic program involving overwhelming sacrifice. Stalin could not provide such a myth in his own person. Lacking the public talents of such contemporaries as Roosevelt, Churchill, or Hitler, he made very little use of such new mass media as gigantic rallies, radio talks, or motion pictures. While his mythological image and published words were disseminated on a grand scale, his actual person and voice were increasingly withdrawn from public display (except for a series of radio addresses during the war and a number of ritual appearances at holiday parades on Red Square). Despite his cataclysmic agricultural program, he never visited a village after 1928. During the war he made no morale-building appearances among the troops whose "marshal" he was. Except for the wartime conferences, which took him as far afield as Teheran and Potsdam, he seems to have spent almost all his time immured in his Kremlin suite, or at his various resorts. Leningrad, the second city of the USSR and the birthplace of the Revolution, he seems to have visited only once after 1929.

Churchill's account of his visit to Stalin's quarters in the Kremlin in 1942 indicates that this official residence was still the simple four-room suite that Stalin had occupied in the twenties, in harmony with the austere tradition of Lenin's time. However, it is also well established that the dictator maintained at least one sumptuous estate near Moscow and a number of villas in the Caucasus Mountains and on the Black Sea coast, although the existence of these amenities was never publicly noted in the USSR. Indeed, the impression left by Stalin's press is that he did not indulge in activities unbefitting a demigod, such as recreation, illness, or even marriage. In 1932 the death of his second wife, Nadia Allilueva, was announced—although no mention was made of the violent circumstances (suicide or murder?) of her demise—and the existence of the two children of this marriage was acknowledged (the boy, Vasili, became an air force general after the war). So little was known about his personal life that it was for years widely believed that Stalin married a third time, to Kaganovich's sister, though this was wholly untrue.

In his years of supremacy Stalin's volume of public speeches and published writings dwindled greatly. Only one of his four speeches, said to have been delivered in 1937, can be considered public, and in 1947 there was not even one. Only two volumes of his official *Works*, planned but never completed, would have sufficed to contain almost all his publishable writings after January, 1934 (it required eleven volumes to contain the works of the previous fourteen years).

The withdrawal of Stalin the man facilitated the fabrication of the myth of Stalin the demigod, who was as ubiquitous as the actual human being was elusive. The rarity of his addresses or writings made it easier to build up gigantic campaigns of acclaim for these "classics." The incessant repetition of limitless praise for his genius was more effective because it was associated not with a human being but with an ikon. The ikonography of Stalin is probably one of the dreariest subjects awaiting historians of art. Its artifacts range from the ordinary cheap print, to massive oils (such as "Stalin and Voroshilov on the

Ramparts of the Kremlin"), to the immense metal statue at the mouth
of the Volga-Don canal, which is probably the largest statue of a living
man ever to be erected anywhere. Of course, the contrast between the
small, sallow, pockmarked man and the radiant, towering figure of the
ikon is striking.

The veneration of Stalin especially emphasized the versatility of the
leader's genius. Stalin's program for Soviet Russia was comprehensive
in scope, omitting no department of life and culture, and it is natural
that an all-embracing program should be directed by an all-round
genius. Stalin's claim to personal mastery of all questions was naturally
founded on his increasingly emphasized "genius" in the fundamental
science of Marxism-Leninism-*Stalinism* (until the thirties Stalin had
been presented only as an expositor of Marxism-Leninism; with deifi-
cation he became the proud possessor of an *ism* in his own right). Although an increasing variety of his works on Communist doctrine was
highly emphasized, the theoretical keystone of his claim to omniscience
came to be the essay entitled "Dialectical and Historical Materialism,"
published in 1938.*

On the base of this alleged theoretical wisdom a superstructure of
genius was steadily raised. Stalin contributed directly to this process by
delivering rare but madly acclaimed pronouncements on such subjects
as history, military science, linguistics, and economics. In numerous
other fields the propagation of his status as "the coryphaeus of the sciences" was left to his publicists. These included not only party propagandists, but all manner of humble and distinguished citizens, from
schoolchildren, factory workers, and peasants (expressing their admiration in letters to newspapers every day), to the members of the Academy of Sciences, who in 1949 published a ponderous volume of essays
describing the contribution of "the pride of Soviet science" (Stalin) to a
multitude of fields of learning.

The historical content of the Stalin myth followed naturally from
his speech at Lenin's funeral in 1924, when Stalin first staked his claim
to the Bolshevik apostolic succession. A large portion of the most
widely disseminated and most blatantly mendacious propaganda of
Stalin's culminating years emphasized that Stalin's Bolshevism was the
only possible sequel to Lenin's work and ideals. The alleged continuity
was based on the highly inventive argument that Stalin was practically
the cofounder of the party and certainly Lenin's right hand throughout the Revolution and Civil War. In 1938 the publication of the *History of the All-Union Communist Party (Bolsheviks)* (authorship of

---

* It was included in the *History of the All-Union Communist Party (Bolsheviks)*,
of which thirty-six million copies were printed, 1938–1948, not to mention millions
of additional copies of the essay appearing in periodicals, as a brochure, or in the
later editions of Stalin's anthology, *Problems of Leninism*.

which Stalin misleadingly claimed in 1946) laid down the outline of this grossly distorted version of the Bolshevik tradition, linked all Stalin's enemies to the capitalists, and lauded his flawless devotion to the work of Lenin. The date selected for the official establishment of the party was 1912 rather than some earlier date, which made it possible to represent Stalin as a member of the first Bolshevik Central Committee (after having been virtually the Lenin of the Caucasus). Despite the volumes of historical works on Stalin, the human side of his biography was scarcely touched upon, thus preserving the impression that he was not entirely mortal.

During the war the military aspect of Stalin's genius naturally received enormous attention. His supporter Voroshilov had prepared the way for this in a little book that fantastically maintained that it was Stalin who led the Red Army in the Civil War. But the full significance of the military cult emerged only after the victory at Stalingrad in 1943 made it seem fairly likely that there were more triumphs than defeats ahead. Stalin, who previously had been a civilian commander-in-chief, then took up the rank of marshal of the Soviet Union and in June, 1945, was "promoted" to the newly devised rank of "Generalissimo of the Soviet Union." Thenceforth most new works of ikonography depicted Stalin not in the unadorned, semimilitary party tunic he had been accustomed to wear, but in full uniform, often bedecked with several medals. To assure that the popular national victory would be associated with Stalin, the decisive Soviet offensives of 1944 were recorded as the "Ten Stalin Thrusts."

Taken literally, the torrent of praise for Stalin's genius is revolting and deceitful. But the very existence of this cult is in a sense the proof of its own validity, for only a genius of a very peculiar sort could conceive and execute so immense a deception and could enforce upon so many people such abject conformity to the absurd. Khrushchev maintains that this cult stemmed from the sickly vanity of one man, encouraged by a few villainous followers. Stalin's appetite for glory probably did exceed the normal by a substantial margin, but this does not exclude the likelihood that the cult of the leader was acceptable and even necessary to a large number of Soviet citizens (and foreign Communists) during a period of colossal sacrifice. And Stalin's own totalitarian vision, which seems to have required an omnipotent demigod, is a logical extension of the Bolshevik tradition.

The glorification of Stalin appropriately symbolized the fate of the party after 1929—that is, its transformation into an increasingly effective vehicle by which one man could exert more and more control over more and more people. Stalin personally took over more of the leading state offices: Chairman of the Council of People's Commissars ("Council of Ministers" after 1946) in May, 1941, a month before the German attack; Chairman of the State Committee of Defense, which served as a kind of war cabinet; People's Commissar of Defense; Marshal and then Generalissimo of the Soviet Union; and in practice, though not in name, People's Commissar of Foreign Affairs (as chief Soviet negotiator, 1939–1945).

It is noteworthy that Stalin's new offices were in the state structure rather than in the party apparatus. Although the two were closely interlocked throughout his reign, with numerous high officials holding major offices in both, it appears that Stalin chose to enhance the role of the state. From the later thirties on, the Communists in the police force intermittently terrorized other Communists, clearly under Stalin's direction. And after 1946 a presidium of the Council of Ministers, composed of Stalin and eight party leaders—but excluding at least two eminent ones (A. A. Zhdanov and N. S. Khrushchev)—seems to have been second to no party organ in policy making. The point is not that Stalin was antiparty, but rather that he could rely on alternative instruments of power to manipulate different situations. Lenin, too, in the last years of his active career, had made major use of such bodies as the Council of People's Commissars, the Cheka, Rabkrin, and Goelro, which were filled with Bolsheviks but did not report directly to the Central Committee of the party. After the passing of Lenin, Stalin had worked to alter this order and concentrate as much power as possible in the bodies that he controlled—the party Secretariat and the Orgburo. Once Stalin had consolidated his power, he returned to a pattern of rule through various party and extraparty organs, which served as a system of checks and balances against any of his more ambitious lieutenants but permitted him to keep one hand on each of the two main levers of power.

Naturally, Stalin retained his accustomed offices in the party apparatus (General Secretary, senior member of the Politburo and Orgburo, until these last two were merged in 1952), but his authority in the party after 1929 did not depend solely on these offices, nor even on the combination of his party offices and his lofty titles in the Soviet apparatus. Stalin's authority, like Lenin's, ceased to be associated with his statutory offices and became an intrinsic part of his personality. The name "Stalin" took on a unique authority of its own; in the Soviet Union he was often referred to neither by official title (e.g., General Secretary Stalin) nor by the normal Bolshevik appellation, "Comrade Stalin," but as "the great Stalin" and "our Leader" (*vozhd'*—often compared with *Duce* and *Führer* in its connotations).

Against this background it was quite appropriate that Stalin's personal secretariat, a body not mentioned in the party statutes or Soviet constitution, increased its practical authority to the point at which it may well have become the most crucial center of power in the Communist world. Although G. M. Malenkov, who became Stalin's heir apparent by 1953, owed his early promotion to service in this body, Stalin carefully kept it segregated from the normal party and state organs, permitting no interlocking membership between the personal secretariat and, let us say, the Politburo or the Council of Ministers. The chief secretary on whom Stalin most strongly relied was a shadowy individual named A. N. Poskrebyshev, who seems to have enjoyed continuous tenure in his uniquely important office from about 1930 until 1953, while Stalin's chief lieutenants in the party-Soviet organization were continually being shifted around the apparatus, moving laterally, vertically—or out. The scope of Poskrebyshev's responsibilities is indicated by his accession to the rank of lieutenant general during the war, the same rank awarded Khrushchev, a member of the Politburo. It is more forcefully implied in the secretary's abrupt disappearance when Stalin died and in Khrushchev's later, bitter remarks about this "shield-bearer" of Stalin. If Stalin really did feel a unique confidence in the loyalty of Poskrebyshev, it was very likely because he was aware that Poskrebyshev knew the Politburo would remove him the day Stalin was gone.

As Stalin increasingly concentrated authority in his person and his personal secretariat, he permitted less and less activity—even purely formal meetings—to the statutory organs of Bolshevism. Of course Stalin had gained effective control of the party congress and conference during the twenties, and in the last twenty-three years of his life presumably could count on mighty ovations and no opposition at these gatherings. Nevertheless, he all but eliminated such meetings, despite their statutory importance. The Sixteenth Congress met in 1930, the Seventeenth in 1934, and the Eighteenth in 1939 (until 1934 the statutes called for annual congresses; after 1934 for triennial ones). After 1939 it appeared that Stalin intended to ignore the congresses entirely, but in 1952, only a few months before his death, a widely proclaimed Nineteenth Party Congress assembled, for the dictator did not want to see the prestige of the party slip too far, possibly creating a dangerous imbalance between party and Soviet apparatuses. Although Stalin's failing health evidently prevented him from delivering the Central Committee report, he asserted his continued interest in the party as such in a brief address which was notable for its omission of any indication that he might have to pass on his mantle to a successor.

During the late twenties the joint meeting of the Central Committee and Central Control Commission, with a combined membership (including candidates) of over 300, served as a sort of substitute congress. But in 1934 new statutes transformed the Central Control Commission into a "Party Control Committee" and thereafter the joint sessions ceased. The Central Committee itself met from one to four times a

year between 1934 and the onset of the war in Russia, but not once
during the war and only on four authenticated occasions from 1946
through 1952 (including two meetings held in close conjunction with
the Nineteenth Party Congress).* As late as 1937 serious discussion
and even resistance to Stalin's policies occurred in this body, but thereafter it dwindled to insignificance before the leader's might.

More surprising is the similar fate of the Politburo, a smaller body
not so bady suited to serve as the kind of council that even a dictator
might find useful. No list of meetings of the Politburo is available, but
Khrushchev claims quite plausibly that Stalin made decisions without
asking the opinion of either the Central Committee or the Politburo.
The State Committee of Defense probably supplanted the Politburo
during the war, and in later years it appears likely that Stalin rarely if
ever formally convened the Politburo. He did, however, utilize a series
of specialized subdivisions that he established among the membership
in the Politburo, such as a so-called "sextet" to deal with foreign affairs. It appears that in practice the supreme council of the Soviet
Union consisted of intimate, vodka-bibbing, all-night dinners at Stalin's villa, attended regularly by such officials as L. P. Beria, Malenkov,
and Molotov and occasionally by others whose special advice was desired.

The culmination of Stalin's process of subordination of the statutory
party organs came at the Nineteenth Party Congress in October, 1952.
New party statutes, replacing those of 1939, disbanded the Orgburo
and the Politburo entirely and appointed a "Presidium of the Central
Committee" in their stead. But this new Presidium was clearly not
intended to make top-level policy decisions, for a majority of its thirty-
five members and candidate members were decidedly secondary figures.
Just how Stalin intended to operate within this new framework is far
from clear. When he died, only five months after the introduction of
the new statutes, it was revealed that an unofficial "buro" of the Presidium enjoyed at least a shadowy existence under the new scheme,
although it is not known whether it ever met or who its members were.
What is generally accepted is that Stalin's last table of organization
served to reduce the power of the lieutenants who had belonged to the
Politburo. That it was Stalin's scheme and distasteful to his lieutenants
is pretty well demonstrated by their haste to abolish the unwieldy Presidium and to reestablish a genuinely potent Presidium of fourteen as
soon as Stalin was safely dead.

* The Statutes of 1934 called for no less than four sessions of the Central Committee per year, while the 1939 statutes reduced the theoretical minimum to one per
year.

9

THE AGE OF STALIN
Terror and Utopia

It is inadequate to explain Stalin's concentration of power in his own hands as simply a reflection of paranoid insecurity or to present the cult of the leader as merely a product of sickly vanity. These oversimplified interpretations miss the intimate relation between Stalin's unquestionable self-seeking and his grandiose utopian drive, which led him to risk his personal reputation and security in vast social and political gambles. The Age of Stalin was characterized by a costly and risky drive, interrupted only by World War II, to extend the scope and intensity of Bolshevik power in Russia far beyond the limits that had existed until about 1929.

At this juncture the Soviet Union was certainly a one-party dictatorship, but it fell far short of Stalin's totalitarian vision of socialism. Not only did dissenters from the Politburo line within the party and Soviet society at large exist, but they expressed themselves publicly. For example, the party archives of Smolensk record that in 1929–1930 dissident party members openly said: "The Five-Year Plan cannot be fulfilled" and "The state farms and collective farms give nothing, but only take," while a nonparty factory worker declared: "Formerly there was one tsar—now a whole lot of them—every Communist is a tsar." Intellectuals too could dissent, despite censorship. For example, when the more or less anti-Bolshevik writer E. I. Zamiatin was criticized by a Communist, another litterateur publicly defended him, maintaining that Soviet writers were gagged. (If this had been wholly true the protest would not have occurred.) A dictatorship existed, but it was not so terrifying or pervasive as to be called totalitarian.

Although factories and mines (except for some small enterprises) were state-owned, the potential force of the party was not yet felt in the industrial economy and a number of the most responsible posts in the organs of planning and administration were rather casually left in the hands of unrepentant Menshevik economic experts. Strikes were illegal (except by permission—which was never granted), but even so they were far from unknown in the late twenties. The countryside was subdued as far as active antiparty organization was concerned, but it could hardly be considered socialized or bolshevized. In June, 1929,

slightly less than 4 percent of all peasant households had been collectivized, and party organizations on the countryside were few and small
(less than one rural citizen in 400 was a party member).

Although Stalin probably never formulated a complete blueprint or
timetable for the development of his model monolithic society, it is
clear that the laxity of the regime in 1929 did not conform to his ideal.
And it is only mildly speculative to suggest that Stalin planned on the
use of a considerable degree of terror in "the construction of socialism." A sociological attempt to explain the role of terror in Stalin's
Russia has suggested an analogy with an electrified fence in a cow
pasture, which serves to condition the inmates to the desired pattern
of behavior. One might also borrow an analogy from psychiatry and
suggest that Stalin used terror on Soviet society somewhat as a psychia-
trist applies electric shock therapy to a patient to weaken accustomed
associations and responses—in the Soviet case, to break down the usual
patterns of human association and mutual trust and to produce the
"new Soviet man," a person who could really be at home in a totalitarian society. Whether or not Stalin ever dreamed of such analogies,
it does seem likely that his campaign of terror had a higher rationale
than mere sadism or political maneuver, that it was integrally related
to forming the "new Soviet man" and achieving the goal of communism. In this light the suffering of innocent victims, from anonymous
peasants to loyal Politburo members, becomes comprehensible as an
attempt to impress all citizens with the power of the leader and the
necessity of obedience. The very arbitrariness and unpredictability of
the terror heightened its physchological impact. N. A. Bulganin, a Politburo member, demonstrated the point when he allegedly told Khrushchev: "It has happened sometimes that a man goes to Stalin on his
invitation as a friend. And, when he sits with Stalin, he does not know
where he will be sent next—home or to jail." At lower levels in society
corresponding reactions have also been observed: former Soviet citizens reported that they kept a small bag of essentials by their bedsides
in the not unfounded belief that the police might come for them any
night.

Stalin also sought to extend the effectiveness of the party as a pervasive elite, to advance his forces from the "commanding heights" that
they held in the twenties into the valleys of society as well. This required enlisting many new recruits and intensifying the devotion and
quality of the elite. The purges that operated in the party fairly con-
tinuously from 1933 to 1939 did not begin as terrorism and in many
cases involved expulsion from the party without any police action, as
had the purges of the twenties. That is, the normal Leninist process of
selecting and rejecting members of the elite—without terrorism—was
a natural part of party life, especially at a time when the extent of

party activity in the economic and social life of the country had been greatly increased. Because this normal process became inextricably entwined with the terrorism of the latter half of the thirties, a good deal of confusion has arisen over the meaning of "purge" in Bolshevism. In one sense it is a permanent fixture of any party of the Leninist type and continued under Khrushchev and Brezhnev, who have acknowledged that unworthy party members must be weeded out at a good clip. In a more limited sense it is the combination of broad social terror and the removal of unsuitable Bolsheviks, which reached its high point in the late thirties and was renounced by Khrushchev.

With or without terrorism, the expulsion of party members in 1934–1938 was so widespread that recruitment failed to offset losses, and there was a sharp downward trend in total membership in those years. On the other hand, the rapid growth in party membership, including candidate members, from 1929 (1.5 million) to 1935 (3.5 million), meant that the size of the elite in Stalin's time was always markedly greater than that of previous years.* Moreover, a substantial share of the field work of the party was undertaken by the young Communist auxiliary of the party, the Komsomol (age limit: twenty-six, according to 1936 rules). This body grew from about two million in 1928 to about nine million in 1939, despite losses during the purges, and its growth constitutes a significant reflection of the expanded role of Bolshevism in Stalin's Russia.

An enlarged Bolshevik vanguard was at no time more necessary than in the early thirties, during which the most drastic changes in the social and economic life of Russia were attempted. Although all parts of the country were drawn into the whirlpool that has often been called the "Second Revolution," the countryside not only underwent economic upheaval but also suffered from the first great terror of the Age of Stalin. The frantic replacement of the peasant family by the collective farm as the basic unit of Russian agriculture, while certainly not economically rational in the short run (nor in the long run, quite possibly), was definitely rational from Stalin's point of view. The new collective farms and the machine tractor stations that supplied them with essential implements provided the foundation for an unprecedented degree of party control in rural areas. Between 1930 and 1934 some 50,000 party members from the cities were sent into the country to man the new outposts, especially the primary party organizations associated with the machine tractor stations. And even though the number of rural party organizations and the proportion of peasants in the

---

* The party membership slipped to somewhat under two million in 1937–1938 (the low point was 1.9 million in 1938), but was over two million in every other year after 1930. In February 1941 it stood at 3.8 million.

party have lagged, the collective farm system has been preserved in essence as a foundation of Bolshevik rule, an enduring monument to Stalin. Although Khrushchev has made some modifications in the system, he never stated publicly that collectivization, even at its most painful moments, was one of Stalin's errors.

An important adjunct to the expansion of the party authority on the countryside as a result of collectivization was the terrorization of the peasantry. This commenced shortly after Stalin's speech of December 27, 1929, calling for "the liquidation of the *kulaks* as a class." In the next few months the full weight of the party, with its police and Komsomol auxiliaries, was set to enforce the rapid reorganization of the peasantry into collective farms, the confiscation of *kulak* property, and the application of terror.

In the first months of 1930 a civil war raged on the countryside between unequal forces: the virtually unarmed and unorganized peasantry and the contemporary version of Lenin's proletarian elite, especially its security forces. In some cases villages were wiped out by military action and in many more cases a portion of the populace was rounded up and shipped off to remote forced labor camps in the dead of winter with practically none of their possessions. Reliable statistics on deportations are unavailable, but it is clear that they were very substantial, as is indicated by the creation in 1930 of a new branch of the police establishment, "The Chief Administration of Camps" (Gulag). This grim organization, with its difficult economic assignments and its chronically high death rate among laborers, remained an imposing, though inconspicuous, reminder of Stalin's terror until he died. Although some forced labor camps existed before 1930 and have continued since 1953, Gulag is chiefly identified with the Age of Stalin.

Orders issued by the party in the Smolensk area forbade the confiscation and deportation of non-*kulaks* among the peasants, and it may be that Stalin did not intend to terrorize the whole rural populace, except by example. However, it is well established that in practice the local party representatives forcibly collectivized or deported peasants of various degrees of wealth (and poverty). Stalin himself stated in March, 1930, that there had been deviations from his intent—cases of "dizziness with success"—and he ordered a temporary relaxation in the collectivization drive. Whatever his original intention, it is clear that he allowed the widespread random terrorization of the peasantry to wreak havoc for a couple of months and that few of the alleged *kulaks* were soon released from their bondage, which proved fatal to many. The terrible famine of 1932–1933 may not have been planned, as some have charged, but it too served to advance the subjugation of the peasantry.

In the early 1930s the urban population was subjected to an equally furious economic drive, but without the massive dose of terrorism.

Once he had gained full power, Stalin set aside the conception of a planned economy, which attempted to nurture a predetermined rate of growth by the rational allocation of resources. After ousting a number of the economists of intelligentsia background, who had prepared the 1927 draft of the Five-Year Plan (several were tried for economic "wrecking" in 1931), Stalin radically altered the character of the Plan. In his hands the Five-Year Plan lost most of its significance as an attempt at scientific economic management and became an adjunct to the myth of the leader. Rationality gave way to immensity as the guiding principle. Production in excess of Plan estimates was considered most desirable, and in an orgy of mythological statistics, the first Five-Year Plan was pronounced complete in 1932—a year ahead of schedule. The party and its Komsomol auxiliary played an essential role in this new conception of planning; theirs was the responsibility for goading the rest of the populace forward toward the shimmering statistical paradise. Before the stalinization of the Five-Year Plan, the party had been well organized in the industrial enterprises of Russia but had not been playing a revolutionary role in the life of the economy. In the Plan era, which has continued to the present (except during the war years), the role of the party as the motivating force behind economic growth has been a primary tenet of Bolshevism.

A particular characteristic of Bolshevik economic planning, as established by Stalin, is the emphasis on heavy industry—the means of production, rather than consumer goods. Stalin explained that this was essential for national defense, which was true, but it appears that his zeal for heavy industry was partly a reflection of his personal taste for the grandiose: the huge tractor, the ambitious canal (Baltic-White Sea, Volga-Don, and others), the immense hydroelectric dam, or the largest building in the world (the Palace of Soviets—planned but never built). Light industry, housing, and agriculture seemed irrelevant, and the last two especially slipped into dangerous condition after the war (and not wholly because of the war). The resulting drastic decline in the standard of living made necessary the most strenuous efforts on the part of the party to suppress dangerous discontent among the people and to encourage continued exertions. There is no doubt that Russia achieved a striking rate of economic growth in the Age of Stalin, and that the basis of this growth was the ability of the Bolshevik regime to maintain a very high rate of investment, made possible by the low standard of living. In short, Stalin required that the "proletarian" elite relentlessly impose discipline upon a peasant-proletarian mass that was toiling mightily for comparatively small returns, a harder long-term task for the "vanguard" than Lenin ever envisaged. It is not surprising that enthusiasm for the seemingly endless Five-Year Plans waned as time went on, for "plan" became synonymous with "all-out drive" rather than "rational allocation." That the Five-Year Plan represented austerity rather than the good life of socialism was implicitly recognized by Stalin in a speech of 1946, in which he attempted to reassure his public with the prediction that three more Five-Year Plans might be enough to secure communism in the USSR.

The first years of the thirties were a real test of strength for Stalin and his regime, but by 1934 it could be said that the crisis was passed. Agriculture was largely collectivized, the worst inefficiencies of the transition from private agriculture had been alleviated, and a good crop had been harvested in 1933. Industrial management had become less chaotic, and in 1933–1934 the rate of growth of industrial production soared from about 5 percent to a remarkable 20 percent. Labor discipline was comparatively well enforced, partly by the introduction of piecework wages and greater wage differentials and partly through the establishment of the domestic passport system in 1932. The intellectuals, too, were more securely controlled; the literary profession, for example, was impressed into a party-directed, "closed-shop" Union of Writers in 1932. The Seventeenth Party Congress, which met in January, 1934, indicated its sense of self-satisfaction by calling itself "the congress of the victors." An ordinary dictator, even one with totalitarian tendencies, might have considered the situation quite acceptable.

In light of Stalin's whole career, however, it appears that he felt that both the party and the populace stood in need of much conditioning before they could be considered fit for the Communist society he visualized. It seems likely that he wanted to expand the application of terror (by executing an alleged oppositionist plotter, M. N. Riutin, for example) at least as early as 1932, but that he ran into opposition from his own cohorts. These "moderate" Stalinists had supported Stalin's ruthless policies in the past and none of them could be considered liberals by any normal standard, but they evidently did not share the full measure of his vision of the "new Soviet man" nor of the educational value of terror.

Although many details remain obscure, it seems reasonably sure that Stalin first joined battle with the "moderate" Stalinists in December, 1934, following a Central Committee meeting in which some of his wishes were frustrated. On December 1 the presumed spokesman for the "moderates," Kirov, was assassinated in his Leningrad party headquarters under circumstances that strongly suggest Stalin's involvement. The death of this member of the Politburo provided the pretext for a serious exercise in terror. Thousands of persons were deported to forced labor camps, and Kamenev and Zinoviev were tried in secret for alleged complicity and sentenced to prison. The sifting of party membership that proceeded in 1935 and early 1936 led to more and more arrests.

However, the repressions following upon Kirov's death were but a dress rehearsal of the full-scale terror that began in the latter part of 1936. In the intervening period Stalin improved the deployment of his newer, tougher Bolshevik bosses (Zhdanov in Leningrad and Khrushchev in Moscow) and further weakened the remaining "moderate" Stalinists. Kuibyshev, a Politburo member, and Gorky, the famous writer who held no major office but presumably influenced Stalin through a personal relationship, are both considered to have been "moderates," and both died in the interval between Kirov's death and the onset of the full terror in 1936. Stalin is suspected of having caused both deaths, but the evidence is not as strong as in the case of Kirov.

It was in August–September, 1936, that Stalin opened his great campaign of terror. In August Kamenev and Zinoviev were hauled out of prison, and with fourteen others were tried for anti-Soviet conspiratorial activities in collaboration with Trotsky and the Nazis. This was the first of the three famous "show" trials, at which a total of fifty-four first- or second-rank Bolsheviks incriminated themselves on the most fantastic charges, involving gross treason to bolshevism over a protracted period. Presumably these ludicrous confessions were extracted by various combinations of brutal coercion, promises of clemency, and appeals to party loyalty. From Stalin's point of view the trials were important not only because they removed his former opponents, but also because they demonstrated that deviation from Stalin's position meant treason and that the party and populace must deal unmercifully with the faintest trace of dissent. Moreover, the absurd charges laid against such distinguished old Bolsheviks as Kamenev, Zinoviev, Bukharin and, most of all, the absent Trotsky provided a matchless exercise in the art of believing (or pretending to believe) the incredible.

Anyone with the slightest knowledge of the Bolshevik past who could believe that Trotsky and others had long been capitalist agents was capable of believing anything that he was told on the authority of the leader. Such a person was properly conditioned, in Stalin's view, for residence in the new "socialist" society that the "Stalin Constitution" of 1936 claimed to be already in existence. It has been said that it was the exiled Trotsky—and not the defendants in Moscow—who was really the one on trial, but in a broader sense the trials represented a crucial test for all party members and Soviet citizens, a test of their willingness to submit their intellectual independence to totalitarian rule.

The first of the "trials" (August, 1936) served a special purpose as the pretext for the general terror that Stalin had wished to apply earlier. A telegram signed by Stalin and one of his toughest new assistants, Zhdanov, in September, 1936, maintained that the necessity for a trial showed that the security forces were "four years behind" in the liquidation of enemies, and it called for the replacement of the incumbent police commissar, G. G. Iagoda, by N. I. Yezhov, the man whose name was to be associated with the wild terrorism of 1936–1938.

It became increasingly clear that Stalin's list of victims was not limited to old Bolsheviks of intelligentsia background, although this group —which had lost control of the party in the twenties—was very nearly wiped out. The wave of terror also engulfed those of Stalin's own lieutenants who failed to pass the credulity test. The last of these who dared speak out made their final stand before and during the Central Committee meeting of February 23 to March 5, 1937. The most distinguished was Stalin's personal friend, Sergo Ordzhonikidze, who died on February 18 (hounded to suicide, according to Khrushchev). At the meeting itself, P. P. Postyshev, a candidate member of the Politburo, frankly said that he did not believe that "an honest party member who had trod the long road of unrelenting fight against enemies for party and for socialism would now be in the camp of the enemies." Postyshev was an excellent example of the newer, ruthless generation of Communist executives raised up by Stalin in the period of the terror on the countryside. Yet he failed to pass the credulity test that was required of "new" Soviet men and, like others who raised objections in the Central Committee, soon found himself under arrest. Stalin's victory in the Central Committee was marked by his one major published statement on the terror, "On Deficiencies in Party Work and Measures for the Liquidation of Trotskyite and Other Double Dealers," delivered near the end of the session. In it Stalin enunciated the dogma that the class struggle must intensify as the Soviet state advances toward communism, and that therefore increasingly ruthless repressions are justified. He particularly warned against the assumption that the apparently loyal and sometimes successful worker cannot be a "wrecker" and that the "Trotskyist counterrevolutionary Fourth International" had large reserves of agents in the USSR.

Having imposed this doctrine on the Central Committee, Stalin was able to expand the terror to include the former leaders of the police apparatus, including former Commissar Iagoda (arrested in April, 1937), and the high command of the Red Army, including Commander-in-Chief Marshal M. N. Tukhachevsky. The military victims, who were liquidated without public trial, were incriminated by the most lurid evidence of all: documents forged by the Nazis and planted in Soviet security agencies through the naïve medium of the Czech government. It is hard to know how much credence Stalin put in this forged material or in the "confessions" that his police interrogators extorted. Various documents released by Khrushchev prove that Stalin knew and approved of the techniques of the interrogators, which would seem to indicate that he realized that ostensible "enemy" strength in the Soviet

Union was an invention. To a victim of intense paranoid delusions, this knowledge might not be relevant, and there is certainly reason to believe that there was a strong element of mental imbalance in Stalin's conduct at the time. On the other hand, his delusions—if such they were—did not prevent his operation as a keen political analyst for many more years, and any "madness theory" must acknowledge that Stalin usually seemed capable of controlling his overt paranoia to suit his political objectives. It is possible that Stalin sincerely believed he was crushing a real conspiracy against himself, even though he knew that the particular accusations of his prosecutors were invented as part of the brainwashing that he was deliberately inflicting on the party and masses. But really adequate understanding of his mental state and motivations might be impossible even if Stalin were alive and willing to submit to a thorough psychoanalysis. As he is not, and as there are only fragmentary hints concerning his inner life, any analysis of his motivation and private beliefs remains highly problematical.

What is clear is that the terror reached its highest peak in 1937–1938 and by 1939 had enveloped 70 percent of the Central Committee members elected at the Party Congress of 1934, about half of the higher army officers, a substantial but unknown proportion of the economic administrators, a very high proportion of the intelligentsia of the minority nationalities, and a wide assortment of individuals who were probably picked up at random or on the basis of the hysterical slander generated by the terror. The last definable group to perish was that portion of the police staff that had been responsible for maintaining the highest pitch of terror; this included Yezhov himself, who was released from office on December 8, 1938, and simply vanished in early 1939.

By this time the terror had subsided. If Stalin really had believed in the threat of conspiracy, he was able to stifle his fears and return to a more realistic approach before the terror began to devour his instruments of power. In 1939 Stalin admitted that there had been excesses and mistakes (a further indication that he probably did not believe his own fabrications) and blamed these on the conspirators themselves and on his own inept subordinates. He attempted to come out of the affair as the benefactor of the populace, somewhat in the manner of the interrogator who offers a friendly cigarette to the victim of a twenty-four hour third degree.

Certainly the affair had cost something, apart from the price paid in human lives. The annual growth of industrial production is estimated to have fallen from about 20 percent in 1935 to about 2 percent in 1939. This decline (partly the result of increased military investment) and the poor showing of the army in the war with Finland in 1939–1940 may be partly attributable to the losses in the military ranks caused by the terror. On the other hand, there is no reason to believe that the terror had adversely affected the power of the governing machinery or Stalin himself. On the contrary, there is much evidence that it had been a real success in conditioning the Soviet populace and especially its "vanguard" to the kind of discipline that Stalin associated with true bolshevism and ultimate communism. It is almost certain that only a very few persons did not feel some of the psychological impact of the terror, and that party members and other persons with comparative responsibility would never again feel secure while Stalin lived. Yet only a man with Stalin's conception of the Communist vision would look back over the terror and tell the Eighteenth Party Congress (March, 1939) that "the weeding out of spies, assassins, and wreckers from our Soviet organization was bound to lead, and did lead, to the further strengthening of these organizations."

The terror on the countryside, which reached its peak in early 1930, and the Yezhov terror of 1936–1938, which raged primarily in the cities, represent Stalin's two major campaigns to condition the party and masses to his new society. It is true that extensive arrests and deportations were inflicted in 1939–1940 on the borderlands acquired through the Nazi-Soviet Pact and again at the close of the war in borderlands that had displayed fairly general disloyalty before the Germans. In fact, the postwar deportations inflicted on the Baltic countries, the Crimean Tartars, and some of the Caucasians might well be considered the most thorough local applications of terror in Stalin's career. Forced laborers and prisoners of war returning from Germany to Russia also received a thorough going-over, with many sentences resulting. And in the postwar years there was a rising wave of bloody purges within the party, mostly focused on various regional organizations. On a countrywide scale, however, Stalin was able to rely on sample doses of terror and verbal reminders to sustain the approximate level of conditioning that had been achieved by 1939. That this was possible is a considerable tribute to the effectiveness of Stalin's prewar terror techniques, for there was a considerable relaxation of Bolshevik rigidity during the war. One reflection of this was the massive increase in party membership in the war years (from 3.8 million in 1941 to 5.7 million in 1945, despite extremely high casualty rates among members in the armed forces and occupied areas). Although many of the new members were weeded out after the war (although evidently with comparatively few arrests), Stalin felt sufficiently secure to permit membership to remain well over six million as long as he lived (it was 6.8 million by 1952).

A number of postwar incidents served to remind these party members that indiscipline would not be countenanced. The most striking was probably the "Leningrad case," a murky episode in 1949–1950, in the course of which N. A. Voznesensky, a Politburo member and head of the economic planning apparatus, was executed secretly. In the months before his death in March, 1953, Stalin seems to have been planning a refresher course in terror, possibly on the same grand scale as that of 1936–1938. The main portent of bloodshed was the "discovery" in January, 1953, of a conspiracy on the part of a number of Kremlin doctors, none of them political figures but most of them Jewish, who had allegedly shortened the lives of two Bolshevik leaders (Zhdanov and a lesser figure) and had planned to eliminate others. This time the class enemy behind the conspirators was said to be a Jewish capitalist organization, indicating that the new terror would have a particularly anti-Jewish direction. Whether or not Stalin really disliked the Jews, he did on several occasions in his career exploit the anti-Jewish feeling which is not without popular appeal in Russia. At the same time, there were signs that others might fall victim, especially those connected with the police, whom the official press charged with "carelessness" (i.e., treason).

Terror was probably Stalin's major instrument for the preparation of the masses for communism, but the use of Soviet Russian nationalism also played a major role buttressing the solidarity of the new society. The Bolshevik attitude toward Russian nationalism had always been ambiguous and at various times, especially during the crisis of the Civil War, the Bolshevik regime associated itself with Russian patriotism. Until the early thirties, however, the official party line opposed certain aspects of Russian nationalism. "Great Russian Chauvinism" was often castigated and the culture of Western Europe was recognized as valuable to Russia and worthy of respectful attention. Although this outlook was reasonably consistent with Marxism, Stalin seems to have understood that it failed to recognize the depth of Russian nationalist feeling and the necessity of utilizing this sentiment in the interests of Bolshevik solidarity. Despite his apparent intellectual crudity, Stalin seems to have sensed that nationalism is an essential social cement in almost any state, and especially in a totalitarian state. Stalin's personal sentiments had long been favorably disposed toward Russian nationalism, and it was no reversal of form on his part to sponsor the revival of patriotism in the thirties. As the new Soviet Russian nationalism unfolded, the historic heritage of Russia was treated with increasing favor; not only were the national heroes of Russia reinstated, but in 1941 an article by Stalin (dated 1934) defended tsarist Russian foreign policy against an attack that Engels had written in 1890. In general, Stalin implied that Engels failed to see that the interests of the Russian nation and those of the world proletarian movement might merge. Russia had become a "socialist fatherland" and Leninism was explicitly declared to be the "highest achievement" of Russian culture. In 1934 Great Russian nationalism (no longer called "chauvinism") was dismissed as a major problem in the Soviet Union, while "local (i.e., non-Russian) nationalism" was designated as "a danger to the state." Although the national republics with their limited cultural autonomy remained, an all-union "Soviet patriotism" was officially inculcated, and the benign authority of the Russian big brother was insisted upon—even retroactively in the centuries of imperial expansion under the tsars. This position probably failed to satisfy some of the intellectuals of the minority nationalities, but few of these survived the purges, and the national groups that wavered in loyalty during the war were thoroughly terrorized afterwards.

The war years were indeed the great test for Stalin's marriage of communism and Russian nationalism, and it is likely that the survival of the regime depended on the success with which it associated itself with patriotic interests. Certainly large portions of the citizenry had no love for the government, but many of the disaffected were willing to set aside their discontent in the interests of national defense, even accepting Stalin in his pose as Russian military leader. This apparent success of the synthesis of Bolshevism and Russian nationalism seems to have encouraged Stalin to carry it to its most extreme development in postwar Russia. In these years admiration for the Russian national heritage was combined with a new, intense xenophobia, for which Stalin's lieutenant, Zhdanov, was the chief spokesman. "Cosmopolitanism" was fiercely condemned, and the autonomy or priority of Russian culture was maintained to an absurd degree, including the fabrication of evidence to support the assertion that the first flight of a heavier-than-air craft occurred in Russia. If such a policy, which reduced to a minimum any cultural exchange with foreign countries, was unpopular with some intellectuals, it may still have been a source of strength in mobilizing mass support for the immensely demanding program of postwar reconstruction. It may be too that Stalin's propagation of nationalism in Soviet Russia helped to foster reactive, anti-Russian nationalism in the Communist world and outside, aggravating a problem that his heirs would have faced in any case. But it is safe to say that the net result in the USSR of Stalin's marriage of communism and nationalism has been greatly to the advantage of the regime and one of his shrewdest strokes.

10

THE AGE OF STALIN
Security and Imperialism

As totalitarian dictator Stalin naturally insisted on exercising supreme authority over the foreign policy of the Soviet state, and he at least attempted to do the same for the world Communist movement. His international policy was inevitably influenced by geographic, military, economic, and political considerations, but it was founded on two tenets of Stalinist Bolshevism. First, he believed that the security of the USSR, the "base" of international communism, was the crucial short-term objective of Soviet foreign policy and the world "proletarian" movement. Second, he believed that enduring security for the USSR and the proletariat could be obtained only through a realization of the universal, historic goal of communism: the establishment of a world-wide Communist order. One important implication of the first principle deserves emphasis: Stalin would not hesitate to set aside the interests of the Communist movement outside the USSR if the security of the "base" seemed to require such a sacrifice. This in turn required that Russian preeminence and Bolshevik discipline be accepted by all branches of the world Communist movement, not only by parties that had yet to take power, but also by Communist states. At times the tension between the long-term and short-term objectives was acute, but Stalin seems to have experienced no difficulty in assigning priority to the current interests of the USSR. For all his caution in this respect, he did not lose sight of the ultimate goal (as Trotsky and various democratic statesmen thought he had), and when comparatively safe opportunities for Communist expansion presented themselves, Stalin was ready and able to exploit them. In short, his guiding principles appear to have provided Stalin with both short-term flexibility of action and long-term stability of purpose, which proved confusing to the so-called capitalist powers.

Stalin in 1927 had stated that "a period of new revolutionary upsurge" had started, which would presumably assure the eventual realization of worldwide communism. During the next fifteen years or so, however, he emphasized the short-term security of the Soviet "base," which could hardly afford to risk overt support of foreign revolutions while it was undergoing drastic internal transformation or, as during the war years, fighting for its own existence. No major effort was made to assist the Chinese Communists, who were forced in 1935 to withdraw their battered forces to the Northwest, there to reorganize under Mao Tse-tung. Clearly, it would have been even more costly and risky to attempt to save the German Communists from decimation at the hands of the Nazis, who had come to power partly because the Stalin regime had ordered the German Communists not to join the Social Democrats in opposing Hitler.

From mid-1934 until at least the latter part of World War II Stalin felt obliged not only to avoid any assault on the capitalist world, but even to seek collaboration with various non-Communist powers, however costly to the immediate interests of foreign Communist parties. In 1934–1935 this collaboration involved entry into the previously much-despised League of Nations and contraction of a defensive alliance with France, and then a general order to foreign Communist parties to form a "united front" with other working-class groups against the Fascist threat. This tactic was formally proclaimed at the Seventh (and last) Comintern Congress, which met in Moscow in August, 1935. However, Stalin's interest in the Comintern—even a highly stalinized one—as an instrument of world Communist policy was even less than in former years. Once he had achieved personal supremacy in the USSR, he attended no meetings of the Comintern executive committee, and in general accorded rather low billing to the Third International.* Evidently foreign Communist parties retained their utility in Stalin's sight, but he preferred to deal with them directly and individually. In 1937 he facilitated this kind of supervision by transferring from the Comintern to the Secretariat of the Bolshevik Party a major share in the responsibility for the administration of international communism. In the same period an increasing number of the European Communist leaders took up protracted residence in the USSR, directly under Stalin's surveillance. This was partly a reflection of the more stringent anti-Communist measures which were being applied in most of Central and Eastern Europe at that time, but it also fitted in with Stalin's presumable desire to train and control directly the area of Communist movement whose field of operations lay in the part of Europe nearest the USSR. When the time came, these "Muscovites" among the Central and East

---

* The "Short Course" on the history of the party, the Stalinist primer published in 1938, pays rather little attention to the Comintern. More striking, Stalin's last major report to a party congress (1939), does not mention the Comintern, except for a sarcastic jibe at "imperialist" propaganda about it, even though the report includes a significant summary of the international situation and the "tasks of the party in the sphere of foreign policy." By this time Stalin had ceased to extend public interviews or congratulatory letters to foreign Comintern leaders, even though he found the time to give numerous interviews to "bourgeois" journalists and to publish congratulatory notes to the participants in the "Moscow-Kara Kum automobile race" and the like.

European Communists played a considerable role in the communization of their homelands, which in most cases they reentered with the Red Army. The Stalinist education that these foreign Communists received included a drastic weeding-out process during the terror of the late thirties (the victims were so numerous among the Communist parties of Poland and Korea that these parties were formally disbanded for a time).

In this period the Spanish Communist Party probably received more pervasive assistance and direction from Moscow than did any other foreign Communist party. Stalin decided to support the Republican forces in the Spanish Civil War of 1936–1939 through a "Popular Front" with socialists and other anti-Fascists (i.e., a broader coalition than a "united front" limited to Communists and socialists), which the Communists were able to dominate to a marked degree. In this struggle the Spanish Communists were directed and given military assistance by Soviet Communists and others dispatched from Moscow. Whether or not Stalin's maximum goal in Spain was the establishment of a Communist-dominated state is still a matter for speculation; his minimum objective almost certainly was to give a temporary check to the expansion of Fascism and to win for Communists the admiration of various anti-Fascist groups abroad. In no case did his interests in the Spanish contest lead him to take any overt steps that would risk the involvement of the USSR in war.

The continued emphasis on the security of the USSR was strikingly demonstrated soon after Franco had triumphed in Spain. Having lost confidence in the utility of cooperation with the Western democracies to protect Russia from the rising Nazi German power (a loss of confidence hastened by the surrender of Czechoslovakia in 1938–1939), Stalin voluntarily sacrificed much of the good will that he had won among anti-Fascists by negotiating a nonaggression pact with Hitler in August, 1939. Although Trotsky (who was to be murdered by a Bolshevik agent in August, 1940) considered this to be an utterly unprincipled act, it may be understood as a calculated (or miscalculated) application of the first of Stalin's principles: the short-term security of the USSR. Since foreign Communist party members had been thoroughly indoctrinated in the spirit of this principle, and the less disciplined ones had been removed by one means or another, the international Communist movement survived the shock of the Nazi-Soviet pact without much loss of composure or fidelity to Stalin (who had not bothered to warn his foreign comrades of the pact, much less seek their advice). For Russia the agreement brought the opportunity to expand the strategic western borderlands during 1939–1940 and to divert German aggression toward countries other than the Soviet Union. The Finnish, Estonian, Latvian, Lithuanian, Polish, and Rumanian territory gained by Soviet Russia with the blessing of the Nazis was incorporated into the Soviet Union under direct Bolshevik control.

The security gained for the USSR was, of course, short-lived. The German invasion of Russia in June, 1941, rendered worthless the sacrifices of international communism, and Stalin was obliged to turn to Britain and the United States for assistance. With the survival of the USSR more severely threatened than at any time since 1919, Stalin emphasized the short-term goal of security far more than the extension of communism on a world scale. The official Soviet line distinguished between the "imperialists" of the enemy camp and the British and Americans, whom Stalin now credited with having "elementary democratic liberties . . . , trade unions . . . , labour parties . . . , (and) a parliament. . . ." He referred to all the Allied forces as "armies of liberation," and promised on behalf of the USSR, "No intervention whatever in the internal affairs of other peoples!" In 1943 this pledge was underscored by the dissolution of the Comintern, although Stalin probably found this no sacrifice since he preferred to maintain bilateral relations with foreign Communist parties. Those in German-occupied territory were asked to undertake difficult underground operations. Moreover, the most successful of these movements, Tito's Yugoslav partisans, was asked to jeopardize its future by recognizing the rights of the exiled King Peter, whom the Soviets thought it politic to support for the moment. In the Far East the Soviets, hoping to divert the Japanese from the Siberian frontier, supported a "united front" (formalized in 1937) of the Chinese Communists and Kuomintang.

Although the perfectly sincere Bolshevik interest in defending Soviet Russia led many persons to conclude that Stalin was no longer interested in world communism, it now seems sufficiently clear that he never ceased to believe that capitalism must be destroyed before the USSR could achieve complete security or the ultimate Communist society could be established. If anything, Stalin's conviction was probably strengthened by the experience of wartime alliance. The delay in opening the second front in France, which Stalin had been led to expect before 1944, quite clearly suggested to him that his allies were attempting to permit the Germans to bleed Bolshevism white. Through such tactics Stalin himself had hoped to weaken the capitalists when he made the pact with Hitler in 1939, and as late as the closing weeks of the war he saw in Anglo-American attempts to arrange the early surrender of German forces in Italy a plot to release these troops for use against the Red Army. Another wartime issue that probably appeared to Stalin as evidence of the continued malevolence of capitalism was the Polish question, and especially the Allied efforts on behalf of a Polish government-in-exile that was not well disposed toward the Soviet Union.

Certainly Stalin intended all along to seek the security of the USSR by at least such steps as the retention of his gains of 1939–1940; he insisted on this in discussions with Anthony Eden in December, 1941, when the very existence of the USSR hung in the balance. But it is hard to say when Stalin came to feel that he could go well beyond the short-term interests of Soviet Russia and undertake the formation of a really large Communist empire as a major advance toward world communism. Ambassador George F. Kennan, an American student of Soviet foreign policy, suggests that "as early as 1943 he [Stalin] was already resolved to exploit a German defeat, if at all possible, for the purpose of expelling the British and Americans from Europe and assuring the early communization of the continent." This may be, since Stalin evidently believed that capitalism would suffer a severe economic crisis following the war and had reason to believe that the United States would withdraw her forces from Europe at the end of hostilities.

On the other hand, it seems more likely that Stalin began the advance beyond the prewar Soviet borders with no definite plan except to see how far he could go, both geographically and in the degree of communization within the territories occupied. His fervent pleas for maximum Anglo-American military efforts on the continent imply that his minimum objective until at least the last months of the European war did not include communization of Western Europe by means of Soviet occupation. Moreover, it is safe to assume that the Stalin regime was far too preoccupied with immediate problems as the war closed to take time to work out a blueprint for an empire. Even had they wished to work out such a plan, the Soviets could not have predicted the operation of such vital variables as American policy, the reactions of various European peoples to communism, the rate of recovery of the Soviet economy, and the internal situation in countries outside Soviet occupation. It seems most likely that Stalin worked out his program of expansion only as these factors gradually became clearer. Despite the tactical errors that he committed in various areas (the attempt to take over northern Iran, the alienation of Yugoslavia, and the Berlin blockade, for example), Stalin's extension of Communist power in the postwar years may be considered a masterpiece of flexibility.

In most cases the future satellite countries, once "liberated," were governed by coalitions of Communist and other political parties; monarchs were permitted to remain for a time in Rumania and Bulgaria. Although the new form of government was described as a "People's Democracy," the 1945–1947 Communist line maintained, even for internal consumption, that this was not a "dictatorship of the proletariat," and the constitutions of the Eastern European states did not at first follow the Soviet pattern. However, as Western unwillingness to offer forceful resistance (except in Greece) and the effectiveness of Communist terrorism, electoral fraud, agrarian reform, and propaganda became apparent, Stalin advanced further. Generally speaking, the first phase of communization had proven successful by 1948, and the second phase began at about that time. In the Soviet-occupied states of Poland, Hungary, Rumania, Bulgaria, and East Germany, and also in unoccupied Czechoslovakia, the Communists took complete control of the coalition governments and imposed Soviet-style regimes, including constitutions based on the "Stalin" model of 1936. These regimes also made at least a start toward collectivization, Stalinist industrial planning, and the police state. In Yugoslavia and Albania approximately the same level of communization had been achieved with almost no Soviet aid by 1945. On the other hand, Marshall Plan aid and internal resistance to communism prevented Stalin from carrying off any coup in France, Belgium, or Italy (unlike Czechoslovakia), despite the strength of the Communist parties of these countries. When both parliamentary tactics and violence in the streets showed that the Communists could not take power in these countries without Soviet intervention—and the risk of war—Stalin prudently avoided overt aggression.

By about 1950 Stalin's new European empire bore the unmistakable imprint of the leader's conception of bolshevism, even though he never bothered to visit any part of it after the Potsdam Conference of July, 1945. The satellite world, even though it was not absorbed into the Soviet federation, was as deeply involved in the Stalin cult—and real obedience to his orders in most cases—as the USSR itself. This control was partly the result of the presence of the Red Army (except in Czechoslovakia, Yugoslavia, and Albania), and partly the presence of Soviet ambassadors (wielding extraordinary "advisory" powers), police officials, and military advisors. But the native Communist leaders, most of whom had resided in the Soviet Union, generally accepted Stalin's direction as a matter of personal subordination. This subordination was tested and strengthened in 1949–1952 by Bolshevik-style purges—complete with preposterous accusations, phony confessions, and real executions—carried out "independently" in the satellite countries. Much less important in the stalinization of East Europe was the Cominform, founded in 1947 as a visible union of the Soviet, French, Italian and East European Communist parties (excluding the German and Albanian parties). Although Stalin definitely had an interest in this body (he is known to have telephoned instructions to the founding session), he appears to have retained the belief that Bolshevik dominance in the international Communist movement could best be achieved without any formal international league of Communists. Operating from headquarters outside the Soviet Union, the Cominform served mainly as a means of disseminating the dogmas laid down in Moscow, and it dwindled in importance even in Stalin's lifetime.

Far from encouraging any real union of satellite Communists, Stalin suppressed discussion of various sorts of federation between these states, notably between Yugoslavia (before Tito's defection) and Bulgaria. While the satellites all were obliged to make bilateral agreements with the USSR, any intrasatellite bloc was prohibited. Not only were the satellite countries isolated from one another, they were also, like the USSR itself, sealed off from the capitalist world. Although Soviet Russia became the military, political, and economic arbiter of the satellite zone, and increasingly its cultural model as well, it does not appear that Stalin intended to integrate his conquests into the USSR in the immediate future. As an imperialist he was content to accept the establishment of personal and Bolshevik party authority over the satellites, permitting them to exist as nominally independent national states. Although the new Communist empire in Europe was beset with serious difficulties, it was definitely a going concern. Established in the face of Western hostility and at little cost to the USSR, by 1950 it possessed the military and political forces to sustain itself against any immediate threat. It was one of Stalin's chief achievements and a major extension of the Bolshevik tradition.

Two portents of future difficulty for international communism appeared in Stalin's lifetime. One was the defection of Tito's Yugoslavia from the satellite bloc in 1948; the other was the addition of the vast Chinese state to the Communist sphere in 1949. Khrushchev, among others, had maintained that the alienation of Yugoslavia was the result of Stalin's clumsy arrogance, and it is certainly true that Stalin did underestimate the will power and domestic strength of Tito and his government. The basic issue, however, as Khrushchev discovered in subsequent dealings with Tito, was not tactfulness but the fundamental principle that all Communist parties must accept Bolshevik discipline under Soviet leadership. Tito was probably ready to accept this condition in the earlier phase of his partisan operations, but a number of developments during and after the fighting seem to have led him to the view that a heroic, self-sustaining Communist party should be respected as a member of the Communist community in its own right, entitled to a degree of autonomy. In 1948, when Stalin attempted to discipline the perpetrator of such heresy, Tito surprised him by demonstrating that an old Communist, who had been eager to declare his state a dictatorship of the proletariat on the Soviet pattern, might nevertheless defy the Bolshevik leader. The immediate result was the loss of a strategic part of the Communist bloc, and the purging of alleged Titoists in other satellites. The loss was infuriating, but not mortal. Most of the other Communist countries, occupied by the Red Army and infiltrated with Bolshevik security forces, were unable even to attempt to follow Tito's example. Nevertheless, the case of Yugoslavia suggested that it might be extremely difficult to communize large areas of the world and retain Russian Bolshevik hegemony at the same time.

In a much broader sense, the victory of the Chinese Communists by 1949 raised the same problem. During the late thirties and early forties, the Chinese Communists under Mao had existed as a virtually sovereign state in at least some portion of China. Although they never openly challenged Stalin's authority, they had not been subject to the more direct forms of Soviet domination. It appears that Stalin did not expect them to overthrow the Kuomintang government in the immediate postwar period and was not very generous in granting military assistance during the Civil War of the late forties. The Bolshevik dictator naturally welcomed the victory of communism in China, but the appearance of a Communist state that was too vast and too proud of its independence to be truly subordinated bore ominous overtones. Nevertheless, no major Sino-Soviet difficulty arose during Stalin's lifetime. Mao tactfully journeyed to Moscow in 1949 to negotiate a bilateral treaty of alliance and aid, and Stalin, with comparatively good grace, assented to the renunciation of Soviet rights in Manchuria (except one port). The apprehensions of both Communist powers during the Korean war of 1950–1953 also served to prevent any outbreak of Sino-Soviet friction in Stalin's time. But the problems of achieving far-flung Communist power in truly Stalinist fashion remained unresolved.

Stalin has been accused of rigidity in the last few years of his life, and it is true that his international policy was highly inflexible in certain particulars, such as his refusal to sign an Austrian state treaty or to permit any capitalist tourism in Russia. But in the main Stalin displayed a clear perspective on world affairs and a flexible tactical line during the last few years of his life. In recognition of the revival of Western Europe in alliance with America (NATO was established in 1949), the Western European Communist parties were ordered to cease their militancy and adopt "united front" tactics in an attempt to block "American imperialist" influence. In 1949 a massive "peace campaign" was initiated, stressing the pacific intent of the USSR and attempting to attract as much non-Communist support as possible. At the same time the USSR diverted a substantial share of its manpower and industrial output, badly needed in the reconstruction, to build up the armed forces to well over five million, a massive peacetime body. Stalin maintained publicly that only combined forces, and not atomic weapons alone, could be decisive in modern war, an inflexible, outmoded theory according to his posthumous Soviet critics. But it must be remembered that the Soviet research leading to a Soviet atomic explosion at least as early as 1949 and to extensive aircraft and rocket development took place under Stalin's regime. Had he not been interested in the potentiality of the new weapons, he surely would not have permitted the massive financial allocations needed for their development. He not only hedged his bet on peaceful propaganda with a military buildup, but also hedged his bets on various types of military forces.

It appears that the Chinese example had stimulated somewhat higher hopes for the immediate future in the Far East. Military operations in South Korea and Indochina continued until after Stalin's death. However, truce talks were initiated in Korea before Stalin's death, and in his last major pronouncement (October, 1952) he set the tone for world policy in stating that war between capitalist powers was more likely than war between the capitalist powers and the Soviet bloc. In December, 1952, he even hinted that he might consent to meet President Eisenhower at a summit conference.

Thus Stalin reacted to the stiffening of "capitalist" resistance and the increased risk of disadvantageous war by shifting away from his long-term objective, world communism, and returning to his short-term objective, security for the zone already communized. By the opening of 1953 this maneuver had already enhanced Soviet security, but it could not realize its full potential while Stalin, by now a symbol of Communist expansionism, remained the supreme leader of the peace movement.

The opening months of the year 1953 found the Soviet Union and its ruling party approaching turning points in various important fields of policy. Although the effectiveness of tactics of "peaceful coexistence" were limited by Stalin's personal presence, the combination of a vast military buildup and maturing developments in nuclear weapons, air craft, and rockets promised to offer the USSR the opportunity to return to a tougher policy. At the same time, the problems of Sino-Soviet collaboration had scarcely begun, and sooner or later Stalin would have had to modify his accustomed authoritarianism—if he could. Within the USSR the recovery and further advancement of industrial production had been impressive, but the continued faltering of collectivized agriculture seemed likely to bring about a crisis if matters were not improved. Since the beginning of the war, there had been a tendency to rely more on Soviet organs—such as the Council of Ministers—and less on party bodies, and the reorganization of the Politburo and Orgburo into a Presidium late in 1952 may have portended a basic transformation of the governing apparatus. Perhaps the key to all these questions lay in the political terror that seemed to be about to break out in early 1953, heralded by the mysterious "plot" of the Kremlin doctors.

Whatever Stalin had in mind, he did not live to realize it. On the night of March 1–2 he is supposed to have suffered a cerebral hemorrhage, and on March 5 he died. Although the timing of his death was certainly convenient to at least some of his frightened lieutenants, whose accustomed moral level was not beyond reproach, there is good evidence that he had not been strong for some years and had previously suffered from a circulatory disorder. At the very end, according to his daughter, "something incomprehensible and awesome happened that to this day I can't forget and don't understand. He suddenly lifted his left hand as though he were pointing to something above and bringing down a curse on us all. The gesture was incomprehensible and full of menace, and no one could say to whom or at what it might be directed." * This final sign of clairvoyance and intimidation was a fitting finale to Stalin's efforts to realize his particular vision of communism.

* From Svetlana Alliluyeva, *Twenty Letters to a Friend,* trans. Priscilla Johnson (New York: Macmillan, 1967).

11

STALIN
AND THE BOLSHEVIK TRADITION

"The Revolution Betrayed"—"Thermidor"—"Grave-digger of the
Revolution"—"You have strangled the party"—"Genghis Khan"—
such were the epithets that the defeated oppositionists of the twenties
hurled at the victorious General Secretary of the Bolshevik Party. Considering the polemical brilliance of some of the vanquished, and the
crude deceptions that Stalin employed in his campaign for power, it
is not surprising that there is considerable support among non-Communists for the theory that Stalin betrayed the Leninist Bolshevik tradition in the years 1924–1929. Lenin himself lends credence to such an
interpretation in his testamentary writings of 1922–1923.

Yet it should be remembered that Lenin qualified and postponed his
attack on Stalin, that the bureaucratization of the party and the prohibition of opposition factions were in large measure Lenin's work, and
that only Lenin himself had the prestige to maintain monolithic unity
in the party without resort to Stalin's more odious tactics. In terms of
the Bolshevik tradition Stalin's best justification—denied him by his
ambition to play the second Lenin—might have been the following
argument: Lenin could not bequeath his unique prestige to his heir,
and Stalin could not afford scruples in his tactics, if the elitist, dogmatic, monolithic character of the party was to be preserved. Stalin had
to compensate for his personal inadequacies by inflating the cult of
Lenin; by making himself its high priest; by exercising immense tactical patience; by deceiving, coaxing, and threatening; and by conceal-
ing as long as possible his vaulting ambition and his peculiar conception of socialism. If, as his enemies said, he was bent on concentrating
power in his own hands, identifying his person and the Bolshevik
cause, this too was the essence of Leninism. Whether or not Lenin
would have approved of his tactics, Stalin preserved the Bolshevik tradition against unfavorable odds, a process that involved some intensification of the authoritarianism and ruthlessness that was inherent in
bolshevism. It is significant that Khrushchev, for all his denunciations
of Stalin's sins, still respected the imperative necessity and the success
of Stalin's victories against the opposition of the twenties.

But Khrushchev, while declining to rehabilitate the reputations of the oppositionists of the twenties, laid charges of equal gravity against Stalin's Leninism. Under his guidance the Party Congress of 1961 resolved:

> To recognize as unsuitable the continued retention in the Mausoleum of the sarcophagus with J. V. Stalin's coffin, since the serious violations by Stalin of Lenin's behests, the abuses of power, the mass repressions against honest Soviet people, and other actions in the period of the cult of the individual make it impossible to leave the coffin with his body in the V. I. Lenin Mausoleum.

This is even less acceptable than the critique by the opposition of the twenties, for the Khrushchev position takes issue with Stalin only after having acknowledged him as the rightful Bolshevik leader until about 1935. This position accepts almost all of the repressive policies of bolshevism before that time and the strangulation of the Trotsky-Zinoviev-Bukharin opposition thereafter, only to wax indignant over the fate of the loyal Stalinists and bystanders who perished in the terror of his later period. Either the party was to accept Stalin as the "Lenin of today" or to take the side of John Stuart Mill against Marx and Lenin and to admit that truth, especially political truth, is nobody's monopoly. In sum, neither the Bolsheviks whom Stalin bested in the twenties nor Khrushchev and his associates have been able to advance a cogent case against Stalin's claim of having continued the main lines of the Bolshevik tradition.

On the other hand, it is less than just to Stalin to present him merely as an imitator, for the practical application of Bolshevik principles was enormously extended in his time and to a very large extent under his personal direction. Most important, Communist rule was transformed from dictatorship to totalitarian dictatorship, thus approaching the completion of the work that Lenin had started. This required an immense and sustained act of will, for the terror on which Stalin's totalitarianism was based was so unbearable that even his select, toughened lieutenants sought to relax this pressure as soon as he was gone. This implicit compliment to the awful strength of Stalin's spirit was far more sincere than the ritualistic praise his henchmen had heaped upon him while living.

It would be a great oversimplification to attribute Soviet economic growth since 1929 directly to Stalin. His agricultural policies probably were retrogressive on the whole, and it is very hard to determine whether Stalin's methods of industrialization were more effective than other alternatives known to history. But from a Bolshevik point of view he deserves acclaim for having impregnated the expanding economy with the authority of the party, surpassing in this respect not only earlier Soviet experience but also contemporary Nazi-Fascist dictatorships.

It would also be an excessive simplification to give Stalin exclusive credit for the expansion of the Communist sphere during and after World War II. The wartime conditions that brought Soviet power into much of Eastern and Central Europe were in large measure the unexpected result of Stalin's miscalculation in signing the Nazi-Soviet Pact; out of catastrophe he fashioned triumph—at a hideous cost that not even he desired. But even though he may have blundered into victory, he exploited his opportunities with undeniable skill and force. And if his new empire suffered from certain basic weaknesses, he nevertheless did add greatly to the international strength of the Bolshevik Party.

Yet Stalin remains not only one of the chief enemies of liberty in the twentieth century, but also one of the most odious persons ever to have attained great power. It is practically impossible to cite any attractive human qualities to relieve the grey horror of his biography, and the moralist can justly appreciate the irony by which only the Albanians, of all his Russo-European subjects, still honor his memory. But the student of politics must recognize his genius, possibly ranking him as the most successful politician of the century. And the Bolshevik leader of today, who stands on an edifice erected largely through the efforts of Stalin, would be doing no more than is just if he restored Stalin's corpse to Lenin's mausoleum and honored his unique contribution to the Bolshevik tradition.

PART THREE
KHRUSHCHEV

12

THE EDUCATION OF
A STALINIST

Nikita Sergeevich Khrushchev was the first of the three major Bolshevik leaders to use his real name rather than a conspiratorial pseudonym in public life. Unlike his two immediate predecessors, his entire connection with the movement had been in the period after the Bolsheviks had seized power, and his whole political career had taken place within a bureaucratic administrative system. The question is: did this lack of prerevolutionary experience and this abundance of bureaucratic service seriously affect the continuity of the Bolshevik tradition?

In some ways it undoubtedly has. Certainly Khrushchev's personal style was far removed from the spirit of the revolutionary intelligentsia or even the quasi-intelligentsia of the earlier twentieth century. The change in the perspectives of generations was at least superficially reflected in Khrushchev's dress: the well tailored, expensive, and comfortable garb of the modern executive had replaced Lenin's professorial black suit and Stalin's stern party uniform.

Contrary to the expectations of some analysts, however, such changes in form did not bring corresponding changes in the foundations of Bolshevism. Stalin's political machine was not only an effective instrument of rule, but also an excellent school for Bolsheviks. All party officials had to study its curriculum in order to survive, and the standards for promotion were high. Khrushchev attended this school for about thirty years, and if he expressed dislike for the principal after graduation, it does not follow that he learned his lessons poorly.

The scanty information available on Khrushchev's early years indicates that his background was more proletarian than that of either Lenin or Stalin. Khrushchev came, as Stalin did, from a humble family, but while Stalin went from the seminary into professional revolutionary work without having been a laborer at any time, Khrushchev took up full-time party work at thirty, after many years as an ordinary laborer. He was born in the Russian town of Kalinovka in Kursk Province in 1894, the son of a peasant who often worked in the coal mines of the Donets Basin, over two hundred miles south in the Ukraine. Young Nikita tended farm animals and received a little education through the parish church—substantially less academic learning than Stalin received before leaving the seminary and incomparably less than Lenin's law degree represents. At fifteen Khrushchev joined his father at the mines of Yuzovka (later Stalino and now—thanks to Khrushchev —Donetsk), where he was to spend most of the next ten years.

In this time he worked at various jobs and apparently acquired sufficient skill as a mechanic and machinery operator to be deferred from military service in World War I. Although hardly prosperous, he was able to marry and support two children, both of whom were born during the war years. There is no indication that he participated in political or trade union activities (although the Donets mines offered plenty of opportunity) until the opening of the Russian Civil War in 1918. By this time mining operations were virtually at a standstill, and it may have been unemployment that impelled the youth Khrushchev to join the Red Guards detachment that was formed in Yuzovka and, later in the year, the Communist Party. Although Stalinist and Khrushchevist accounts later credited him with a vaguely important role in the Civil War, it does not appear that he attained any special distinction as a soldier-Bolshevik. But at least he had attached himself securely to the winning side, and after demobilization he was able to return to the mines in 1920 or 1921 as some sort of minor foreman and a member of the local Communist organization. His next step was to improve his inadequate formal education by entering the local "workers' faculty," an emergency secondary school for ambitious proletarians. This may not have contributed very much to his formal education, but it did lead him into Communist administrative work, first on a part-time basis as secretary of the school's party group, and, after leaving school in 1925, as full-time secretary of a largely rural district in the Donets Basin. This type of executive work was Khrushchev's principal occupation for the rest of his active career.

From 1925, when his professional executive career began, until 1939, when he became a full-fledged member of the Politburo, Khrushchev's advance through the ranks was undoubtedly brilliant. From his district post he moved back to Yuzovka and thence to the party offices in Kiev, meanwhile attending both Ukrainian Union Republic and All-Union Party Congresses as an elected delegate. In 1929 he went back to school, this time the J. V. Stalin Industrial Academy in Moscow, where he again used the office of party secretary of the school as a steppingstone to higher responsibilities. His chances for advancement were probably improved by his acquaintance with Kaganovich, who headed the Ukrainian party machine in the early days of Khrushchev's career and directed activities in the Moscow area while Khrushchev was enrolled at the industrial academy. Instead of finishing the three-year course, Khrushchev was in 1931 given the secretaryship of one of the districts within the large Moscow party machine. Such an assignment usually is a severe test for the rising Bolshevik bureaucrat, who at this level is a crucial link between the higher authorities who formulate policy and the rank and file who must produce results. There is usually a high failure rate, possibly 50 percent, but Khrushchev passed the test in two districts within Moscow. His success led to his promotion to Second Secretary (Kaganovich was First Secretary) of the whole city of Moscow only a year after he had left the academy. He remained in Moscow until 1938, succeeding Kaganovich as First Secretary of the city and the surrounding region in 1935.

Khrushchev's technique as a field leader of the party was already marked by the style that later distinguished his dictatorship. In a manner reminiscent of the typical tough but able American political boss, he continually toured his territory, making himself known to his subordinates as a man capable of both exuberant comradeship and ruthless demands. Evidently the technique paid dividends, especially in contrast to the office-sitting, bureaucratic aloofness that is proverbial in Soviet officialdom. In particular Khrushchev devoted considerable personal attention to the most highly publicized urban monument of Stalin's new order, the Moscow Metro, which was completed with great speed through the constant pressure of the party organization and its Komsomol auxiliary.

Having made good in the Moscow territorial command, Khrushchev was promoted in January, 1938, to the secretaryship of the Ukrainian Union Republican organization, the biggest job of this sort and one that carried with it fairly certain membership in the Politburo (Khrushchev became a candidate member in 1938 and a full member the next year). He remained in the Ukrainian command until the very end of 1949 and did not receive any further definite promotion until after Stalin's death.

Since hyperbolic condemnation of the victims of Stalin's terror, along with equally hyperbolic praise for Stalin, was the general rule for some years, it is hard to say that Khrushchev really distinguished himself as a conformist to the absurdities of the party line. But such statements as the following, taken from a January 30, 1937, speech by Khrushchev, indicate that he at least lagged behind nobody as a chanter of hate and praise:

> These murderers (the accused in the January, 1937, trial) aimed at the heart and brain of our Party. They have lifted their villainous hands against Comrade Stalin. . . .
>   By lifting their hands against Comrade Stalin, they lifted them against all the best that humanity possesses. For Stalin is hope; he is expectation; he is the beacon that guides all progressive mankind. Stalin is our banner! Stalin is our will! Stalin is our victory!

And he lagged behind nobody in benefitting by the purge: his promotion to the Ukrainian secretaryship and the Politburo became possible precisely because Stalin liquidated the previous secretary (a Politburo member), S. V. Kossior, and needed a reliable, ruthless replacement, who would inevitably have to finish the bloody cleansing of the party bureaucracy. Khrushchev not only carried out this task but also avoided the dangerous backlash that overtook many other purgers when Beria directed the removal of those guilty of "excesses."

In his twelve years in the Ukraine Khrushchev directed the party apparatus through purge, expansion into the "western Ukraine" (taken from Poland in 1939), Nazi invasion, Soviet counterattack, and postwar reconstruction. Although Kaganovich took over the post for a few months in 1947 (for reasons that remain obscure), Khrushchev became identified with mature Stalinist rule over the second largest national group in the USSR, the forty-odd million Ukrainians. In some ways his method was, though on a smaller scale, very much like that of the General Secretary. Khrushchev fostered a regional cult of his own leadership (Soviet and satellite leaders were permitted to do so, provided they deferred to Stalin's clearly superior position in the Bolshevik hierarchy). During the war he became a lieutenant-general (and collected about as many medals as Stalin did) and took on the chairmanship of the Ukrainian Republican Council of People's Commissars (after Stalin had become the head of the All-Union Council). Khrushchev applied terror both to the genuinely disaffected, including the newly conquered western Ukrainians and wartime collaborators, and to the innocent. He applied all possible pressure to spur progress toward the economic objectives of the party—a vital task in a region that contained the principal granary and ferrous-metallurgy center of the country.

On the other hand, Khrushchev, even while conforming to Stalinist etiquette, showed something of his own style of political leadership. As in his Moscow days, he spent much time in the field, even accompanying military units into his new domains in the western Ukraine, and cultivated the image of a personable, approachable leader—a task made easier by his ability to speak Ukrainian at least moderately well. Although he kept a relentlessly firm hand on the machine, he observed the statutory norms for meetings of party bodies. Moreover, his technique as a general and member of the council directing the "front" or army group in the Ukrainian area made it possible for him to continue his usual close contact with his party subordinates and with the common folk.

For the last three years of Stalin's life (December, 1949, to March, 1953) Khrushchev served in Moscow, resuming the secretaryship of the party organization in the capital city and the surrounding district, to which was added for the first time a place in the Secretariat of the All-Union Central Committee (Stalin was one of the other four secretaries). Khrushchev specialized in the field of agriculture, and he associated himself with the consolidation of collective farms into fewer, larger units (with the establishment of "agricultural cities" as the ultimate goal). This last proposal had to be withdrawn after adverse criticism which evidently stemmed from his colleagues, but Khrushchev held a leading place at the Nineteenth Party Congress of October, 1952. His speech to this body ranked second to Malenkov's—discounting Stalin's brief appearance on the rostrum—and was devoted to the presentation of revised party statutes.

Khrushchev's education in Stalinism had been rigorous and quite diverse. He was thoroughly familiar with the central and regional administration of the party, with the military establishment, and with agricultural and industrial affairs. His main deficiency was in foreign affairs, for he had never left the borders of the USSR and never received any assignment in this field. His long sojourn in the Ukraine probably helped to develop a more independent approach to Bolshevik politics than was common among the officials who lived under Stalin's immediate scrutiny through almost their entire career (Malenkov and Molotov, for example), but Khrushchev had satisfied Stalin with his subservience and there was no reason to consider him a dissenter in any sense.

13

THE TRIUMPH
OF THE FIRST SECRETARY

Despite his undoubted success in the Stalinist hierarchy, Khrushchev
did not appear likely to become a central figure in the history of bolshevism following the death of Stalin. In March, 1953, he was almost
fifty-nine years old; he alone among the party leaders had never held a
major post in the central state organization; and he was not nearly as
widely known as at least a half-dozen others. In the first post-Stalin distribution of offices, announced on March 7, Khrushchev stood behind
Malenkov, Beria, Molotov, and Voroshilov in the new, ten-man Presidium of the Central Committee. In the Secretariat Khrushchev was
overshadowed by Malenkov, and he lost his command of the Moscow
regional party organization, a potentially useful basis of support. While
Malenkov succeeded Stalin as Chairman of the Council of Ministers,
and Beria, Molotov, Bulganin, and Kaganovich joined to their Presidium membership the title of "First Vice-Chairman of the Council of
Ministers," * Khrushchev still lacked any major post in the state organization.

This raises the crucial and perplexing question of party-state relations in the post-Stalin era. Despite the eventual appearance of a so-
called "antiparty group," there is no reason to think that any of the
leading politicians desired to demolish the party organization or to depart from the dogmatic ideological foundations of Bolshevism. All the
important leaders were members of the party Presidium, which they
obviously regarded as a council of great importance. In March, 1953,
they reduced its membership from thirty-six, including candidate members and Stalin's vacant chair, to fourteen members and candidates.
Even more indicative of the leaders' recognition of the lofty status of
the Presidium was the intense rivalry to control it during the five years
following Stalin's death, and herein lies the crux of the party-state
problem.

In the Bolshevik tradition, the dominant member of the inner council of the party (the Central Committee, later the Politburo, still later

---

* Mikoyan was simply "Vice-Chairman," the only holder of this slightly tarnished
dignity.

the Presidium) had come to this position of leadership as a party organizer—Lenin as the founder, Stalin as General Secretary. Whatever offices he might acquire outside the party, the dictator of the inner council arrived at this eminence by virtue of his ascendency in the party. After the death of Stalin there was a good chance that this tradition would be shattered, with incalculable consequences for the future of the party.

At first Malenkov seems to have made an effort to succeed Stalin as head of the Presidium, party Secretary, and Chairman of the Council of Ministers; this was in keeping with party traditions, since Malenkov had long been a major figure in the party Secretariat. But on March 21 it was announced that a Central Committee meeting of March 14 had "granted" Malenkov's "request" to be "released" from his duties on the Secretariat. The change was of major importance because it changed the terms of the competition for control of the Presidium. The three most likely candidates for supremacy, Malenkov, Beria, and Molotov, were leaders whose main duties and sources of authority now lay in the state organization, in the ministerial structure, not in the party apparatus itself. If, as seemed probable in early 1953, any of these (or Bulganin, Kaganovich, or Mikoyan) had gained supremacy in the Presidium, the Lenin-Stalin tradition would have been broken. The new dictator would not have been the main party organizer of the day. The Council of Ministers of the state would have been used to gain control of the party and not the reverse, as was traditional. This would have meant a renunciation of the "legitimacy" on which Lenin and Stalin rested their claims to supremacy, and it might have led to serious erosion of the party as the organizing, driving force in the country and as the infallible font of ideology.

How far-reaching a transformation might have occurred will never be known, for Khrushchev saw to it that the new dictator was the man who stood directly at the head of the party organization: Nikita Sergeevich himself. When Malenkov stepped down from the Secretariat, Khrushchev became the leading secretary among five (soon reduced to four), and the only one who was a member of the Presidium. In the new situation he was the only contender who could reaffirm the traditional supremacy of the party leader. He was well suited to this task by his long, almost exclusive association with the party machine and by his self-interest in the face of rivals who banked on the power of the ministries, not the party. His rivals for supremacy probably thought of Khrushchev as a "safe" executive who would subordinate the party machine to the ministerial leaders in the Presidium (Malenkov had a personal representative, N. N. Shatalin, on the Secretariat), but they underestimated Khrushchev's intense ambition and tactical shrewdness.

The first break came in June, 1953, when the "collective leadership" of the regime discovered that the second-ranking member of the Presidium, Beria, was a "British agent." This, at least, was the charge when his expulsion was publicly revealed by a Central Committee meeting in July. A much more plausible report attributed to Khrushchev has it that the Presidium determined that Beria, who directed the police apparatus, including crack security troops, was planning to seize power from his colleagues. Although he was officially tried and "executed" only in December, 1953, the report cited indicates that the Presidium had him shot during the meeting at which he was seized. The political significance of this act of gangland justice was to remove from the Presidium one potential dictator whose stronghold was in the ministerial structure rather than in the party itself. Directly or indirectly this helped Khrushchev to advance the Secretariat and his own status.

In September the Central Committee met for the fifth time in 1953 and Khrushchev emerged as a serious contender for supremacy. His triumph lay partly in the acquisition of the title "First Secretary of the Central Committee" (not "General Secretary," as Stalin has been called) and partly in the delivery of a major address on the deplorable situation in agriculture, an address which adopted a tone contrary to the official line of Stalin's day. Since this speech, and its counterpart delivered by Malenkov a month earlier, were clearly the most important policy statements since Stalin's death, it appeared that First Secretary Khrushchev had taken Beria's place, standing slightly behind Malenkov and ahead of Molotov. Moreover, Khrushchev soon began to demonstrate that the head of the Secretariat still controlled patronage within the party. In November, 1953, F. R. Kozlov, who supported Khrushchev at this stage, replaced V. M. Andrianov, probably a Malenkov supporter, as First Secretary of the important Leningrad regional party organization. And in March, 1954, I. V. Kapitonov, who supported Khrushchev to at least a fair degree, was named First Secretary of the Moscow regional party organization (five years later Kapitonov was demoted, but not before he had served Khrushchev in several crises). At the same time the lower party organizations were drawn closer to the Secretariat by the appointment of additional secretaries,* even beyond the limit prescribed by the 1952 statutes.

Evidently Khrushchev assumed, not unreasonably, that the manipulation of personnel was not by itself a sufficient guarantee of success in

---

* As prescribed by the 1952 statutes, on each of the four levels below the central party organization there was a "buro," roughly analogous to the Presidium on the national level, and a secretariat. Each secretary was an *ex officio* member of the buro of the regional party organization of which he was secretary. Thus, by increasing the number of secretaries, Khrushchev was increasing the number of his appointees and subordinates in the local buros in preparation for a similar procedure in the Presidium of the Central Committee.

his campaign for power. Some dramatic, popular policy had to be associated with his cause if he were to emerge with the stature of supreme leader. Unlike Stalin, who maneuvered for years before committing himself to massive collectivization and industrialization, the aging Khrushchev could ill afford to wait.

On March 2 he made his bid. A meeting of the Central Committee adopted Khrushchev's personal proposal for dealing with the chronic agrarian weakness: a costly and risky plan to put under cultivation by 1956 a vast amount of "virgin land" in Kazakhstan. The initial goal was an area twice the land surface of England; later this was increased to an area half again as large. In light of the competition between the First Secretary of the party and the principal ministers of the state, it is significant that this program, the most dramatic innovation since the first Five-Year Plan, was initially published as a party decision on the initiative of the First Secretary against the wishes of his main rivals. They probably considered it unsound but could not carry the day in the Central Committee. The case illustrates not only Khrushchev's forcefulness but also his willingness to gamble, for the lands in question were largely semi-arid areas where drought and dustbowls were a constant threat. If, after about two million laborers and vast quantities of capital had been assigned to this project, there was a bad run of weather, the project and its propagator would be highly vulnerable to the waiting critics. Fortunately for Khrushchev, the harvest was good in 1954 (although much of it was lost through inadequate storage and transport), which enabled him to ride out a bad crop in 1955; for the next seven years his luck held fair to good. In retrospect, the virgin lands plan seems to have succeeded in gaining the initiative for Khrushchev and the party in matters of agrarian policy, quite apart from its debatable success in solving the long-term problem of per capita food production in the Soviet Union.

In October, 1954, Khrushchev enhanced his prestige by taking up another major problem: relations with Communist China. While Malenkov and Foreign Minister Molotov remained at home, Khrushchev, accompanied by Bulganin and Mikoyan, conferred with the highest Chinese officials and negotiated a new bilateral treaty (generally favorable to China) concerning economic assistance and questions of territorial occupation.

Although the façade of "collective leadership" had been maintained since the fall of Beria (the rivals even vacationed together in August, 1954), an open rift began to develop at the end of the year. The issue which gave rise to the controversy was the allocation of investment between heavy industry (the means of production) and light industry (consumer goods). Although the actual budget that Malenkov supported did not involve a radical de-emphasis of investment in heavy industry, it seems likely that there was a real difference of opinion among the oligarchs and that Malenkov was unable to gain the backing of Khrushchev, Molotov, or other major leaders (Mikoyan, Minister of Trade, probably backed the change at first, but shrewdly withdrew before the showdown). In November and December, 1954, it appeared that Malenkov was holding firm and defending the consumer goods orientation through "his" mouthpiece, *Izvestiia* (the newspaper published by the Soviet state), despite critical articles in "Khrushchev's" *Pravda* (published by the Central Committee of the party). The campaign against Malenkov culminated in a meeting of the Central Committee in January, 1955, during which Khrushchev evidently felt confident enough to launch the final attack. While any defense that Malenkov may have offered remains unpublished, *Pravda* (February 2, 1955) reported that the First Secretary had castigated the consumer-goods priority program as "contradicting the laws of Marxism-Leninism and slandering the party, a belching forth by the right deviation [of views] that in their time were preached by Rykov, Bukharin and their ilk." Although he forebore to mention the name of the chief culprit, Khrushchev had implicitly identified himself with Stalin and his opponents with the "enemies of the people" who had opposed Stalin and were soon liquidated by him.

On February 8, Malenkov was obliged to submit his resignation as Chairman of the Council of Ministers. Significantly, this unspontaneous request to be "freed" from the chairmanship emphasized its alleged author's "inexperience" in "various sectors of the national economy" (industry?) and his "guilt and responsibility for the unsatisfactory state of affairs in agriculture" at a time "when the Communist Party of the Soviet Union and the workers of the country are concentrating all their energies for the further upsurge of agriculture" (the virgin lands campaign?), and assured the Supreme Soviet that in his new, unspecified post he would work conscientiously *"under the leadership of the monolithic and unified Central Committee of the Communist Party of the Soviet Union"* (emphasis added).

Malenkov's resignation (he became a "vice-chairman" of the Council of Ministers) indicated that for the moment there was little danger that supremacy in the Presidium could be obtained through the Council of Ministers of the state. The new chairman, Bulganin, was the former Minister of Defense and a first-deputy chairman, a less forceful figure who was evidently well disposed to collaborate with Khrushchev on terms of formal equality. Khrushchev was able to wring further advantage from the new circumstances by assigning Malenkov's former watchdog in the Secretariat, Shatalin, to a post on the shores of the Pacific. However, the First Secretary could not yet assert his own authority in the Presidium. Membership in this crucial council remained unchanged after the crisis of January–February, 1955, and the members of the Council of Ministers who also sat on the Presidium would have held a majority against the First Secretary, had they been provoked to unite.

Shrewdly, Khrushchev did not challenge them as a group, but, having isolated and undermined Malenkov, he applied the same tactics to the next in line: Molotov. Since 1939 this old Stalinist had specialized in foreign affairs, and it was in his own field that Khrushchev chose to tackle him. Judging by subsequent accusations from Khrushchev's camp as well as Molotov's usual demeanor, the minister of Foreign Affairs felt that the Soviet cause could only suffer in negotiation with the capitalist world. Khrushchev felt otherwise and evidently sensed that he could win a majority in the Presidium and Central Committee on this issue, at the same time enhancing his own role through the practice of highly personal diplomacy. In the course of 1955 the Khrushchev line was reflected in such events as the signing of a treaty with Austria and the withdrawal of Soviet forces from that country; the diplomatic recognition of West Germany; the inconclusive but highly publicized Geneva summit meeting of Bulganin, Khrushchev, Eisenhower, and Macmillan; and the almost equally glamorized visit of "B & K," as the apparent diarchy was then called, to India, Burma, and Afghanistan. But for the internal conflict in Russian communism, the most important development was almost certainly the renewal of "normal" relations with Yugoslavia. Despite Molotov's insistence that this rapprochement was still essentially wrong, Khrushchev and Bulganin went to Belgrade in May, 1955, on the exceedingly un-Stalinist errand of apologizing to Tito for the breakdown of "fraternal" relations. This they blamed on the defenseless Beria, a gambit that frustrated and annoyed Tito, who wanted a sensible apology. Khrushchev's confidence in his personal diplomacy was eventually shown to be overly optimistic with respect to Tito, who knew the Russian Communists, but for a time Soviet-Yugoslav relations were improved, much to the discomfiture of Molotov. He brought the issue to a head in a Central Committee meeting in July, 1955, but, according to reliable reports, found not only Khrushchev and Bulganin but also Kaganovich, Mikoyan, and a rising younger leader, D. T. Shepilov, against him.

The session not only administered a stiff setback to Molotov but also adopted a number of personnel changes which served Khrushchev's interests: a former associate in the Ukrainian party machine, A. I. Kirichenko, and a member of the Secretariat, M. A. Suslov, were promoted to full membership in the Presidium, while three new, pro-Khrushchev Communists were added to the Secretariat.

The July meeting of the Central Committee officially called for the convocation of the first post-Stalin party congress, the twentieth, clearly a major event in the struggle for supremacy. The months leading to this event in February, 1956, were full of subtle bargaining and maneuver, in which the major issue was Stalin. Ever since the old man's death his status had been ambiguous. His bemedalled corpse had been placed beside Lenin's in the public mausoleum, under the direction of mortician Khrushchev ("Chairman of the Commission for the Funeral of Joseph Vissarionovich Stalin"), and remained enshrined in statue, picture, book, and toponymy. But his sanctity had been called into question in a number of implicit but fairly clear respects. The first and one of the most important reversals of Stalinism was the retreat from rule by terror; although his heirs had all participated in and benefitted from the liquidations, they evidently did not share Stalin's faith in the efficacy of this technique either as a means of approaching the ultimate society or of maintaining their power. On March 28, 1953, the regime published its first amnesty, which began the liberation of many of Stalin's living victims and the posthumous vindication of many others. Stalin's final security crackdown, the "doctors' plot," was explicitly debunked on April 14. Even though the "trials" of Beria and many of his agents, a process stretching into 1956, recalled the great purge of the thirties, the destalinization of the political prisons continued steadily, bringing to light such an embarrassing number of innocents that statistics on the subject have not been released, and undoubtedly producing volumes of confidential reports on the atrocities of Stalin's reign.

Other developments also implied criticism of the late dictator: the revelation of the pitiful agrarian situation cast doubt on Stalin's policies and propaganda in this field; the renewal of relations with Yugoslavia discredited Stalin's charge of heresy; and the so-called thaw in intellectual life added to the sense of reaction against Stalinism. Undoubtedly there was a good deal of popular support for this shift, but at the same time there is reason to think that many or most citizens, including high party members, still regarded Stalin as a great leader. Moreover, his association with the regime had been so intimate for so many years that it seemed doubtful that any successor could risk an open attack on Stalin without incriminating himself and demoralizing the party.

The ambiguity of Stalin's posthumous stature was manifest in the uncomfortable, inconclusive shiftings of the official treatment of the subject. At times Stalin was ignored (on his birthday in December, 1953, for example); at times he was criticized in all but name (as in an article of 1953 attacking the idea that "eminent personalities" make history); at times he was praised with something approaching the old adulation (as in a *Pravda* article commemorating his birthday in 1954). Such confusion continued to the eve of the party congress of February,

1956. In January the imminent publication of the fourteenth volume of Stalin's *Works,* one of his most important monuments, was announced, but on Voroshilov's seventy-fifth birthday (February 4) the official greeting for the first time omitted mention of Stalin, whose "comrade-in-arms" Voroshilov had been since the Civil War. It is difficult then to ascertain which living leaders favored an open campaign against Stalin and which did not. At various times at least several of the rivals for power had found occasion to appeal to Stalinist tradition: Malenkov had briefly attempted to continue Stalin's dictatorship by simultaneously serving as head of the Council of Ministers and the Secretariat (March, 1953); the several opponents of Malenkov had appealed to Stalin's emphasis on heavy industry (January, 1955); Molotov presumably appealed to Stalin's authority on the Yugoslav question (July, 1955); and Khrushchev had in 1954–1955 steadily attempted, though not without resistance, to gain acknowledgment of the supremacy of the First Secretary in party affairs.

On the other hand, none of the leaders was likely to be guided by sentimental affection for the deceased dictator, and it was evident by early 1956 that the accumulation of implied criticisms of Stalin and secret files of incriminating evidence could be put to explosive political use—though not without risk to the man who detonated the charge.

The Twentieth Party Congress opened on February 14, 1956, and until the closing session on February 25 the only speaker to raise any specific criticism of Stalin was Mikoyan, whose loyalties within the Presidium at that moment are still not entirely clear. Khrushchev's public report on behalf of the Central Committee, delivered on the opening day of the congress and presumably approved in advance by the Presidium, evaded the crucial issue, and when he finally launched his outright attack on Stalin nine days later, the session was postponed until six hours after the scheduled time.

According to Khrushchev a majority of the Presidium, including Molotov, Kaganovich, Malenkov, and Voroshilov, opposed delivery of the speech and meant to "gain the upper hand in the Party"—to place control of the Presidium in the hands of the ministerial Communists at the expense of the First Secretary.* It seems likely that the crisis occurred in the six hours before midnight, February 24, when Khrushchev launched into the secret speech that originally had been scheduled for 6:00 P.M. It was probably in this period that Khrushchev broke the opposition by threatening to ask the Congress itself whether or not it wished to hear the speech, for that is his version of how he

---

* Khrushchev avoided explicit admission that he was in a minority at this juncture, but he listed four opponents and said that there were "others" (at least two), making a total of at least six out of eleven voting members. Pervukhin and Saburov, both economic administrators, were almost certainly the "others."

finally carried the day. It is also a remarkable admission that in normal practice a party congress—supposedly the highest authority—cannot decide for itself what it will hear of the politics in the inner circle. That Khrushchev emerged on the rostrum to assault the Stalin myth is a triumph of his superior will.† Khrushchev's action was a striking violation of the "intraparty democracy" and "collective leadership" that he claimed to admire, but it was in keeping with Lenin's practice of defying the majority of his Central Committee whenever it suited him. It is not necessary, however, to conclude that Khrushchev had been consistently favorable to an attack on Stalin in the preceding weeks or months, or that his opponents opposed *any* attack on Stalin. Khrushchev seems to have wavered in his attitude toward Stalin and definitely took a turn in Stalin's direction in December–January, 1956–1957. His opponents, or some of them, may well have favored some sort of critique of Stalin, but objected to the venom of Khrushchev's draft or to its cunning implication of themselves in Stalin's misdeeds. Also, the issue of secrecy probably caused dissension. Khrushchev delivered the attack at a meeting that was closed even to foreign Communist observers. This unusual step probably represented a concession by Khrushchev to his opponents, or rather a ruse, considering that the speech was leaked to the Americans several months later, causing Khrushchev no visible displeasure.

The speech itself attacked Stalin for his vanity, arbitrariness, brutality, and blundering—an apparent rupture with the tradition of the succession of leaders and disciples. But it may also be perceived as an implied tribute to Stalin, an expression of confidence in his efforts to create a party whose members believe whatever their leaders tell them. Stalin tempered the credulity and discipline of the party by insisting that all believe in the guilt of the "Fascist" agents who had been Lenin's close collaborators. Khrushchev did not deny this, for it was not the old oppositionists whom he rehabilitated. Moreover, he went Stalin one better by insisting (as the party still does) that all Communists believe in the infallibility and moral rectitude of party leadership which, by his own statement, had lied and sinned monstrously for twenty years. When a more or less accurate idea of the speech seeped through the party hierarchy to the public, it appears that there were

---

† To succeed in his bluff, Khrushchev depended on the noninterference of the police, which appeared to be controlled by the Council of Ministers, not the Secretariat, at this time. In 1961 Khrushchev's political police chief of the moment reported that in the crisis of June, 1957, Bulganin personally disposed of at least some part of the police force, and it is probable that he did so in 1956 as well. Since all indications are that Bulganin favored Khrushchev in the crisis of February, 1956, it appears safe to say that the First Secretary was protected (or at least relieved of danger) by his colleague, the Chairman of the Council of Ministers.

many who were seriously shaken by the revelation, and in non-Communist countries some party members and fellow-travelers left the movement. But by and large Khrushchev was proven right in counting on the survival of Stalinist discipline (i.e., Leninist discipline intensified), and in 1961 he was able to extend the disparagement of Stalin without secrecy or popular objections. Because the party congress and the First Secretary had pronounced that Stalin's evil works did not change the essential rightness of the movement, and since political opposition to the party still led to arrest, the authority of the regime was never in danger. Molotov and the others have been referred to as "Stalinists," but in a way it was Khrushchev who showed the keenest appreciation of Stalin's ideal of the disciplined party.

Khrushchev did not dare to discuss openly the rift in the Presidium, but he took advantage of the attack on Stalin, especially the brutalization of loyal Communists, to imply that his opponents had been Stalin's accomplices, while he had been innocently working in the outlying areas, frequently trying to correct Stalin's outrages. Molotov, Kaganovich, Malenkov, and Voroshilov were all associated with some aspect of Stalin's misdeeds, while Mikoyan, Bulganin, and Khrushchev received only sympathetic mention in the secret speech. Here Khrushchev confronted his opponents with a nice dilemma: they could defend themselves against his imputations only by debating the relative sinfulness of all major figures, a morbid process that could only increase the very revelations they wished to avoid. Or, they could accept the implied opprobrium and try to hush up further attacks. This, according to Khrushchev, is what they attempted to do in the coming months, a plausible assertion in the light of a Central Committee resolution (June 30, 1956) against the "cult of personality." This was a comparatively mild attack on Stalin, the sort of thing that might have been desired by Khrushchev's opponents at the start of the year. It was not as hard on Stalin—it was certainly less vivid—and did not mention any living Russian Communists.

On the whole, Khrushchev had made an impressive show of strength at the Twentieth Congress, daring to tackle the sorest subject of the hour. He had thwarted and embarrassed his opponents, but he had not finished them. Unable to make the final blow, Khrushchev waited and deployed his forces against the future. The congress elected a new Central Committee, the first such election since 1952, and it was clear that Khrushchev gained heavily. Many of the new members were officials in the territorial organization of the Secretariat, to whom Khrushchev was not only boss but also a protector. Had he not come up through their ranks, and did he not express horror concerning Stalin's crimes against such officials? The new Central Committee met almost immediately after the congress and proceeded to enact Khrushchev's tactical program. The crucial issue, the voting membership of the Presidium, was ignored, but one Malenkovite was dropped as a candidate member, while five pro-Khrushchev candidate members were appointed. Of these, four had lately been associated with the Secretariat and the fifth was Marshal G. K. Zhukov, the war hero whom Stalin had disgraced and Khrushchev had restored. At the same time the Secretariat was expanded from six to eight members, and a separate "Buro of the Secretariat for the RSFSR" was established, headed by Khrushchev and presumably improving his control over the politics of the union republic in which about half the Soviet population lives.*

In April–September, 1956, Khrushchev and Bulganin worked steadily to reduce the power of Molotov and Kaganovich in the Council of Ministers. In April the Cominform was dissolved, removing a standing insult to Tito and thereby administering a rebuff to Molotov. A visit to England by "B & K" in the same month accomplished little abroad but was favorably publicized in the USSR and probably added to the humiliation of the Foreign Minister. When a Yugoslav delegation, headed by Tito, arrived in Moscow on June 1, Molotov resigned as Foreign Minister, perhaps as a gesture of protest, perhaps at the insistence of the Presidium members who rejected his attitude toward Yugoslav communism. In any case, his ministerial portfolio passed to his former critic, Shepilov, and the negotiations led to a published pronouncement recognizing that "the path of socialist development varies according to country and conditions," a momentous retreat from the Stalin-Molotov approach. In the same week Kaganovich was somehow obliged to relinquish the chair of a major economic committee of the Council of Ministers.

In September Khrushchev and Tito exchanged apparently friendly visits at one another's villas and gave the impression that they were collaborating in the transition from Stalinism to a more relaxed order in Eastern Europe. But in October the accumulated effects of the anti-Stalin campaign and the slogan of "separate paths to socialism" produced upheavals in Poland and Hungary. These countries had not been sufficiently assimilated to the Bolshevik tradition, and when their Communist leaders followed Khrushchev's cue and acknowledged the fraudulent character of the Stalinist terror, especially the purge following the "heresy" of Tito in 1948, the authority of the leadership was seriously shaken.

The Polish crisis was potentially more menacing because of the size,

---

* The party machine in the vast Russian republic previously had been directed from the All-Union Secretariat. In establishing a special secretarial "buro" for the Russian republic, Khrushchev probably gained in efficiency and, as he alone served in both the All-Union Secretariat and the new Russian-Buro, added to the security of his personal control of the secretarial machinery.

location, and military strength of the country and the shrewd firmness
of Gomulka, who had been imprisoned in Stalin's time and emerged
to lead a reformation of Polish communism. By mid-October the Russians were thoroughly alarmed by the signs of popular unrest, the Polish attitude toward Russian troops, the increasing influence of Gomulka, and the reluctance of the Polish leadership to come to Moscow
for consultation. On October 19 an uninvited Russian delegation flew
to Warsaw to force a discussion with the Polish Politburo. While
Khrushchev had excluded his opponents from his previous junkets, he
shared this precarious excursion with both Molotov and Kaganovich,
whose earlier warnings now seemed justified. The Polish Communists
insisted on regaining a measure of real sovereignty but professed loyalty to the Communist bloc, and when the Russian leaders hastily
withdrew in less than twenty-four hours, the deployment of Soviet
troops indicated that a recourse to arms was quite possible. But the
cost of this solution would have been high, not only in military terms
but in its impact on other Communist parties; Tito would surely have
taken mortal fright at such a war, and there is good reason to believe
that the Chinese Communists urged moderation on the Soviets. The
result was that the Poles were promised pretty much what they wanted
and came to Moscow on November 15, led by Wladyslaw Gomulka, to
negotiate an agreement. The affair was a shock to Khrushchev's prestige as would-be arbiter of international communism, but a far more
painful experience had been avoided.

But, the apparent Soviet willingness to accept Gomulka touched off
an explosive reaction in Hungary, where previous Khrushchevite tute-
lage (especially a visit by Mikoyan in July, 1956) had failed to replace
the intensely unpopular Stalinist remnants with more flexible Communists. Mass demonstrations, led by students, occurred in Budapest
on October 23, and in the ensuing chaos neither the divided Hungarian
Communists nor the Soviet leadership seemed to know what to do. At
the request of one Hungarian politician, Soviet troops undertook to
repress the rising demonstration. Meanwhile, a new, anti-Stalinist Hungarian Communist government emerged under Imre Nagy and Janos
Kadar, and on October 28 negotiated a cease-fire. On the same day
Khrushchev's emissaries, Mikoyan and Suslov, arrived in Budapest and
promised the withdrawal of all Soviet troops from Hungary (the troops
actually were withdrawn from Budapest on October 29). If Khrushchev
hoped to achieve an agreement similar to that negotiated with Poland,
he was frustrated, for the Nagy faction in the Hungarian leadership,
backed by a substantial portion of the populace and the army, aimed
at a higher level of international and domestic freedom. Nagy publicly
advocated Hungarian neutrality and the establishment of a multiparty
political system—a clear challenge to the Bolshevik tradition. This

ended whatever conciliatory tendencies Khrushchev may have had, and on November 4 Soviet troops began the offensive against the Hungarians. The attack was allegedly in support of the Hungarian "government"—the Kadar faction, which defected from the Nagy government and formed a rival regime on the same day. Despite heroic Hungarian resistance and appeals to the UN, the Red Army soon reestablished Russian Communist control throughout the country, and followed this by ruthless punitive measures, including the abduction and execution of Nagy, who had attempted to leave the sanctuary of the Yugoslav embassy on a "guarantee" of safe conduct.

Khrushchev seems to have come off pretty well. Although the Western world was shocked and there were some embarrassing moments in the UN, the non-European neutralists generally swallowed Soviet excuses, partly because of their preoccupation with the concurrent Suez crisis. Tito could hardly have been pleased, but he was willing to sanction the second, decisive Russian intervention in Hungary. Although Khrushchev's ideas of a new, more permissive Communist order in Eastern Europe had been sacrificed, he had shown both satellite and Soviet Communists that he could be as tough as Stalin when he chose, and it may be that the resulting respect for his ruthlessness was really worth more than the myth of "popular" or "national" communism. Khrushchev's domestic rivals may have gained briefly from the upheaval: Molotov received a new ministerial portfolio and the sixth Five-Year Plan was revised, perhaps against Khrushchev's wishes. At the February, 1957, meeting of the Central Committee Kozlov, who proved to be an ambitious, troublesome hardliner, was elected candidate member of the Presidium.

At the end of March Khrushchev launched a major administrative reform, which was aimed as much at diminishing the political strength of the ministerial leaders as it was at improving efficiency. This was a plan to reduce sharply the number of economic ministries of the central state machine and transfer a large share of authority to a network of 105 "soviets of national economy" (*sovnarkhozy*). Most of these economic units correspond to a region (*oblast'*) in the party machine, and in practice the *sovnarkhozy* seem to be subordinate to the party secretary of their region. If, as seems probable, Khrushchev expected that this tactic would gradually render impotent his ministerial opponents in the Presidium, he got more than he bargained for. According to his later version, the Molotov-Kaganovich-Malenkov-Voroshilov opposition —quiescent since the Twentieth Party Congress—"activized" itself after the decision on "reorganizing the management of industry and construction" and won over Bulganin, M. G. Pervukhin, and M. Z. Saburov. Pervukhin and Saburov had probably opposed Khrushchev to some extent in 1956 and simply rejoined the ministerial opposition in the spring of 1957, but the addition of Bulganin was crucial. Most likely he had been willing to support Khrushchev on the basis of equality between the Chairman of the Council of Ministers and the First Secretary of the party, but now he was willing to believe that Khrushchev meant to subordinate the authority of all ministers. The group, now holding a seven-to-four majority in the Presidium, conducted "secret meetings" in Bulganin's office in preparation for "seizing the leadership of the party and the country" (i.e., remove Khrushchev from the Secretariat and place full control of the Presidium in the hands of the ministerial leaders). With this apparent superiority they won the support of Shepilov, who was only a candidate (nonvoting) member of the Presidium but a full-fledged member of the Secretariat, and therefore represented an important beachhead (or intelligence outpost) in Khrushchev's territory. In retaliation for this treachery, Khrushchev suggested that Shepilov's opposition and his alone was motivated solely by a desire to be on the winning side.

The climax of the affair came at a Presidium meeting of June 18–22, the details of which are still enshrouded in a good deal of mystery. Evidently a critique of Khrushchev's policies was combined with the accusation that he was attempting to establish himself as supreme dictator. The aim of the opposition was to enable the Presidium majority "to confront the members of the Central Committee and the whole party with a *fait accompli*," the resignation of the First Secretary, we may presume. Even though the meeting place in the Kremlin office buildings had been placed under special guard by Bulganin, according to Khrushchev's later police chief, the First Secretary would not capitulate, and the majority in the Presidium could not bring itself to use more or less the same technique that they had applied to Beria when he had been in a somewhat similar position four years earlier. It may well be that the attitude of Marshal Zhukov, a nonvoting member, was decisive on this question. In any case Khrushchev successfully insisted on calling a special meeting of the Central Committee, which opened on June 22 and lasted for a week.

In this arena Khrushchev was the master. Although he had taken pains to arrange the Central Committee membership in his favor, it was not clear that he could depend entirely on its support, and it seems likely that his victory was determined in some measure by his debating skill. Molotov, Kaganovich, and Malenkov are officially reported to have given two speeches each, which were later described as "a platform for further struggle," but plainly failed to convince the body. At some point in the session, possibly at the beginning, members of the anti-Khrushchev Presidium majority began to defect, according to their later apologias. Only Molotov, Kaganovich, and Malenkov remained in the end, and of these only Molotov demonstrated his defiance by abstaining from the vote on a resolution of June 29 condemning the "group."

Very likely Khrushchev had hoped to avoid so dangerous a confrontation with his enemies, but the point was that he had defeated them. After four years he had ended the danger that control of the Presidium would, contrary to Bolshevik tradition, pass into the hands of ministerial Communists.

As might have been expected, the new Presidium was heavily secretarial, including seven members of the central Secretariat and three regional secretaries, and it was also the largest Presidium since Stalin's day: fifteen voting members and nine candidates. On the other hand, Khrushchev was constrained to move slowly in settling scores. Kaganovich, who had been perhaps the closest observer of Khrushchev's methods since the twenties, evidently assumed that the victor would deal ruthlessly with his victims. According to Khrushchev's later report, Kaganovich telephoned the First Secretary after the June meeting and pleaded: "Comrade Khrushchev, I have known you for many years. I ask you not to let them treat me in the vindictive way people were treated under Stalin." To this Khrushchev supposedly made a more-Leninist-than-thou answer, but it is by no means clear that the comparative clemency of the dictator resulted from principle as much as from his obvious reticence to reveal the number of eminent leaders who opposed him. There is also some likelihood that members of the Central Committee and Presidium had a keen awareness that their own welfare depended on the prevention of a revival of a purge atmosphere. Even though some delegates to the Twenty-second Party Congress advocated harsh punishment for Molotov, Malenkov, Kaganovich, and Voroshilov, who by then had been implicated in veritable murder, no criminal charges were laid. The political police remained under the Committee of State Security, headed by second-rate figures, and evidently were kept on the fringes of intraparty affairs. Presumably the Committee form of executive in this organization, which came into force the year after Beria's downfall, made it more difficult for any individual, even the First Secretary, to use the police against the Central Committee. This is not to suggest that the police ceased to be an important instrument of party control over the populace. One notable trend in party propaganda after the attacks on Beria and Stalin was the attempt to assure the masses that the new police were true "Chekists" in the loftiest tradition of Lenin and Dzerzhinsky, whose fame was especially revived. This campaign had the side effect, perhaps intentional, of demonstrating that the police were still very much alive. At one point an interview between various journalists and leading police investigators was published to show what fine fellows the present-day Chekists are, arresting only *real* imperialist agents. Unfortunately the tone of the session was set by the comment of the general in charge: "This is an unusual situation for us. As a rule it's the investigator who does the questioning, . . . but today you're welcome to ask the questions that interest you."

In any case, Khrushchev was able to remove his leading adversaries from active politics following the four-year struggle. Molotov, Kaganovich, Malenkov, and "Shepilov-who-joined-them" (the usual formula) were neutralized right after the Central Committee meeting of June, 1957. Saburov and Pervukhin were allowed to recant in July and thereby retain their membership in the Central Committee until the Party Congress of 1961: Pervukhin even served for a time as a candidate member of the Presidium. Bulganin's complicity was revealed only in December, 1957, and he remained Chairman of the Council of Ministers until Khrushchev took over that post in February, 1958. Voroshilov remained Chairman of the Presidium of the Supreme Soviet, a largely decorative position, until 1960, and it was only at the Party Congress of 1961 that his misdeeds before and after 1953 were revealed. Marshal Zhukov, an opponent of the antiparty group but a potentially dangerous ministerial leader (Minister of Defense and quite possibly the most popular man in the USSR in 1957), was at first promoted to full membership in the Presidium and then, in October, 1957, removed and shoved into retirement. His successor, Marshal R. Ia. Malinovsky, alleged that he had reduced the authority of the party over the army and had exaggerated his role in the Russian victories in the World War.

Khrushchev succeeded not only in achieving the triumph of his personal interests, but also those of the party. His success in 1957 and even his defeat seven years later (at the hands of the party Central Committee) demonstrated that the supreme authority in the USSR was the party, not one of its "transmission belts," as Stalin had called the soviets and other public organizations.

14

KHRUSHCHEV'S COMMUNISM

Between the defeat of the "antiparty group" in 1957 and the surprising "retirement" of Khrushchev in 1964 lay seven years in which a single leader again directed the party and state. In the end it was revealed that his regime suffered from a fatal flaw—insufficiently ruthless and vigilant discipline in the top ranks. But until some dissatisfied and ambitious lieutenants of the leader dared test this flaw, it appeared that Khrushchev had had his way and succeeded in creating his own brand of communism within the framework of the Bolshevik tradition.

In its attitude toward the conception of the leader, the Khrushchev regime was both traditional and distinctive. Lenin was revered as intensely as in former years. Of the countless daily appeals to his memory, none was more striking than a speech by a Madame Lazurkina at the Twenty-second Party Congress in 1961. A party member since 1902, who had worked directly with Lenin and had served fourteen years in Stalin's jails, she expressed horror at Stalin's alleged perversion of Leninism, yet managed to exceed even the mystical tone of Stalin's funeral oration of 1924: "Yesterday evening I counseled with Ilyich [Lenin]; it was as if he stood alive before me, and he said: 'It is unpleasant for me to lie side by side with Stalin, who brought so much harm to the party.'" Impressed by this necromancy, the assembled scientific socialists approved a resolution to move Stalin's corpse to a relatively modest plot outside the Lenin mausoleum.

While demolishing the cult of the individual who preceded him as dictator, Khrushchev advanced his own glorification to an imposing level and with a style that was very much his own. Where Stalin withdrew to Olympian majesty, Khrushchev was constantly in the public eye, visiting foreign countries the world over, addressing the UN General Assembly and small Russian villages with equal gusto, appearing on Soviet television and in all manner of Soviet writings, including his own, which filled over twenty volumes as they were published in anthologies. Conscious that he could not claim credit for such historic achievements as the founding of the party, the seizure of power, the transformation of the national economy, or the winning of a world war, Khrushchev attempted to compensate by referring to his virgin lands program as "an achievement that will live through the ages," by magnifying his role in the Battle of "Volgograd" (Stalingrad), by associating himself with Soviet space exploits as closely as possible short of orbiting the earth himself, and by producing a plan for the attainment of completed Communist society within the life span of the contemporary generation.

Of all the varied emanations of the Khrushchev cult, the most highly publicized was his extended visit to the United States in 1959. The Soviet public was treated to a publicity campaign in which Khrushchev was shown as a welcome and honored guest at Camp David and among the common folk as well. His own comportment was meant to convey an image of a peacemaker and a patriot who would stand up for his country and for communism in case of argument. The capstone of this propaganda exercise was the publication of a 678-page book entitled *Face to Face with America*. This was prepared by an editorial team of which Alexei Adzhubey and P. Satiukov were the most eminent members. The editors of the two principal Soviet newspapers, they were among a number of journalists whom Khrushchev drew to his personal staff, in preference to party secretarial types. Adzhubey was his son-in-law and increasingly became the First Secretary's chief assistant. His responsibilities expanded rapidly in the 1960s, and in 1964 his intended dispatch on a top-level diplomatic mission to West Germany was one of the grievances of the party regulars (and career diplomats) against Khrushchev. Unlike the career men of the party apparatus whom Khrushchev had patronized, these confidants and cult-builders were dismissed from their positions shortly after the retirement of their boss.

Of the various manifestations of the cult of Khrushchev, the one most directly linked with major policy decisions was the publication of his sketch of the future Communist society and the path to it. In both of the party congresses dominated by him the main focus was on this progression to utopia, taking the form of "control figures" for a new "Seven-year Plan" at the Twenty-first congress in 1959, and the adoption of a new party program, the first since 1919, at the Twenty-second in 1961. This stress on the achievement in the USSR of the ultimate aim of communism was timely. It gave Khrushchev an opportunity to present himself as a master of Marxist-Leninist scientific vision, which was necessary to his attempt to don Lenin's mantle. It was equally important as assurance to the mass of party members and ordinary Soviet citizens that their toil and suffering, even under Stalin, had not been in vain, that the legitimacy of party rule was still justified by the great regards at the end of the road. And it was essential for the Soviet Communist Party to restate its claim to primacy in the advance to Communist society at a time when its predominance in the world Communist movement was sorely tried.

Khrushchev depicted a society characterized by rigorous egalitarianism, collectivism, and conformism. According to Khrushchev, it will be democratic but "highly organized and centralized. . . . Communist society, more than any other, needs a single system for planning the economy, organized distribution of labor, and regulation of working time." The old Marxian slogan "To each according to his needs" will be realized but with qualifications: the free distribution of goods will be limited to "wholesome consumption commensurate with the needs of a cultured person, . . . not whims, nor claims to luxury." The twenty-year plan envisaged in the program of 1961 resembles Stalin's Five-year Plans in having more significance as an inspirational myth than as economic rationalization; it was in effect an attempt at one final exhortation to economic heroics.

Unfortunately for Khrushchev, it was not enough to signal the storming of the final obstacles on the path to communism. Agriculture, which Khrushchev regarded as a personal specialty, was especially disappointing. Far from overtaking the United States in per capita consumption of meat, eggs, and dairy products, the USSR even experienced serious difficulties in grain supply in 1963–1964 and had to import substantial stocks from the capitalist world. Beset with this and other problems of production, Khrushchev twisted and turned in search of new technical and administrative measures that would carry the day. In a revealing memorandum to the party presidium in September, 1962, he acknowledged in effect that the command economy of the USSR could not achieve balanced and diversified production at the desired levels. The existing technique, he admitted, suffered from "campaignism," the habit of throwing massive human and material resources first into one great drive, then into another, as if a perpetual state of emergency were normal. Noting that Russia had developed sufficiently numerous and experienced managers and technicians to work on a more stable basis, it almost seemed that Khrushchev was on the verge of recommending the reduction of the command function of the party in the economy. But the memorandum concluded with a magnificently bureaucratic panacea: reorganize the party as a more effective medium of economic control by adding more boxes to its administrative chart. More specifically his plan created separate party bureaus for agriculture and for industry on the *oblast'* and *raion-gorod* levels; for the first time in party history the basic organization of the apparatus implied that its prime function was economic. The new party administrative system was approved by the Central Committee in November, 1962. It is unclear what effect it had on production, but, in view of the speed with which the Central Committee rescinded this plan after removing Khrushchev in 1964, it is safe to say that its operation was anything but a personal triumph.

Meanwhile, Khrushchev retreated from his commitment to the *extensive* development of agriculture, as in the virgin lands, and, in a great outburst of "campaignism," sought to break the agricultural barrier by greater *intensification*, especially the use of more chemical fertilizer. He had early shown a partiality for the chemical industry and by 1964 was recommending it as a nostrum—rather like Lenin's infatuation with electrification and Stalin's with tractors and shelter-belts. This involved vast new industrial investment, implying consumer sacrifice somewhat beyond the levels planned a few years earlier.

Along with these economic measures, Khrushchev made a number of gestures in the direction of the kind of political and social transformation required to achieve his version of fully developed communism. In 1961 he proclaimed that the dictatorship of the proletariat had been replaced by the "state of the entire people." This was partly a merely proclamatory achievement, comparable to the attainment of "socialism" under Stalin. In some new and specific ways, however, Khrushchev's regime did attempt to engage more people in public activities under party direction. For example, the police received the assistance in some routine work, such as traffic control, of "people's teams for the defense of public order," which are voluntary, part-time bodies, numbering several millions by the end of the Khrushchev era. In addition, much was made of the alleged revival of Lenin's ideal of popular control of the state through the Khrushchevian movements called "Under the control of the masses" and "Komsomol Searchlight," which were intended to uncover and correct inefficiency and abuse in the lower levels of the administrative order.

Such steps presumably lead toward the withering away of the state under completed communism, but they do not imply the replacement of the party. According to Khrushchev it would be "the highest form of sociopolitical organization," and none of his policies was aimed at diminishing its role. The total size of the party was expanded from 7.2 million members and candidate members in 1956 to 9.7 million in 1961 and no doubt more thereafter, for the number of candidate members more than doubled in that five-year period. While aiming at a more massive party, Khrushchev evidently thought that its elitism could be maintained or improved by a regular rotation of personnel in elective offices in the party. According to the party statutes of 1961 party committees on the union republican and *oblast* levels must replace at least one-third of their members at each election, while a turnover of one-half is to occur at lower levels. Moreover, members of the Presidium and All-Union Central Committee are normally to serve no more than three consecutive terms. One might suppose that Khrushchev was too successful for his own good in preaching the virtues of replacing old hands in the party apparatus. However, this ruling was not mentioned in his case, and a statutory loophole permitting exceptions for outstanding individuals in practice offered secure tenure to anyone with the right connections.

More important was his management of the Central Committee, the body to which he owed his survival in 1957 and his removal in 1964. He convened this body regularly and gave due honor to its meetings. The character of the Central Committee proceedings, however, was designed to prevent really serious policy discussion. The proceedings of most sessions were published, and hundreds of "guests" were invited by the First Secretary—regional Soviet officials, agriculturalists, and others. Khrushchev also attempted to manipulate Central Committee membership. The Party Congress of 1961 increased the former membership of the Committee by one-third to 330 members and candidate members. Only half the Committee of 1956 was reelected, giving the impression that the First Secretary had shrewdly packed this authoritative body. And so he had, if his success in ramming through the agricultural-industrial bisection of party bureaus in 1962 is a fair test. But eternal vigilance is as much the price of authority as it is of liberty.

If Khrushchev was distracted from the risks of a palace revolt, the growing tribulations in international Communist relations must have been partly to blame. According to the party program, "The experience of the peoples of the world Socialist community has confirmed that their fraternal unity and cooperation conform to the supreme national interests of each country." But the very congress that adopted this program in 1961 witnessed a sharp outburst of interparty antagonisms, with Chou En-lai demonstratively decorating Stalin's grave and walking out on the congress, and, from that time until the fall of Khrushchev, relations within the world Communist community steadily worsened. Surely Stalin deserves some of the blame for this serious development. By scuttling whatever chances the Comintern ever had as a genuine forum for sovereign national Communist parties, and by treating the non-Soviet Communist parties as pawns, Stalin laid up a store of problems for his heirs.

Despite the proclamatory confirmations of fraternal tranquility in the early years of his dictatorship, Khrushchev demonstrated in practice that he realized that international communism was faced with fundamental problems. One of Khrushchev's methods of meeting this challenge was, characteristically, a continuing whirl of personal visits with foreign Communist leaders, initially to attempt to achieve general harmony, later to line up support against the Chinese. But he must have realized that this could not wholly compensate for the absence of any specific international Communist organization, and in various ways he attempted to develop multilateral Communist institutions. In November, 1957, the fortieth anniversary of the Bolshevik revolution served as a pretext for convening the thirteen Communist parties that held power in their homelands, a procedure that was no doubt odious to such large and influential parties as the Italian and the Indonesian, which do not hold power. Their interests were recognized in the next gathering of "fraternal" parties in Moscow, November–December, 1960. On both occasions the conference produced declarations to the world that expressed deathless proletarian unity, while resorting to generally vague wording to assuage underlying disagreements. Even at that the Yugoslavs were too affronted by the rejection of "revisionism" and the "peaceful path to socialism" in 1957 to sign the proclamation, and the Italians, while signing in 1960, acknowledged that they were troubled by much the same issue at that time.

Despite Soviet talk about a "commonwealth" (*sodruzhestvo*) of Communist states, no definite institutions or rules of conduct emerged from Khrushchev's efforts to stabilize multilateral Communist relations. Non-Soviet parties were cool to Khrushchev's suggestions concerning an international secretariat; the "Council of Mutual Economic Assistance," which involves only the USSR, Mongolia, and some East European Communist states, found both Albania and Rumania in defiance; and the use of various national Communist party congresses for consultation among visiting "fraternal" delegates proved futile.

Unfortunately for Khrushchev, the absence of rules and machinery to draw Communists together coincided with the sharpening of disagreements on particular issues of policy. The most serious of these were the interconnected disputes on foreign and domestic policy between the USSR and China. The interpretation of Khrushchev's slogan of "peaceful coexistence" was central to the increasingly sharp dispute. Such a slogan was certainly not a total innovation in Bolshevik policy. Stalin had instigated a massive "peace" drive in his last years, and the attacks on him by the Khrushchevians had never suggested that his enmity to "imperialism" was one of his faults—quite the contrary. Moreover, Khrushchev even claimed that all Soviet foreign policy since 1917 had been based on "peaceful coexistence," and was at great pains to demonstrate how Lenin himself had founded this line. This stress on continuity indicates that to a considerable extent Khrushchevian coexistence was quite compatible with acts that non-Communists might with reason regard as aggressive, such as the invasion of the Georgian Republic in 1921, of Finland in 1939, and of South Korea in 1950—as well as the deployment of Soviet missiles to Cuba in 1962. The party program of 1961 frankly asserted that Communists must be ready for "*all forms* of struggle—peaceful and nonpeaceful. . . . The possibility of a *nonpeaceful transition to socialism* must be kept in mind" (original emphasis).

Notwithstanding the militant potentialities of "peaceful coexistence," it appears that Khrushchev really did acknowledge that the destructiveness of nuclear weapons requires the avoidance of general war if at all possible. Although the threatened use of Soviet nuclear strength might be used as an umbrella for some foreign revolutionary regimes, as a threat to relatively small allies of the United States, or even to the United States itself if a major tactical advantage could be gained (as in the Cuban gamble), Khrushchev acknowledged by the withdrawal of the rockets in Cuba that nuclear weapons could not settle the fate of "imperialism" as long as the balance of weapons was fairly even. Generally his conception of the victory of communism on a world scale was gradualist, foreseeing that the encouragement of "national liberation" movements and the expansion of the "zone of peace" in Asia, Africa, and Latin America would eventually leave the "imperialists" isolated and ready to capitulate.

Ironically, the Chinese Communists, who exploded their first atomic device only at the time Khrushchev was removed, maintained that Khrushchev's strategy was anti-Leninist "revisionism." Khrushchev's conferences with Western leaders excluded and irked the Chinese; the Soviet decision not to send nuclear and other advanced weapons to China was an equally sore point. These two issues met in Khrushchev's willingness in 1963 to sign the agreement with Britain and the United States ending nuclear tests in the atmosphere. This implied a rebuke to any country such as China that regarded its own nuclear development as essential to national security, and even suggested that Khrushchev was teaming up with "imperialists" to preserve the existing balance of power. The shortcomings of Soviet military aid to China were paralleled by dissatisfaction with economic support. Even though Khrushchev supported increases in aid to China—mostly on a loan basis—it was not enough to satisfy the Chinese, especially after their "great leap forward" ran into serious difficulties in 1959. The Chinese maintained that Soviet deliveries had fallen short, and as the entire dispute gained momentum Khrushchev sought to apply pressure by withdrawing Soviet technical advisers to China in 1960. Meanwhile, Sino-Soviet differences concerning non-Communist former colonial countries further embroiled the two. No doubt Soviet aid that was channeled to such projects as the Aswan Dam in Egypt would have been appreciated in China, and the supply of Soviet military aircraft to India during a Sino-Indian border dispute in 1963 was downright provocative.

The Chinese response to these disputes was to campaign for the support of all Communists, even to the point of conducting a leaflet campaign based on the Chinese embassy in Moscow. Khrushchev's counter-campaign included the circulation of stinging diatribes against the Chinese Communists and such intolerable auxiliary techniques as booing down the attempt of a Chinese representative to address an international Communist gathering in Berlin in January, 1963. The result was deadlock, as was amply proved by the failure of a meeting of top-level Chinese and Soviet party ideologists in Moscow in July, 1963. The Chinese could not be disciplined, and even succeeded in splitting numerous parties in other countries. Khrushchev, no doubt angered by the personal character of Chinese invective, determined to settle the issue in true Leninist style: to convene a world Communist assembly organized on Soviet terms, and there to excommunicate the heretics. A preliminary meeting was set for December, 1964, and in the Soviet press an almost daily feature was an article castigating the "schismatic" Chinese. But Khrushchev's outlook was bleak as well as blustery. Other Communist leaders, including some who were not inclined to follow Mao Tse-tung, were reluctant to see the "commonwealth" split and feared the extension of such purge tactics.

With the international showdown approaching, the world was stunned to learn on October 14, 1964, that "the Central Committee of the Communist Party of the Soviet Union approved the request of Comrade Khrushchev N. S. concerning his release from the responsibilities of First Secretary of the Central Committee of the CPSU, member of the Presidium of the Central Committee of the CPSU and Chairman of the Council of Ministers of the USSR in connection with old age and declining health." A full explanation of this abrupt desire to retire—even to disappear from party history, one would gather—may be a long time coming. Clearly the imminent fiasco in international communism undermined Khrushchev's position (for Chou En-lai was invited to the anniversary of the October Revolution in November, 1964), and the party administrators clearly disliked his scheme of divided agricultural and industrial party bureaus (for these were reunited with comparable haste). With diligence one could compile quite a long, and perfectly valid, list of ways in which Khrushchev had failed or had made enemies. But the crucial point, both for the man and the party tradition, seems to have been his insufficient concern for the foundations of his personal power.

In 1964 Khrushchev's position was comparable to that of Stalin in 1934. Both men had triumphed over their major opponents several years earlier, had filled the Politburo or Presidium and the Central Committee with their own appointees, and had imposed their personal policies on the party. At this juncture both Stalin and Khrushchev were vulnerable to criticism concerning their less successful policies and had to contend with the objections of energetic young lieutenants, especially Kirov in 1934 and Brezhnev in 1964, both of whom were members of the party secretariat. Stalin met this situation by arranging the assassination of Kirov (it appears) and then undertaking a reign of terror that cowed the survivors for the rest of the dictator's life. Khrushchev, forgetting Machiavelli's dictum that men love at their own free will but fear at the will of the Prince, apparently left much of the secretarial responsibility in the hands of Brezhnev, while undertaking an ambitious schedule of foreign visitations and receptions. He was innocently vacationing on the Black Sea when the blow fell. The fate of Khrushchev demonstrates that Stalin's ferocious purges, and especially the butchering of his own appointees, can be considered politically rational from the dictator's point of view.

15

KHRUSHCHEV
AND THE BOLSHEVIK TRADITION

Khrushchev tried to destalinize the Soviet system without debolsheviz-
ing it. In some ways he succeeded. For example, the cult of Stalin was
dismantled and police terror on a massive scale was enormously diminished. On balance he failed, and paid the price. Stalin had built too
solidly. The institutions that he left behind, for all their problems,
worked too well to be fundamentally changed without endangering
party rule. In the crucial matter of the party Khrushchev may be considered a *re*stalinizer, and a successful one, at least until 1958. Stalin
was the main builder of the party apparatus, and never intended to
destroy it, but in his later years his reliance on his personal authority
and the institutions of the Soviet state (including the police) did represent a threat to the future of party supremacy. Khrushchev led the post-
Stalin campaign to reverse this trend and to assert the primacy of the
Communist Party of the Soviet Union in all matters. This return to
"Leninist norms" might equally well have been called a return to the
norms of Stalinism as it was until approximately the Second World
War. Khrushchev did succeed in this kind of restalinization. There was
a revival of the formal institutional activities of the party, such as the
holding of regular Central Committee plenums. The intervention of
the police within the party ceased. The secretarial hierarchy was restored as the critical instrument of authority on every level, and at the
top the party institutions (especially the Presidium of the Central Committee) regained control of decision making. For this Khrushchev deserves at least a modest statue on Red Square.

On the other hand, Khrushchev moved away from reliance on the
party machine after he had assumed the chairmanship of the Council
of Ministers in 1958. His tendency to rely on his personal authority
and Soviet state institutions could even be considered another kind of
restalinization, a return to the trend of the great dictator's later years.
This trend never developed as far under Khrushchev as under Stalin.
The party leaders in the Presidium were able to keep his power in
check, to advance the careers of men opposed to Khrushchev (such as
Frol Kozlov), and ultimately to depose him. In becoming the victim of
his party colleagues, who recognized the threat to themselves and party

supremacy, Khrushchev unwittingly made his final contribution to the vitality of party predominance.

Khrushchev's failure to destalinize the system is rooted in ideas as well as institutions. He was a sincere Communist, and must be given some credit for attempting to revive the egalitarian ideals of communism, even at the price of considerable unpopularity. For example, he attempted to change the educational system so that the children of ordinary workers and peasants would have the same opportunity as those of the administrative-technical elite, which had grown up under Stalin. For all his political toughness Khrushchev seems to have really believed that "true" Marxism-Leninism could be determined fairly simply and that it would easily attract most right-thinking people. In his own attack on Stalin and his willingness to encourage Soviet intellectuals, such as Alexander Solzhenitsyn, Khrushchev apparently did not anticipate that people might "go too far," that even a modest degree of freedom of expression would soon lead to the appearance of all manner of non-Bolshevik and even anti-Bolshevik concepts. The same kind of error is manifest in his dealings with foreign Communists. By offering what he no doubt regarded as reasonable fraternal relations, Khrushchev sought to build noncoercive relations with the other Communist states. But Mao Tse-tung in China and Imre Nagy in Hungary, in very different ways, responded with their own ideas, which were far from agreeable to Khrushchev. Both at home and abroad, then, Khrushchev left his successors a morass of hostilities that he had not invented but had unwittingly aggravated.

Khrushchev was not a historic figure of the magnitude of Lenin or Stalin. Because of his visibility and personal color he probably cut a larger figure with the non-Communist world public than he deserved. His years in power were relatively few, and the power was subject to serious restraint much of the time. But he made significant contributions to the persistence of the Bolshevik tradition: through his success in restoring the primacy of the party, and also in demonstrating, by his failure, that the party must enforce its ideology just as the leader must enforce his authority.

PART FOUR
BREZHNEV

16

THE UNGRATEFUL PROTÉGÉ

Like Stalin and Khrushchev, Brezhnev did not seem very formidable or durable as a leader when he was first elected head of the Central Committee Secretariat. True, tradition had endowed this post with lofty authority, but Malenkov's case had demonstrated that in a succession crisis the initial claimant to the title might not keep it long. It was widely believed that Brezhnev represented some kind of short transition, an undistinguished organization man who would merely keep the shop until some new leader or institutional arrangement emerged. The very fact that he had been heir apparent for some time before October 1964 was reminiscent of Malenkov and suggested weakness. An heir chosen by a leader in power is likely to have been chosen because he does not seem to be a formidable rival. At the same time the heir is likely to line up opposition from would-be leaders who have an interest in stopping the front-runner. In Brezhnev's case it is reasonable to surmise that his selection as Khrushchev's successor in the Secretariat owed much to innocuous appearance and to the fact that the conspirators against Khrushchev could not fight openly for the succession. That he accepted a diarchy in which Kosygin seemed easily his equal and that he was not particularly eminent in public in his first months in power reenforced the impression that Brezhnev was more a temporary regent than a real successor of Lenin, Stalin and Khrushchev.

Quite likely some Kremlinologists *in* the Kremlin shared this misperception with foreign observers. If so, it can be said that underestimation of a "mere" party secretary served to protect Brezhnev in the early phases of his consolidation of power, just as it had protected Stalin around 1922–1925 and Khrushchev around 1953–1955.

But if there were reasonable grounds for questioning Brezhnev's prospects as a leader in 1964, these did not include his experience in party affairs. His career to 1964 was in most respects a model of what a person should do to succeed in the business of the CPSU. Brezhnev was born twelve years after Khrushchev and like him was the son of a Russian who had moved into one of the grim new industrial settlements of the Ukraine in search of a livelihood. The place was then called Kamenskoe, later renamed Dneproderzhinsk in honor of the River Dnieper and Lenin's first police boss, and the date was December 19, 1906. Leonid, the son of steelworker Ilia, presumably had some sort of elementary education at the expense of the tsar's government. At least the timing of his birth suggests that he could have completed the basic four-year elementary program shortly before the revolution of 1917 began an era of great disruption to such programs. As a boy he witnessed and somehow survived the marching and countermarching of German, Red, and White armies and the still more deadly invasion of famine and pestilence. Rescue came in the form of Lenin's New Economic Policy, which began the restoration of the economy and enabled the fifteen-year-old Brezhnev to obtain some kind of unskilled industrial job in his home town. Two years later his political career began in a modest way when he joined the Komsomol. This enabled Brezhnev to go on to secondary education, a land surveyor's course, and this in turn enabled him to enter public administration in 1927. For four years, the critical ones for Stalin's policy toward the peasants, Brezhnev served in rural soviet administrative jobs, moving from Belorussia, to Kursk, to the Urals. He was one of the tough proletarians whom the party sent into the countryside to impose its will on the peasantry, and he must have proven his reliability. In 1931 Brezhnev was taken into the party and entered the metallurgical institute in his home town, which he completed four years later. Brezhnev is, then, a qualified engineer, the first supreme party leader since Lenin to have a higher education. He stayed on in Dneproderzhinsk, working in the steel mills for two years, then entering the full-time political career that has been his life ever since. For a year he served as deputy chairman of the city soviet, then in May, 1938, Brezhnev joined the party apparatus as "director of a department" in the Dneproderzhinsk organization. Five months earlier Khrushchev had gone to the Ukraine as first secretary of its party, which had lost many of its former officials, especially ethnic Ukrainians, to the purge. Brezhnev was one of the non-Ukrainian beneficiaries of this process. Quite possibly he was interviewed by Khrushchev before getting the party job. The two certainly had met by the time Brezhnev became secretary of the whole Dneproderzhinsk *oblast'* in February, 1939. No doubt Khrushchev could see much of himself in the younger man, and from this time until October, 1964, Brezhnev was a protégé of Khrushchev.

For the next decade Brezhnev worked closely under Khrushchev in the Ukraine. With the outbreak of war Brezhnev followed Khrushchev into the party system of political control over the military, and served first on his staff, then under him as political commander of an army. Brezhnev emerged as a decorated major general and was kept in political-military work for over a year after the war, helping in the ruthless pacification of the Carpathian military district, the last refuge of anti-Communist Ukrainian nationalists. In 1946 Khrushchev moved him back to regular political work, in charge of the Zaporozhe, then the Dnepropetrovsk *oblast'* organizations of the party.

Success on this level led to promotion in 1950 at the age of 43 to the full responsibility for the party organization in the Moldavian union republic. This relatively small area, annexed from defeated Rumania, was unofficially a tributary of the Ukraine, but the status of command of one's "own" republican party organization is an excellent and perhaps essential experience for a party leader in the post-Stalin era, something akin to having captained one's own capital ship in a naval career. This status brought Brezhnev to Moscow in 1952 as a delegate to the Nineteenth Party Congress, which elected him to the Central Committee, a routine dignity for the head of a union republic party organization. What was not routine at this point was Brezhnev's transfer from the provinces to Moscow for the first time in his career. Stalin's expanded Politburo, renamed Presidium, needed members in Brezhnev's age group, so he drew this assignment along with membership in the Secretariat, where mentor Khrushchev was highly influential at this time.

This speedy ascent from *oblast'* secretary to party secretary and Presidium member was reversed by Stalin's death. The heirs quickly demoted their unwanted junior colleagues, and Brezhnev was relegated to the unimposing position of chief political commissar for the navy. But Khrushchev was growing stronger, needed reliable supporters and remembered Brezhnev. He was sent to Kazakhstan, the scene of the virgin lands campaign, as second party secretary in 1954, taking over the first secretaryship the next year. The success of this agricultural program was essential to Khrushchev, who was leaning heavily on the party to expedite it. The harvest of 1956 was excellent, confounding the opposition, and Brezhnev was brought back to Moscow, the party Presidium and the Secretariat at the Twentieth Party Congress. Khrushchev was counting heavily on him in the combat with the "antiparty group," and Brezhnev did not disappoint him. With his wide contacts in the party secretarial hierarchy and the armed forces, Brezhnev must have played a vital role. In the reshuffling in 1958 after Khrushchev's victory there was not much left with which to reward Brezhnev, although he did become a deputy chairman of the Buro of the Secretariat for the RSFSR. At this point Brezhnev seemed Khrushchev's number one protégé, but very much dependent on his boss. Too long a time in this sort of status can type a person as second-ranker. Perhaps it was a blessing in disguise for Brezhnev that a party apparatus man, Frol Kozlov, sent Brezhnev's career on a detour in 1960. Kozlov was covertly challenging Khrushchev himself and wished to move aside the boss's number one lieutenant. The shooting down of a secret American spy plane deep in Russia in May, 1960, just as Khrushchev was about to embark on a demonstratively friendly meeting with Eisenhower in Paris, provided Kozlov and other critics of the leader with a chance to insist on some personnel changes. Brezhnev was moved out of secretarial work, which had helped to assure his own and Khrushchev's control of the party apparatus. He was too powerful to be simply demoted, so he was given the honorific post of chairman of the Presidium of the Supreme Soviet, the largely decorative "presidency" of the USSR.

It is a tribute to Brezhnev's determination and shrewdness that he not only survived this setback but even gained something from it. The position for the first time exposed him to foreign affairs, enabling him to travel abroad and to meet both capitalist and Communist dignitaries. He was also able to keep a finger in the civil and military rocketry program, which would not have been likely had he stuck to the administration of the party secretarial network. While he was still regarded as a Khrushchev man, the presidency gave Brezhnev a somewhat more independent image—at least he was not specifically a lieutenant on Khrushchev's staff.

His political survival is also a tribute to his luck. Kozlov might well have been the one to succeed Khrushchev, had not a stroke ended his political career in April, 1963. This enabled Brezhnev to move back into the party Secretariat in June. Since Khrushchev had taken on broad responsibilities in the party and state and was indeed devoting much of his time to administration *through* the state machinery (in contrast to his tactics in the first years after Stalin's death), Brezhnev was in effect the most powerful party secretary. It was not necessary for him to fan discontent concerning Khrushchev. The First Secretary and Chairman of the Council of Ministers had spread his responsibilities too wide and had offended too many influential interests. Those offended were not terrorized, and what was needed by 1964 was a catalyst to precipitate a *coup*. Brezhnev would almost surely be the immediate beneficiary of such a move, at least with respect to the title of First Secretary. Thus it was that he could bide his time and do hypocritical honor to the boss in 1964, beamingly taking part in the ceremonies honoring Khrushchev's seventieth birthday and nonchalantly going off on a business trip to Berlin on October 5–11, when the plot was about to go into action. Probably Brezhnev did not even speak at the Central Committee session that "accepted" Khrushchev's "request" for retirement.

Many of those who voted for Brezhnev that day may have thought of him merely as a transitional figure. If so, they missed some significant points about his career to age fifty-seven. Brezhnev was a survivor. Any Russian male born around 1906 stood an excellent chance of dying in the famines, epidemics, wars and purges of their times. There could not be much talent left to face Brezhnev among his age-peers, and anyone left in this group must have learned a few things about surviving. Doubters of Brezhnev also should have noted his determination and ability to rebound after his setbacks in 1953 and 1960. They should have noted, too, his range of experience in the party secretarial apparatus, both in the provinces and the center, not to mention his extensive work with the armed forces both during and after the war. Not the least of his political assets was a point demonstrated in the October, 1964, *coup*: that Khrushchev's protégé possessed the ambition and ingratitude to participate in the bloodless assassination of Khrushchev.

17

DEKHRUSHCHEVIZATION

It was a kind of tribute to Khrushchev that the men who deposed him felt it necessary to devote several years to the undoing of much of his work. Antagonism toward the man they had deposed was the main thing that held this disparate collection of Communist politicians together, and they agreed on nothing so strongly as their antipathy to Khrushchev's personal style as leader. This was manifest in the unprecedented treatment that he received in retirement. He was not physically abused, for the new leaders were too keenly aware of the possible consequences of using physical force in settling intraparty quarrels. Indeed, one of the grounds for dissatisfaction with Khrushchev was his inclination toward carrying destalinization to the point of bringing capital charges against the defeated Stalinists in the "antiparty group." Thus the defeated Khrushchev was permitted to enjoy a pension, apartment, country house and car with chauffeur for the rest of his natural life. But if his physical treatment was humane, his political fate was stern. The party tacitly sentenced Khrushchev to join the ranks of the unpersons, a punishment hitherto reserved for the dead. Or perhaps Khrushchev was the first authentic unperson, for the likes of Kamenev, Zinoviev and Trotsky had at least been dishonored by thoroughgoing public condemnation before their names were allowed to lapse into near oblivion. With Khrushchev, however, there was not even the publicity of being declared a major devil. His shortcomings were explained in a number (really a rather small number) of allusive remarks about "subjectivism" and "harebrained schemes." Even when he was being criticized, however, it was taboo to mention his name. As for his unchallenged achievements, such as his role in ending Stalin's terror, only the Soviet critics of the regime remembered. All kinds of publications that were favorable to Khrushchev were quietly suppressed or revised, including the basic text on party history, one edition of which was hastily withdrawn and cleansed of Khrushchev's name. Only when an American magazine published a taped memoir by Khrushchev in 1970, did he surface briefly to obey the masters of the land by producing a denial of the memoir's authenticity. His death in 1971 brought no reprieve to his reputation. The funeral was private and he was buried in ground hallowed by the

Orthodox Church, not the plot along the Kremlin wall sanctified by the Bolshevik party.

If Khrushchev was consigned to oblivion, what of the party leaders, dead or still living, whom he had castigated? Was there to be a new wave of "rehabilitations" of the "victims" of Khrushchev to give the new succession process a further parallel to the one that followed Stalin's death? Only in one significant case, it seems. Old Marshal (and sometime Politburo member) Voroshilov was implicitly cleared of crimes in the Stalin era or of support for the antiparty group of 1957. He again appeared on the Lenin mausoleum, he published his memoirs, and when he died in 1969 he received full party and military honors. This was an understandable concession, for Voroshilov had been quite aged in 1957, and his sins in the Stalin era were conformist rather than creative. But Molotov, Malenkov, Kaganovich, and the other losers of 1957 were not pardoned. Evidently the Brezhnev-Kosygin leadership regarded the 1957 confrontation as one of their own victories over heresy.

Moreover, rehabilitation of surviving lieutenants of Stalin (apart from Voroshilov) would have been difficult to envisage apart from the resurrection of Stalin himself. This was, of course, a key question for the new regime. Much has been said of "restalinization." If Stalinism is understood to include the entire political culture of the Soviet Union during his generation in power, then the Brezhnev-Kosygin era can rightly be considered Stalinist in a number of important respects. So can Khrushchev's administration. But with respect to the "cult of personality" in the most immediate sense, the Brezhnev-Kosygin leadership resisted the temptations to launch a full-fledged campaign of restoration. There must have been many party officials, and even ordinary Soviet people, who were permanently antagonized by the anti-Stalin campaign, which struck at the faith of a generation and called into question the very legitimacy of the party. If the anti-Stalinist section of party and public opinion was to be upset in any case by the denigration of Khrushchev, why not at least lay claim to the awe inspired by Stalin's name, which was surely a mightier part of the Bolshevik tradition than Khrushchev's? There must have been arguments in this direction in the top leadership, and they probably reached a peak in early 1966. The first post-Khrushchev party congress, the twenty-third, met in March of that year, and the preceding months provided various signs of an impending rehabilitation of Stalin. Many leading Soviet intellectuals and artists believed that the congress might take a serious step in this direction, and a letter bearing twenty-five signatures was addressed to the congress to dissuade it from rehabilitating Stalin. (Could they exhume the body and replace it beside Lenin's? When Stalin had been removed from the Lenin mausoleum in 1961 no announcement concerning cremation had been given. For that matter, it is not guaranteed that the expertly embalmed body was actually interred, since no ceremony was held. It could be in cold storage, awaiting a change in the political climate.)

The intellectuals' apprehensions turned out to be mistaken. Stalin was not an explicit issue at the congress. This could scarcely be attributed to the pressure of the intellectuals alone. Evidently they had underrated the forces of anti-Stalinism (in the personal sense) in the leadership. Obviously the gains of rehabilitation would have been offset by some serious debits. The revelation of Stalin's misdeeds had been a shock and a strain for the party and people. A new reversal of this line in 1966 would have been at least as bad a wrench, enforceable only by the kind of police regime that Stalin admired and his heirs found too hazardous for their taste. Especially at the time when the leaders were attempting to keep any one person from gaining too much power, there were potent arguments against reviving the Stalin cult.

In place of Khrushchev's anti-Stalin campaign or the decisive rehabilitation of the dictator's image, a compromise was reached. It was admitted that Stalin made "mistakes," and the posthumous rehabilitation of some of his victims (such as A. P. Smirnov, a codefendant in the Zinoviev-Kamenev trial) was continued for several years after 1964. But it was considered poor form to dwell on these matters, as the historian A. M. Nekrich found after he had succeeded in publishing in the Soviet Union a book about the military catastrophe of June, 1941, and Solzhenitsyn reconfirmed in 1974 when he published abroad his book on the Gulag system. Basically the compromise position of the Brezhnev-Kosygin leadership was that the Twentieth Party Congress had *collectively* cleared up the question of Stalin's errors, which were really not as bad as some ill-intentioned persons alleged. Stalin had served the country well in many ways, they said, his wartime leadership being the most prominently cited example. Now that the matter was cleared up, let us revere Lenin, desist from ostentatious pro- or anti-Stalinism and go about the business of building communism. As if to set its seal on the whole matter, Stalin's grave was dignified with a bust in 1970. In keeping with the compromise position, there was no ceremony to mark the occasion, and it was not a grandiose statue—nothing like the monstrosities that had been dismantled—but it was the largest in the row of second-rank party heroes flanking Lenin's mausoleum.

The hero memorialized by the mausoleum was even more emphatically and repetitiously glorified under the new leadership than under Khrushchev, no small feat in itself. This was partly a response to the political situation of the new leadership. They had to demonstrate their legitimacy and orthodox ancestry, and they chose not to claim descent from Stalin. Khrushchev was "harebrained" and "subjectivist"

—hardly a suitable Bolshevik ancestor. The task of increasing the production of the Lenin cult was made easier by the occurrence of the fiftieth anniversary of the October Revolution and the centennial of Lenin's birth within the first five years of new leadership. Any country would have organized some sort of anniversary observance of roughly analogous mythic events, and anyone could have predicted that the Soviet approach to such events would have been excessive. Even so, the propaganda machine outdid itself in monotonous, numbing incantations in honor of Lenin in 1967 and 1970. By late 1970 even hardened ideologues seemed to suspect that there had been too much of a good thing. A Lenin centennial theme in chocolate cakes was officially criticized as going too far. It would be a mistake, however, to dismiss these protracted rituals merely as predictable bores. They were that, but they also set the tone for the period and its leaders—a respect for the traditional and suspicion of experimentation or radicalism.

This spirit was evident in the new leadership's dismantling of many of Khrushchev's innovations. In the field of party internal affairs it was clear that the career party workers found almost none of Khrushchev's changes agreeable. The bifurcation of party administration on the *oblast'* and lower levels was ended only weeks after Khrushchev was overthrown. The more or less open meetings of the Central Committee, with published stenographic reports and hordes of "guests" were ended in 1965. The statutory requirement that a portion of the party executive personnel on each level be replaced at regular intervals was scrapped in 1966. The Buro of the Secretariat for the RSFSR, which had been introduced in 1956, was also abolished in 1966.

The party program of 1961, Khrushchev's main ideological monument, was quietly downgraded. This document had been officially adopted by a party congress, after all. While the party admitted implicitly that individual leaders who strayed from the path of collectivity might make serious errors, it would be heresy to suggest that the highest symbol of the party's collective will, the congress, could go wrong. Yet the program not only reminded people of Khrushchev but also contained a number of unrealistically ambitious goals. As with the Stalin problem, the new leadership disposed of an awkward matter mainly by ignoring its existence. The program was never attacked and was not withdrawn from libraries or bookstores. But it ceased to be emphasized in propaganda and was overshadowed by a series of ephemeral pronouncements, such as theses on the fiftieth anniversary of the revolution.

The program reflected Khrushchev's tendency to take seriously some of the socially radical, egalitarian goals of classical Marxism. One immediate result of this drift was the educational reform of 1958, which attempted to advance social equality by requiring all entrants to higher education, regardless of their origin and secondary schooling, to serve in the ordinary labor force. That such a scheme was needed if the tendency toward privilege was to be uprooted in Soviet society was demonstrated by the pained reaction of the administrative and technological elite. Even under Khrushchev the educational reform had been diluted. Under his successors its egalitarian points were quietly buried. In the same spirit the new leadership reversed Khrushchev's policy on private automobiles, which he considered a prime example of the bourgeois ethos and an economic drag on the push toward the provision of a decent *minimum* of material welfare for all citizens under Communist society. Again the criticism of his policy from the ranks of the well-to-do confirmed his point. Yielding to these interests, particularly the party and industrial hierarchy, Kosygin in 1966 proclaimed that it was a mistake to say that large numbers of passenger cars were unnecessary, and a major program of small car production was undertaken, based on a contract with the Fiat company. (As if to remove the taint of their capitalist origin, the city in which these Italian vehicles of the bourgeois spirit were made was named for the lately deceased Italian Communist leader Togliatti. This irony was compounded by the fact that Togliatti's political testament consisted of a cutting attack on the Soviet leaders.) The idea of the withering away of the state itself withered under Brezhnev and Kosygin. Khrushchevian attempts to begin the transfer of state functions directly to "the people" were abolished or allowed to stagnate. The "people's teams" to aid the police suffered the latter fate.

To be sure, the central question of the program and the transition to communism was perceived as rapid economic growth, embodied in a twenty-year plan. This was highly embarrassing to the Brezhnev-Kosygin leadership, both because it implied the regime's responsibility for an unrealistic rate of growth and because a number of the particular economic tactics designed to attain this growth were not working well. Khrushchev's last great campaign, the "chemicization" of the country, was a prime issue, affecting industry in its massive reallocation of investment away from the traditional steel and machinery area, and agriculture in that chemical fertilizer was to lead to such improvements as would enable the country to catch up with the United States or at least to avert another harvest as calamitous as the one in 1963. The new leadership could hardly deny that the chemical industry needed more emphasis, and the propaganda on chemicization was not dropped with embarrassing abruptness. But the investment plan was revised in favor of more traditional proportions, and the idea that the chemical industry was a panacea was allowed to taper off.

Chemicals were only the last of Khrushchev's attempts to solve the chronic agricultural problem by some sort of major campaign. There was too much invested in the virgin lands program in Central Asia to dismantle it, but the new leadership ceased to treat it as a solution. The corn-growing program, as a basis for the overtaking of the United States in meat, dairy and egg production, also suffered deflation, and corn-growing was limited to areas that were more or less appropriate climatically. Khrushchev's passion for the large-scale in agriculture had led him to drastic restrictions on the private-plot agriculture of collective farmers, with serious effects on the marketing of such foods as potatoes, vegetables, and meat. The new leadership included liberalization of this highly unpopular and doctrinaire policy in their first months in office.

In departing from Khrushchev's tactics in promoting economic growth the new leadership did, however, make a major move toward a radical departure of their own. Or at least Kosygin was able to persuade Brezhnev and other party figures to go part way toward embarking on a plan of reform in industrial administration. This was the plan often associated with the economist E. G. Liberman, which attempted to replace the Stalinist elements of a central "command economy" with economic planning based on market indicators. In large measure the decision making was to shift to the factory managers themselves, who would determine their mix of products on the basis of the demand for this or that product. If there was little demand for glass bottles but a high demand for drinking glasses, to use a crude example, it would be unprofitable for a Soviet factory to make bottles, although they might have been ordered to do so by the ministry or the *sovnarkhoz* under the administrative systems of Stalin or Khrushchev, respectively. Such a change had serious implications for the party. The party stood to lose much of its role in industrial life. Ever since the First Five-Year Plan, there had been a strong assumption that the success of a planned socialist economy depended on the active intervention of the Communist Party to supplement economic incentive with ideological push. Ever since Stalin's intervention in the First Five-Year Plan, "drive" or "campaign" had in many respects been the chief characteristic of the Soviet economy and an implied justification for the central role of the party in economic life. The advocates of reform in the sixties argued that the complexity of an advanced economy required a different approach, in which market indicators would replace to a considerable extent the commands of planning bodies, and managerial specialists would achieve a high degree of independence of party officials. Contrary to some impressions in the West, there was no question of "capitalism" replacing socialism, but rather a challenge of market economy socialism (in which heretical Yugoslavia had pursued the most far-reaching experiments) to the command economy under direct party control.

Theoretical debate and limited experimentation with this change in industrial administration had started during the Khrushchev period, but he had shown no personal enthusiasm for it. But the declining rate of industrial growth in the Soviet Union in Khrushchev's last years provided a powerful argument in favor of making some change. The attempt to decentralize the command of industry to *sovnarkhozes* did enhance the authority of *oblast'* party officials, but it had never been popular with administrators who had been obliged to leave ministerial jobs in Moscow to take up provincial *sovnarkhoz* posts. The Kosygin reform went hand in hand with the reestablishment of the economic ministries that Khrushchev had decentralized, so bureaucratic official-dom could find considerable attraction in the reform, even if many were not genuinely attracted to its key ideas.

The decision to adopt the reform was taken only eleven months after the removal of Khrushchev (an indication of the sense of urgency that must have existed concerning industrial growth rates), but the com-plexity of the change required that the transition of individual enter-prises be phased over five years (1966–1970). This period revealed that many officials in the ministries and the party apparatus were unready to transfer as much latitude to the factory directors as the theoreticians of the reform had envisaged. Moreover, although there was much talk of stress on consumer goods from the beginning of the Brezhnev-Kosygin administration, the Ninth Five-Year Plan, beginning in 1971, maintained the kind of heavy emphasis on investment in the means of production that has been traditional since Stalin's day. Incidentally, the new plan also dispatched to oblivion Khrushchev's notion that seven years makes a better span for planning than Stalin's five.

Another area in which dekhrushchevization no doubt seemed attrac tive to the new leadership was artistic and intellectual life. Having ended the reign of terror and having encouraged some frank depiction of it, Khrushchev found that dissent concerning Bolshevik orthodoxy was getting out of hand. His successors tried getting tough with the dissenters, but this only seemed to add to the problem. The first major effort of the new regime, departing from Khrushchev's practices, was a crude but widely publicized trial of the writers Andrei Sinyansky and Yuly Daniel in 1966, the first in a series of such events. Unlike Stalin's show trials, these did not involve capital accusations, produced no confessions, and did not intimidate despite the usual sentences of hard labor which led to the death of several thought-criminals. Tough-ened survivors of Stalin's camps, such as the writer Solzhenitsyn, were not to be intimidated, certainly not by a regime that would not coun-tenance a general wave of terror for fear of its possible toll within the party. The dissenters were even emboldened to hold some small pub-lic demonstrations and to develop underground *samizdat* ("self-publi-

cation," usually in typescripts with carbons), which soon included not
only literary but specifically political writing. In 1968 the *Chronicle of
Current Events* appeared, an underground newspaper which featured
objective reports on political persecution. The first nonparty political
organizations since Lenin's day also emerged, underground or even in
the open, such as the Action Group for the Defense of Civil Rights
(1969). Granted, the leaders of these activities often disclaimed any
political intent, but in truth the KGB (the latest incarnation of the
secret police) was right to think otherwise. Given the party's traditional claim to a monopoly on truth and political organization, any
challenge to this position is a profoundly political act, even if it is in
the name of the Soviet Constitution, as was usually the case in the later
sixties. In this period the critics of the regime were generally members
of no organization, their total numbers were not imposing, and their
ideas extremely diverse. But the tide seemed to be moving in the
wrong direction, from the party's point of view.

The Brezhnev-Kosygin administration opened with a dramatic effort
to dekhrushchevize Soviet relations with China. The removal of the
outspoken enemy of Maoism and the immediate curtailment of anti-
Chinese propaganda gained Brezhnev and Kosygin enough credit in
Peking to induce Premier Chou En-lai to visit Moscow for the observance of the anniversary of the October Revolution only a few weeks
after the new regime was installed. Evidently the new Soviet leaders
were willing to call off the intended international showdown in the
form of a world Communist meeting, which Khrushchev had intended
as the formal condemnation of the Maoist heresy. Soviet prestige was
salvaged by holding a consultative meeting of eighteen Communist
parties in March, 1965, but no anathemas were issued. All of this failed
to placate the leadership in Peking. Evidently they insisted on some
kind of ideological agreement on their terms and probably concessions
on military and economic assistance. The Soviets evidently felt that
they had conceded enough in turning away from Khrushchev's confrontation. Mutual recriminations were resumed in 1966 and in 1968
the Khrushchevian aim of holding a worldwide anti-Maoist Communist conference was again revived. It was indeed a "harebrained
scheme," again evoking the resistance of many foreign Communist parties as well as Chinese indignation. By 1969 the Sino-Soviet confrontation reached its most serious point, as border fighting and menacing
words flared. Brezhnev and Kosygin had started with the intention of
undoing Khrushchev's errors but had in fact repeated them.

A similar pattern applied to relations in Eastern Europe. Khrushchev's attempts to replace Stalinist oppression with a greater degree
of voluntary cooperation, without undermining Soviet predominance,
had led to the Hungarian uprising, the Albanian defection to the

Chinese camp and the drift of Rumania toward economic, military and diplomatic independence. The new Soviet leadership did not seem to have any specific program for the improvement of the situation when they came to power, but they probably blamed some of the difficulties on Khrushchev's personal mistakes and hoped that a steadier, more reasonable approach would help consolidate their East European clients around Comecon and the Warsaw Pact. Surely they wanted to avoid the risk and stress of another Hungarian situation, but this was approximately what they faced in Czechoslovakia in 1968. Having been "liberal" in permitting reformist Communists to remove the old Stalinist party leader Novotny, Brezhnev and Kosygin found that even their personal attempts to guide the new Dubcek leadership in Czechoslovakia could not prevent the country from turning more and more unbolshevik. The removal of the police control of the populace, and particularly the media of communication, seems to have been the crucial point. Leninist unity of political ideology and with it the dominance of the party elite yielded rapidly to a highly pluralistic forum of ideas, many of them openly critical not only of Stalin but even of the immortal Lenin. The prospect of a system of competing political parties was bad, but the prospect of a Czechoslovak Communist Party devoted to "socialism with a human face" was worse. The slogan implied too much about the face of Soviet socialism and offered far too attractive an alternative to other Eastern European countries.

Thus it was that in August, 1968, the Red Army invaded its ally, following a series of negotiations in which the Soviet leaders failed to persuade the Czechoslovaks to mend their ways. The operation was carried out much more decisively and efficiently than Khrushchev's bloody repression of Hungary. This was partly because the victim had no illusions about the consequences of resistance. Soviet military and diplomatic preparations were also better. The worried conservative Communist governments in East Germany, Poland, Hungary and Bulgaria were willing to participate in this rescue of the Czechoslovak state from the clutches of an imperialist plot. The absurdity of this pretext, matching anything that Stalin had asked loyal Communists to believe, cost the Soviets little. There were a few defections or protests among Communists in non-Communist countries, but most of those who were outraged were not admirers of the Bolshevik tradition. The Brezhnev-Kosygin leadership almost repeated Khrushchev's unnecessary harshness in abducting and executing Imre Nagy. Dubcek was spirited off to Moscow, but Brezhnev was persuaded to repatriate him and even to return him to office temporarily. Thus the transition from "socialism with a human face" to something more familiar could be carried out in an almost bloodless transition lasting many months. On balance, it was a good performance in Bolshevik terms. While it did represent an approximate repetition of Khrushchev's troubles of 1956, the encore was much better than the original performance. It brought Soviet troops into the Czech salient in capitalist Europe for the first time since the end of the World War. The success emboldened Brezhnev to enunciate in the fall of 1968 the ominous doctrine that when socialism was threatened in one country, other Socialist nations had the right and obligation to intervene to quash the threat. This exacerbated relations with China, Yugoslavia, Rumania, Albania and some Communist parties not in power, but it also demonstrated strength and self-assurance.

This spirit of militant, orthodox communism was also manifest in the Brezhnev-Kosygin reversal of Khrushchev's policy on the long-festering warfare in Southeast Asia. While the former leader had sought to avoid major involvement here, particularly at the cost of damaged relations with the United States, his successors undertook a major program of military aid to North Vietnam. While this harmonized with the spirit of the regime at this time, it is probable that the United States and China gave Moscow little option. American military intervention in the Indo-Chinese war represented an open challenge to the Soviet Union's supposed role as the patron of Communist and nationalist struggle against imperialism. To back away from this challenge would have given the Chinese a magnificent opportunity to demonstrate the rightness of their charge that the Soviets were no longer revolutionaries but revisionists in league with the imperialists. One can therefore speak of dekhrushchevization of Soviet policy toward the United States in the period of increasing American involvement during the Indo-Chinese war, with the qualification that both Moscow and Washington took pains to delimit their antagonism.

A degree of dekhrushchevization also occurred in Soviet policy toward the third world. As in the case of Southeast Asia, this was not the result of a deliberate initiative in Moscow. The leading "national democracies," on which Khrushchev had hoped to rely as active allies in the struggle with imperialism, proved to have weaknesses that were beyond Soviet control. Ben Bella of Algeria, Sukarno of Indonesia and Nkrumah of Ghana all were ingloriously deposed by domestic opponents of less pro-Soviet inclinations in 1965–1966. Nasser's Egypt was humiliated in the six-day war of 1967, despite massive Soviet military aid. Soviet strategic interest in the third world, particularly the Near East and India, survived, but talk of "national democracy" waned. The Soviet role in these countries was framed much more in terms of conventional great-power interest, bolstered by a greatly expanded high seas fleet.

Throughout the first years of the Brezhnev-Kosygin leadership, the supreme authority was in practice diffused among a small number of politicians, following the pattern of earlier succession crises. The Central Committee plenum of October, 1964, not only chose to assign the leading party and state posts to two different persons, but probably passed a resolution against the principle of the concurrent possession of the two supreme posts by one person.* There was even an attempt to keep the power of the party Secretariat divided. Khrushchev had sought to enhance his own authority while keeping his lieutenants divided by partitioning secretarial authority between the Secretariat and the "Buro of the Secretariat for the RSFSR" (Russian federal republic). The old man headed both these secretarial bodies, but when he was forced to resign, nothing was published about the Buro of the Secretariat for the RSFSR. Clearly Khrushchev had not been permitted to keep this powerful post, but in the fall of 1964 it was equally clear that Brezhnev could not get it. That he wanted it was demonstrated by the quiet attribution of the office to Brezhnev in an encyclopedia yearbook published over seven months after the October upheaval. Later, when Brezhnev had established himself more securely, he followed a party tradition by improving history. A biographical article published in an encyclopedia in 1971 awarded him the office as of November, 1964 (the first Central Committee plenum after the one that dumped Khrushchev), while a capsule biography published in an encyclopedia yearbook in 1972 determined that history could be made better yet, and pushed the award back to the October, 1964, plenum. In reality Brezhnev had merged the Buro with the Secretariat proper in 1966, but the memory of the humiliating constraints on his power in 1964 and early 1965 still rankled years later.

Because two previous chief party secretaries had tried, with different degrees of success, to establish their personal dictatorship, it was reasonable for the new oligarchy to pay special attention to the containment of Brezhnev's power. For about five years following the deposition of Khrushchev this worked fairly well. Personally Brezhnev was not permitted to dominate the propaganda media. In party politics he certainly did not have things his own way. An unofficial "executive committee" of the party Presidium (again called Politburo after April, 1966), consisting of Brezhnev, Kosygin, Podgorny and Suslov, replaced any one leader as *de facto* head of that council. The composition of the Presidium was changed partly in Brezhnev's favor, partly against it in the period 1964–1969. Three men who were ill or old were removed (Kozlov, Mikoyan and Shvernik) in 1964–1966, but this did not substantially bolster Brezhnev's position. Two men who were certainly not favorably disposed to him, P. E. Shelest' and A. N. Shelepin, were

---

* No such resolution has been published but T. H. Rigby has noted that a Soviet scholarly work published in 1967 certainly seems to imply that an explicit decision was taken in October, 1964.

added in the same period. Shelepin, who could boast an exceptional career in the party apparatus to this point, was seriously regarded as a possible rival to Brezhnev.

The first post-Khrushchev party congress, the twenty-third, met in April, 1966, but did little to enhance Brezhnev's visible power. True, his office was officially renamed General Secretary, rather than First Secretary, and the party Presidium was renamed Politburo. These were symbols of party tradition, rather than any assertion of Brezhnev's authority. In fact, the title General Secretary had been conferred on Stalin during the supposed collective leadership of the 1920s rather than during the thirties and forties when he was at the height of his powers.

Not only was Brezhnev's visible power kept in check for about five years, Kosygin's personal role was strong in this period. Not since Lenin had any chairman of the Council of Ministers (or People's Commissars) played so eminent a role in Soviet politics, without simultaneously commanding the party apparatus. Kosygin should not be suspected of wishing to subvert the party, but he did represent a strong claim to power by the Soviet state organs, which inevitably raised the question of a long-term decline of the party as the supreme political organization. Personally Kosygin represented the many important Soviet public administrators who were party members and considered themselves good Communists, but whose careers had been mainly in the Soviet state apparatus, including economic organs. Their experience with full-time party officials often led them to the notion that the country would function better if the party played a less direct role in such matters as economic administration. It is significant that Kosygin, and not Brezhnev, presented to the party and country the 1965 plan of economic reforms that would tend to enhance the role of factory managers and diminish that of party Secretariat in industry. It also appears that Kosygin and others thought it more appropriate that the leading role in summit diplomacy should be played by the chairman of the Council of Ministers rather than the party head. In the first five years after Khrushchev it fell to Kosygin and not Brezhnev to mediate the truce between India and Pakistan in 1966, to visit the United Nations and see President Johnson in 1967, among numerous diplomatic trips in the non-Communist world, and even to make the most important flying diplomatic visits to Asian Communist countries: North Vietnam, China and Korea. Kosygin was not aiming at establishing his personal dictatorship but he seemed to represent a trend in Soviet politics toward the primacy of nonparty officials and nonparty administrative organs. In the absence of a powerful General Secretary this trend could be ominous for the future of the party as a dominant force, a Leninist vanguard.

18

THE PRIMACY
OF THE GENERAL SECRETARY

Those who believed in October 1964 that the Brezhnev-Kosygin leadership was merely transitional were in a sense right. The new collective leadership was a transition to the predominance of Brezhnev. His primacy cannot aspire to the level of personal dictatorship in the manner of Stalin, and unlike Khrushchev, Brezhnev has not sought to aggrandize his power by taking on the chairmanship of the Council of Ministers. Nor is it possible to cite any particular event in factional politics, such as Stalin's victory over the right opposition or Khrushchev's over the antiparty group, as the beginning of Brezhnev's predominance. Nevertheless, one can say that from approximately 1970 the General Secretary has overshadowed Kosygin and all other contenders. In so doing he has reestablished the primacy of the party as the key institution in Soviet politics.

The personal image of the party leader has certainly assumed preeminence. Although it would be exaggerated to refer to a cult of Brezhnev, he has been accorded not only the largest volume of coverage in the media but also certain symbolic acknowledgments that have very special significance in the traditions of the party. In 1970 his speeches (be they ever so pedestrian) were collected and published in two volumes, the first of many. These works are not called "classics" or "collected works," but they have been given wide dissemination in many languages and are the first such works by a living Soviet politician since Khrushchev's retirement. Summit diplomacy, and there has been a good deal of it since 1970, has featured Brezhnev. According to diplomatic protocol, Brezhnev should yield to Kosygin or Podgorny in such activities because he is a party, not state, official. But the Politburo (and for that matter Indira Gandhi) accepted the practical fact that the party leader is the top man in the country. In 1973 Brezhnev was able to arrange an event that gave special prominence to his authority. An "exchange of party documents" was instituted, meaning that all members would be subject to a review, with undesirables getting no new party membership card. This not only reminded one of the continuity of Lenin's concept of the party as an elite, it also provided the occasion for a ceremony in which Brezhnev occupied the limelight as he issued party card number one to V. I. Lenin. If it seems presumptuous for Brezhnev to approve Lenin's Bolshevik orthodoxy, it was even more so for Brezhnev to receive party card number two. The same relationship between the founder and the present party leader was made in a major art exhibit in early 1974, at which Lenin's portrait was flanked by one of Brezhnev—more modest in size (and painted by Stalin's favorite portraitist).

By 1974 formal announcements of awards to federative units of the USSR consistently referred to "the Politburo of the Central Committee of the Communist Party of the Soviet Union, headed by General Secretary of the Central Committee of the Communist Party of the Soviet Union, Comrade L. I. Brezhnev." There is no "head" or chairman of the Politburo according to the party statutes, but the very fact that Brezhnev has acquired the authority to get this presumptuous formula published repeatedly proves that it is quite realistic. A similar manipulation of the press to enhance Brezhnev's image was introduced in 1974 by the practice of conferring the dignity of "assistant to the General Secretary of the Central Committee" on the relatively obscure men who are the heirs of Poskrebyshev. This title does not exist in the party statutes and they hold no other high rank, but the press mentioned them just behind Politburo members in reportage of such events as the summit meeting with President Pompidou.

Brezhnev's personal style as leader is generally rather ponderous on public occasions. He aspires to calm dignity, which he achieves pretty well, but with a sense of boredom rather than charisma. His excruciatingly long major addresses are relieved only by the quality of his speaking voice. There is, however, another Brezhnev who appears in small groups and serves as a useful complement to the rather slow and stuffy public figure. This is an energetic, tough, very political man of some real force and a distinctly unleninist taste for Cadillacs, Lincolns, Mercedes, and Citroëns. He owns one of each. Unlike Khrushchev, Brezhnev seems to be able to keep his public and private personalities in their proper zones most of the time. This team of the two Brezhnevs seems pretty successful, stronger than the former Brezhnev-Kosygin combination.

Brezhnev's authority was accumulated gradually, patiently, and not without setbacks. Over ten years he maneuvered to arrange the composition of the Politburo and Secretariat in his favor, overcoming the inclination of many leading Soviet politicians to prevent just that. Probably Brezhnev's willingness to concentrate his efforts in his party posts, rather than try to replace Kosygin, has been an asset in his long campaign. Khrushchev spread himself too thin, and his protégé learned from his example. Brezhnev also has avoided Khrushchev's (or Stalin's) open confrontations with groupings of opponents. Although there undoubtedly have been critics and rivals of the General Secretary since 1964, they have been unable to coalesce into a group that can force a showdown, even a losing one. The Politburo as a whole evidently has agreed that open clashes are damaging to the internal security of the system, and the losers have been picked off individually by Brezhnev. All have been quietly shunted aside without any public reproach, and in return they have made their exits quietly. This tacit understanding that there should be no open opposition or campaigns against opposition at the top level draws on a good Leninist tradition and is a great asset to Brezhnev.

The same tacit understanding conceals the inner workings of Soviet politics from the outside observer to an even greater than usual degree, but a number of the main steps in Brezhnev's modification of the leading organs can be discerned. First, the removal of Podgorny from the party Secretariat to the chairmanship of the Presidium of the Supreme Soviet in 1965 greatly diminished the potential of this rival. The control of the party secretarial apparatus, in which Podgorny had played a major role, was now mainly in the hands of Brezhnev and his closest associate, Kirilenko, who was added to the Secretariat in 1966. It may have been helpful to Brezhnev that the Podgorny move was coupled with the retirement of Mikoyan from the Politburo. The Armenian veteran was not a plausible rival to Brezhnev, but was ultra-experienced in maneuver and could have played a role in organizing Politburo membership against anyone's predominance.

An equally important advance for Brezhnev was the transfer of Shelepin in 1967 from the Secretariat to the chairmanship of the trade union organization. The way for this change had been paved by the abolition of the joint party-state inspectorial apparatus in 1965. This body was Khrushchev's creation, one of the many that his heirs found unsuitable. Shelepin had been head of this potentially powerful organization. He seems to have resisted the attack on his power base, but failed and was therefore ripe for transfer out of the Secretariat.

While removing Podgorny and Shelepin from the Secretariat, Brezhnev arranged a number of new appointments to this body: Ustinov, Kulakov, Kapitonov (1965); Kirilenko, Solomentsev (1966); Katushev (1968); and Dolgikh (1972). It is not necessarily the case that each of these were strictly Brezhnev's choices, but he at least must have approved each and is to some extent their patron. The Secretariat stands at the head of the regional party secretarial hierarchy, in which Brezhnev spent so much of his own career. Like Stalin and Khrushchev, he was able to use this apparatus, which is more purely political than any other component of the party-state machine. Persons in the higher levels of the regional secretarial apparatus could be removed if they opposed Brezhnev or were simply found wanting. The outstanding case in point was Shelest', who was first secretary of the Ukraine, until he was removed in 1973.

On the basis of his strengthened control of the secretarial apparatus, Brezhnev was able to manipulate the composition of the Politburo after 1970. Three regional party secretaries (Grishin, Kunaev and Shcherbitsky) became full members of the Politburo, and a fourth (Romanov) became a candidate member in 1971–1973. The Central Committee Secretariat also enhanced its representation in the Politburo. One secretary, Kulakov, joined as a full member in 1971 and two became candidates (Solomentsev and Ponomarev) in 1971–72. In addition, a former Central Committee secretary, Iu. V. Andropov, who had been assigned to the security apparatus in 1967, was promoted to full Politburo membership in 1973. In that year Brezhnev also succeeded in removing from the Politburo two men who clearly were not his supporters: Shelest' and Voronov. Their departure was balanced by the appointment of two men who did not represent the party secretarial apparatus, Defense Minister Marshal Grechko and Foreign Minister Gromyko. If this was intended as counterweight to Brezhnev's expanded authority, it was feeble. Neither Grechko nor Gromyko had any real political base, and the Marshal was a personal friend of Brezhnev from his days in military-political work.

All told, the Politburo of 1974 was much more solidly in the hands of the party secretarial apparatus than it had been five years earlier, and it is most probable that this interest regarded Brezhnev as their leader and representative. Of the added members of the Politburo since 1964, all but a few had been promoted with Brezhnev's personal support and had some reason to be grateful to him—though his behavior toward his patron Khrushchev shows how right Machiavelli had been about the ultimate reliability of love as a political bond.

The management of the Central Committee also demonstrated the strategy of patience and restraint. Brezhnev did not emulate Stalin or Khrushchev in attempting to remove a large proportion of this important body for real or imagined factional activity. He had successfully avoided the formation of open factions on the Politburo level and had no need to alarm the elite of Soviet politics by threatening their security. About 80 percent of the full members of the Central Committee elected in 1961 were reelected in 1966, and 78 percent of the 1966 group continued in the committee following the Twenty-fourth Party Congress in 1971. A few close personal adherents of Khrushchev were among those not elected, but age and normal mortality appear to be responsible for most of the departures. Since Brezhnev was unable and probably unwilling to return to Stalin's terror within the political elite, it made sense for him to cultivate rather than intimidate this key group, which in theory could deal with him as it had with Khrushchev.

As in the Politburo, the easiest way to modify Central Committee membership is to expand it. This Brezhnev did, raising the complement of full members from 175 to 195 in 1966 and from 195 to 241 in 1971. Again as with the Politburo, one cannot assume that all these newly elevated politicians are unconditionally loyal Brezhnevists, any more than Brezhnev and the Central Committee of 1961 were wholly reliable Khrushchevists. But in the politics of patronage the General Secretary certainly has tried to gain some favor among the 66 additional members of the committee, not to mention the replacements for the 78 members who had departed the committee.

Brezhnev's cultivation of the Central Committee also has involved calling regular meetings, but he has kept them fairly rare (usually three a year). The vanity of the membership has been flattered by holding these meetings in secret, and it appeared that a new meeting place was being prepared in 1973, a windowless marble auditorium, attached to a handsome high-rise building housing improved offices for the Secretariat. At the same time, Brezhnev appears to have maneuvered the Central Committee away from much exercise of real power or even the opportunity to debate at length. The meetings are usually very short, one or two days at a time, and the published reports of their work suggests that the committee membership spends most of its time listening to long-winded speeches by the top leaders.

The party rank and file continued to grow under Brezhnev's supervision, but with a greater concern for "quality" (meaning orthodoxy, reliability). In the five years from 1961 to 1966 (most of it under the Khrushchev administration), there was an increment of 2.7 million members and candidates (from 9.7 to 12.4 million), but in the interval between 1966 and 1971 the increment was down to about two million. The total represented 9 percent of the adult population of the country, a really large "vanguard," perhaps too large in the opinion of the General Secretary. In his reports to the Party Congress of 1971 he announced that the exchange of party documents would take place to deal with the question of quality in the party. Although the members were assured that this would not be a purge, it was clear that it could lead to considerable pruning of the organization. Apparently there was some real apprehension and foot-dragging in the ranks, because the actual beginning of the exchange did not occur until 1973, two years after Brezhnev's announcement to the Twenty-fourth Party Congress.

One of the sensitive areas that the scrutiny of party members had to deal with was the social composition of the party. Despite repeated orations about the need to base the party on the peasants and workers, it seemed difficult to overcome the tendency for the white-collar class to dominate. In 1971 official figures showed that almost 45 percent of the membership was drawn from this class. This represented a decline of less than two percent over five years in which there supposedly had been a campaign to increase the proportion of workers, which rose from 38 percent to 40 percent. As usual, the peasantry brought up the rear with only 15–16 percent, a very slight decline.* If, as seems likely, Brezhnev is enough of an orthodox Bolshevik to believe in the importance of trimming the total size of the party and increasing the proportion of workers in it, there could be real grounds for unease among the white-collar members. This is especially true concerning any party members who have shown any sympathy for the intellectual critics of the party leadership. A number of such liberals, including an outspoken *kolkhoz* chairman and a defense attorney in the political trials, had been expelled before the exchange of party documents.

The primacy of Brezhnev brought with it a determined effort to suppress the rising tide of political dissent, which was mainly outside the party. The "democratic movement," as it is sometimes called, was far from being an organization or a cohesive body of ideas, but its challenge to the fundamental myths of the party was intolerable. At first glance it might seem simple for the immense resources of the regime to crush a few thousand dispersed critics who lacked even a single printing press, legal or illegal. But there were two serious risks for Brezhnev: the possible spread of police control into the party and the possible spread of sympathy for the critics among ever larger circles of the populace.

In dealing with this problem Brezhnev demonstrated considerable patience and shrewdness, with enough ruthlessness to suit the needs of the situation. He entrusted the operational responsibility for the repression to an experienced party administrator, Iu. V. Andropov, who was moved from the Secretariat to the chairmanship of the Committee on State Security in 1967. At the same time Andropov was given candidate membership in the Politburo, the first police boss to sit in this body since Beria. For his success, Andropov was promoted to full member in 1973 and received conspicuous accolades on his sixtieth birthday in 1974. This careful linkage of the party apparatus and police work no doubt was intended to keep the repression under party control, and it did.

The techniques utilized by the KGB were equally successful in excising dissent without spreading the infection. Three principal tactics were utilized: criminal prosecution, forcible commitment for so-called psychiatric treatment, and emigration abroad (permitted or enforced). The first tactic yielded poor or even unwanted results at first, but the arrests continued and the tough treatment of some of those convicted

---

* One must bear in mind that the official figures on peasants likely include a number of managerial and technical personnel, and the definition of "worker" is always pretty broad in Soviet usage.

in "strict regime" camps (hard labor, cold climates, inadequate food) gradually began to have its effect as a deterrent. Ironically, the underground periodical *Chronicle of Current Events* assisted the police in their campaign of intimidation by publicizing the harsh penalties for active dissidence. The official press could scarcely report the injustice and brutality of the police, and it is quite possible that Andropov deliberately allowed the *Chronicle* to carry on in order to disseminate the bad news to the appropriate readers without distressing the masses.

For the edification of the masses some trials were reported in the press. While the speeches of the defendants were unreported in the legal media, the message of the prosecution, always approved by "spontaneous" letters to editors, came through loud and clear. Interestingly, it did not stress ideological deviation from true communism, but rather emphasized themes that the authorities deemed more reliable in mobilizing public opinion: Soviet patriotism and personal morality, especially on the treatment of sex in literature. Only with the trial of Viktor Krasin and Petr Yakir in 1973 did the Stalinist stage devices of the full confession and specific intervention of "foreign agents" reappear.

The tactic of compulsory "psychiatric" confinement ran into difficulties in one notable case, in which an eminent biologist, Zhores Medvedev, was released in the face of widespread protests from the scientific community. The regime was willing to bide its time and make minor tactical retreats to avoid an open break with a useful branch of the elite. On the whole, however, "psychiatric" treatment did serve to keep many dissenters in a state of drugged apathy without creating the atmosphere of growing police terror. For the gullible among the Soviet masses, and there were many, this tactic seemed to suggest that only the sick could become upset with a society that was successfully building communism.

The tactic of permitting or imposing emigration was more risky. It could lead to a serious brain drain, and the long-term results of developing a large and talented community of anti-Bolshevik, ex-Soviet citizens remain imponderable. The movement founded by the political emigrant Lenin has cause to ponder this matter. In the short run, however, emigration proved to be a splendid device for ridding the country of the critics who were too well known in the world to be clapped into a labor camp or psychiatric ward. Once abroad, the new wave of Soviet emigration was fairly effectively deprived of communication with masses whom they wished to seduce. The emigrants received scant sympathy from their countrymen to whom they were depicted as unpatriotic types who had sold out to the capitalists. Even their friends abroad had to grant that foreign residence was more humane than martyrdom in the Soviet Union. The climax of this tactic came in early 1974 when the chief moral leader of the protest movement, Solzhenitsyn, openly challenged the authorities to kill him for his convictions. They responded by putting him on a plane for West Germany, condemned to be a wealthy man, free to live in almost any country except a Communist one. In the long run the stormy encounter of the Russian intelligentsia with the government is not over, but Brezhnev's regime of the 1970s appears to have successfully quashed the upsurge of protest of the 1960s.

Brezhnev also succeeded in reasserting party primacy, and his own, in economic affairs in the seventies. There was no sweeping change, but the tradition of party initiative and control was reasserted against the trend toward ministerial authority or plant autonomy, which had appeared in the early post-Khrushchev years. That there were serious tensions in this matter was evident in the postponement of the Twenty-fourth Party Congress from 1970, when it should have met according to statute, to the following year. In this watershed period Brezhnev asserted himself forcibly in favor of traditional ideas of the party's role in economic affairs on at least two major occasions, Central Committee plenums of December, 1969, and July, 1970. His address of December, 1969, has remained secret, probably because it contained harsh criticism of the recent economic performance of the country, which at least implied a dig at Kosygin and the ministries. Since the reported participants in the "discussion" consisted of regional party secretaries and three ministers of heavy industries, it is likely that the thrust of the session favored orthodox emphasis on the primacy of heavy industry, under party supervision. The published Brezhnev speech of July, 1970, dealt with agriculture, criticizing lax control and emphasizing the necessity of closer party supervision.

The economic reforms of 1965 were quietly shoved into the background. Brezhnev and most party secretarial personnel generally ignored them in public addresses in the seventies. In the party congress of 1971 Kosygin indicated that reform had not been implemented fully enough, but Brezhnev ignored the matter, and by this time he was clearly encroaching on Kosygin's control of economic policy. Some technical changes in the planning, pricing and accounting system had occurred, but the main pillars of Soviet economic administration remained from the Stalin era. Among these were campaigns and competitions, which still replaced individual economic incentives to a substantial extent. Under Brezhnev such historic occasions as the centennial of Lenin's birth and the fiftieth anniversary of the Soviet Constitution (1972) provided the pretext for special drives to increase production, and in the absence of such convenient commemorations, new labor competitions, drives, and pledges of heroism were proclaimed anyway (as at the opening of 1974). The *subbotnik* (day of volunteer, unpaid labor) was revived in the name of Lenin. Even Kosygin, speaking in 1971, agreed that it would be erroneous to base the economy on the *market*. If something was to be imported from the capitalist world, it was credit, technical know-how, and actual factories. Brezhnev not only accepted this trend in Soviet economic practice, but even associated his own prestige with it on foreign junkets, especially to West Germany and the United States.

Traditional problems remained in agriculture. Despite the increase of chemical fertilizers, production of farm machinery, and changes in the price system, per capita production lagged. In 1972 there was a bad drought and crop failure. It is a demonstration of Brezhnev's success in fortifying his political position that this kind of calamity did not seem to weaken his authority, as it had Khrushchev's in 1964. Perhaps Brezhnev even got some of the political credit for the exceptionally favorable terms that Soviet buyers wangled in the United States when buying grain to make up the shortages at home. Or perhaps one should stress Brezhnev's shrewd avoidance of personal association with this or that agricultural theory, learning once again from the mistakes of his political mentor.

On balance, Brezhnev's impact on the economic life of the average Soviet citizen has not been dramatic. The Stalinist verities concerning the importance of the means of production and the necessity of strong party exhortation and supervision have remained. Real progress has been made in slowly raising the average standard of living, as has been true fairly consistently since the hard times at the end of the Second World War. But whatever the proper label for the Soviet economy may be—"command," "socialist," "planned"—it is neither "market" nor "consumer."

The General Secretary's leadership in foreign affairs also became more marked in the seventies. One obvious indication was his eminence as a host and guest in summit diplomacy. Brezhnev appears to enjoy immensely the status of peer with the heads of the capitalist powers, and it was Brezhnev, not Kosygin, who visited the United States, West Germany, France and India in the 1970s (not to speak of his numerous visits to East European Communist countries and a demonstratively important visit to Cuba in 1974).

Another indication of Brezhnev's primacy in this field relates to his report to the Twenty-fourth Party Congress in 1971. As is customary, it contained a survey of international affairs, and this was paraphrased and approved in a resolution of the congress. It was not regarded by foreign observers as a particularly striking restatement of Soviet ideas on foreign affairs, and it was accorded no unusual status by the congress. In the next several years, however, Brezhnev's report was repeatedly hailed in Soviet media as the party's "Program of Peace." This brazen puffery not only enhanced the rather routine contribution of the General Secretary at the congress, it also implied that some kind of new "program" had superceded Khrushchev's party program of 1961.

One of the points in Brezhnev's report was a firm but not belligerent stance on the Chinese problem. Mao is ideologically wrong, according to Brezhnev and his press, and the USSR will not yield on territorial questions. An imposing military concentration on the Sino-Soviet border underlines that. But he has learned not to attempt to "settle" the question by another international convention of Communist parties and is willing to see some relaxation of relations between the *states.* In this context the party-state distinction is shrewdly upheld by Brezhnev, who does not wish to involve his personal prestige in negotiations with the Chinese.

While the Chinese problem has been stabilized rather than solved, the Soviet Union has made some real gains in other parts of Asia: India, Vietnam and the Near East. Granted that Brezhnev's personal responsibility for the successes can be debated, but there is an important connection through the Soviet military. Brezhnev's career before 1964 provided him with strong ties in the high command, and it appears that he has been sensitive to their interests, particularly at budget time. The Indian smashing of Pakistan in 1971 must have been an immensely satisfying success for Soviet arms, particularly against an American-armed and Chinese-supported foe. The standoff in Vietnam, in which Soviet weapons cost the vaunted United States Air Force dearly, and the improved showing of the Arabs against Israel in 1973 must have demonstrated to the Politburo the value of a big and diversified armaments industry. In his consciousness of the importance of high priority for the military, Brezhnev has avoided Khrushchev's mistakes, and it is probably another area in which Kosygin's priorities were set aside in favor of Brezhnev's.

While favoring a big arms budget to support war by proxy, Brezhnev nevertheless was able to avoid a dangerous deterioration of relations with the United States or other Western powers. As already noted, his globe-trotting fostered the impression that this was partly due to his personal diplomacy, which combined political and economic overtures. Whoever had supplied the underlying ideas and backstage arrangements, the General Secretary seemed to be shrewd or lucky in simultaneously playing the militant, orthodox "anti-imperialist" and the beaming supporter of "peaceful coexistence," or "normalization," to use the term more in vogue under Brezhnev.

On balance, then, Brezhnev has done an unexpectedly successful job of reasserting the primacy of his office. This is not to say that he has established a personal dictatorship. The Politburo has remained to a degree a functioning oligarchy, which the General Secretary can manipulate but cannot intimidate or ignore. The level of success that Brezhnev has achieved is partly a reflection of his personal shrewdness, drive and luck, partly the need of the system to have an ultimate buck-stopper and adjudicator of disputes. Brezhnev has played his hand much more skillfully than did his mentor and predecessor, particularly in his concentration on the party and its Secretariat as his seat of authority. This enables the General Secretary to identify his own interests with those of the secretarial apparatus throughout the country, which has reason to see him as the guarantor of the party's continued dominance in the entire political system.

Primacy of this sort has real roots, but it is vulnerable. A few bad choices on policy matters, and the oligarchs, including those appointed by Brezhnev, could consign him to Khrushchev's fate. Some of the members of the Politburo who are younger than Brezhnev, but not so young that they can wait indefinitely for him to depart, have a motivation to organize a retirement conspiracy. Against this, it is probable that the party elite would prefer to avoid the embarrassment of once again kicking out its leader. The difficulty that any conspirators would encounter in reaching agreement on a successor to Brezhnev also should tend to obstruct such an ending to his administration. He has avoided any implied designation of an heir apparent. The finale, then, seems much more likely to come through natural mortality. Brezhnev has led a gruelling life, has been ill (including a heart attack before 1964, his wife told Ambassador Foy Kohler). He was looking all of his sixty-eight years as he approached his tenth anniversary as party leader. Sudden death, incapacitating illness or voluntary retirement in the face of seriously impaired health will probably oblige the Central Committee to choose its fifth major leader around the mid-1970s.

19

THE BOLSHEVIK TRADITION IN PERSPECTIVE

Ours is a turbulent century. Any political institution that can claim continuous existence since 1900 may be counted as one of the more stable and durable features of the landscape of contemporary history. The Bolsheviks are such a body, and this in itself is a powerful argument in favor of the continuation of Communist Party rule. The party leaders themselves appear to be keenly aware of this. While much of the symbolism of their propaganda looks to the future (the handsome worker, or Lenin, gazing with heroic determination toward some glorious horizon), there are few if any political cultures in the world that are more insistently devoted to the cultivation of its own past. The very stress on the glorious future is, of course, a deeply traditional myth, and one that no longer has much practical reference to the future, especially after the retreat from Khrushchev's program for the building of communist society by 1980. The omnipresent Lenin cult is the most obvious and fundamental monument to this past-mindedness. However boring and unpersuasive the Lenin myth may be, the party leaders cannot imagine themselves running the country without it. But it is not merely the Lenin cult. In recent years there has been no country that can match the USSR in its obsession with anniversaries. In addition to the Lenin centennial there was the fiftieth anniversary of the October Revolution, followed by the anniversaries of all sorts of institutions that were established shortly after the Bolsheviks came to power, including the secret police and the Soviet federal constitution.

In addition to these specifically Bolshevik commemoratives, official imagery lays enormous stress on World War II, not just the twenty-fifth anniversaries of victory over Germany and over Japan, celebrated in 1970, but a continual memorialization, including an unceasing program of the construction of truly monumental shrines. Many countries have reason to contemplate the experience of World War II, to mourn its tragedy or to celebrate its heroism, but only the Soviet Union promotes such an enormous effort to keep this memory vivid. This is by no means merely a reflection of the great suffering in the USSR during the war. The cult of World War II is permitted to vie with the cult of Lenin (and to surpass it in the size of the permanent monuments) precisely because the party leadership senses that it needs to fuse its sectarian tradition with a broader, nationalistic one.

One perspective on this stress on tradition is that communism is a moribund myth in the Soviet Union and its united front with Russian nationalism will in time lead to fundamental change in the public ideology. This is what Alexander Solzhenitsyn frankly advocated in his "Letter to Soviet Leaders" in 1973—an authoritarian nationalist government without Marxism-Leninism and with an Orthodox Christian background. But the leadership that replied by deporting Solzhenitsyn is by no means ready to give up the faith of their political fathers. This is not only a matter of habit, but also a reflection of some fundamental realities about the idea of legitimacy of the present political system in the USSR. The basic justification for party hegemony is the Leninist idea that the key to social scientific knowledge reposes in this body. The party and only the party is "armed with Marxist-Leninist theory," which enables it to know the true interests of the masses. There is simply no alternative idea of legitimacy that can be applied to party rule. Certainly not divine right, certainly not democratic election, for the nonparty masses do not even have a token vote for the Central Committee or the General Secretary. The traditions of the party may be synthesized with nationalism, as they have been for years, but they cannot be given up without inviting dissolution of the whole polity.

The sensitivity of the leadership to this point is underscored by their reluctance to alter the forms in which party ideology is conveyed to the masses. There is awareness that the media of agitation and propaganda, including the press, television, posters, fiction, film and song, are a good generation behind the techniques of mass persuasion of the capitalist countries. In Khrushchev's time, under the influence of his journalist son-in-law and staff assistant, Adzhubei, there were some tentative efforts at enlivening the propaganda media. But little came of this and less has happened in the Brezhnev decade. This conservatism in matters of form is not merely a matter of the age of Brezhnev or Suslov, but a shrewd appreciation that there *is* an important connection between the medium and the message. Leninism, the image of the all-wise party, cannot be modernized without seriously undermining the venerability of the party tradition, on which the continuity of the whole system depends.

If this credibility is already finished with some elements of the intelligentsia of Russia, there are millions in the party, or merely in positions of some status in the system, who have a big personal stake in political continuity. That Leninist ideology is ossified and uninteresting is largely irrelevant. Most people who count in the Soviet Union have a big personal stake in the party and reason enough to conform to traditional norms that it sets. And what is the alternative leadership? Certainly not the intellectual dissenters of various ideological persuasions, who cannot be imagined, even by their best friends, as a substitute leadership.

The Bolshevik tradition, then, is both necessary and functional, regardless of its absurdities and apparent obsolescence. It is both a body of ideas and an institution, which have a high degree of continuity running back to the opening of this century. The dogmatic attitude toward "scientific" truth in matters political and social has changed little since Lenin's day. The history of the party is still built on the theme of struggle with the enemy, who always turns out to be not only the admitted capitalists but *especially* the wrong-thinking socialists, from the *narodniks* and the "economists" of Lenin's youth to the Maoists and revisionists of Brezhnev's day. The passage of three-quarters of a century does not seem to have prepared the Bolsheviks to think of disagreements on politics as natural and inevitable. Rather, dissent is pernicious and perverse, and no amount of preachment from the present generation of Russian liberals seems likely to change this.

Along with this intellectual dogmatism, another great tradition of the party is its elitism. Granted, the actual appearance of party membership has changed enormously from the time when it was Lenin and a few dozen or hundreds of followers. The growth and bureaucratization of the party in power has in many respects transformed it into an unwieldy collection of persons who want social respectability or advantageous careers. Against this, the party has continually struggled to maintain at least some kind of meaningful elite within the party through a hierarchy of kinds of members. On the lowest level are the candidate members (in Stalin's day, for a time, there was a lower level of "sympathizers"), then the full-fledged members. In recent years these have been so numerous that the party has come to rely less on these millions than on the *aktiv*. This is a loosely defined collection of the more motivated and reliable party members, especially those who have been elected to nonprofessional committees in party organizations or who hold responsible posts in the nonparty leadership. No specific figures on the size of *aktiv* are published, but it appears that 10–20 percent of total party membership would account for this level of the elite. Still narrower is the circle of responsible *apparatchiks,* the professional party administrators, and especially the secretaries, who are the best trained and have the greatest stake in the continuity of the elitist tradition. For all its difficulties, it appears that this approach to politics rests on some pretty realistic assumptions about human behavior and is in no immediate danger of degenerating. The institutionalization of the elite in the party is, at minimum, a continuing success in maintaining the monopoly on political organization, which Lenin and Stalin so painstakingly established.

If the recruitment of an adequate elite seems to be continuing successfully, what about the supreme leader? The case of Brezhnev is highly instructive in this matter. His survival at the head of the party for a decade seems to demonstrate that the institution tends to need a single man at the top and that it can turn up persons capable of filling this role. The very fact that there is no statutory office of party head may assist this process. The head of the Secretariat has come to inherit some powerful advantages, but he is not automatically vested with the authority of a pope, president or supreme commander. The ambiguities of his status imply that the new head is a "candidate," in keeping with the practice of having candidate members of the party and its administrative committees. The probationer may flunk, as Malenkov did. Or, considering the arduous testing that any "candidate General Secretary" has undergone in reaching that eminence, there is a good chance that he will be able to make the grade. Khrushchev and Brezhnev both did, despite general expectations to the contrary, and despite the absence of truly historic personal gifts. In short, the party seems to have evolved practices adequate to the continuation of supreme leadership, accommodating intervals of collective leadership when a new boss is on trial or periods in which a proven leader is in the fullness of his power. In Stalin's later years this power was personalized to an extent that threatened the continuity of party predominance, but the destalinization campaign, the taming of the police, and the dismissal of Khrushchev all go to show that the party has learned much from the experience and has developed fairly effective checks against another threat from its own leader.

Three-quarters of a century after its inception the party founded by Lenin faces formidable problems. To some extent its problems arise from changes in the world to which the Russian Communists have had trouble adapting themselves. If they prove insufficiently adaptable in the next generation, they might not make it, as an institution, to the centennial of the First Party Congress. On the other hand, it would be a serious mistake to underestimate the force of tradition in politics, and the Bolshevik tradition is one of the most imposing in the world today.

SUGGESTIONS FOR FURTHER READING

The books in Section A preceded by an asterisk are recommended for their pertinence to the theme of the present book. The rough chronological divisions into which this list is divided do not work equally well for all books and should not be taken too literally.

A. GENERAL

*ARMSTRONG, JOHN. *The Politics of Totalitarianism: The Communist Party of the Soviet Union from 1934 to the Present.* New York: Random House, Inc., 1961.

BRZEZINSKI, ZBIGNIEW K. *The Permanent Purge.* Cambridge, Mass.: Harvard University Press, 1956.

————. *The Soviet Bloc. Unity and Conflict.* Cambridge, Mass.: Harvard University Press, 1967.

*CARR, EDWARD HALLET. *A History of Soviet Russia* (Six volumes with four more planned; vols. I–III are subtitled *The Bolshevik Revolution 1917–1923*; vol. IV is subtitled *The Interregnum 1923–1924*; vols. V–VII are subtitled *Socialism in One Country 1924–1926*; and vols. VIII–X are tentatively subtitled *Foundations of a Planned Economy 1926–1929*). New York: Macmillan Co., 1951– .

CENTRAL COMMITTEE OF THE ALL-UNION COMMUNIST PARTY (Bolsheviks). *History of the All-Union Communist Party (Bolsheviks).* Moscow: Foreign Languages Publishing House, 1938.

*CONQUEST, ROBERT. *Power and Policy in the USSR.* New York: St. Martin's Press, Inc., 1961.

CONYNGHAM, WILLIAM. *Industrial Management in the Soviet Union: The Role of the CPSU in Industrial Decision-Making 1917–1970.* Stanford: Hoover Institution Press, 1973.

*CURRENT DIGEST OF THE SOVIET PRESS, *Current Soviet Policies.* Vol. I. *The Documentary Record of the Nineteenth Communist Party Congress and the Reorganization after Stalin's Death.* New York: Frederick A. Praeger, Inc., 1953. Vol. II. *The Documentary Record of the Twentieth Communist Party Congress and Its Aftermath.* New York: Frederick A. Praeger, Inc., 1957. Vol. III. *The Documentary Record of the Extraordinary Twenty-First Congress of the Communist Party of the Soviet Union.* New York: Columbia University Press, 1960. Vol. IV. *The Documentary Record of the Twenty-Second Congress of the Communist Party of the Soviet Union.* New York:

Columbia University Press, 1962. Vol. V. *The Documentary Record of the Twenty-Third Congress of the Communist Party of the Soviet Union.* Columbus: American Association for the Advancement of Slavic Studies, 1973. Vol. VI. *The Documentary Record of the Twenty-Fourth Congress of the Communist Party of the Soviet Union.* Columbus: AAASS, 1973.

*DANIELS, ROBERT VINCENT. *The Conscience of the Revolution: Communist Opposition in Soviet Russia.* Cambridge, Mass.: Harvard University Press, 1960.

————, ED. *A Documentary History of Communism.* Two vols. in one. New York: Random House, Inc., 1960.

DEGRAS, JANE, ED. *The Communist International 1919–1943.* Vol. I: 1919–1922; Vol. II: 1923–1928. London: Oxford University Press, 1956.

DJILAS, MILOVAN. *The New Class.* New York: Frederick A. Praeger, Inc., 1957.

DMYTRYSHYN, BASIL. *USSR. A Concise History.* New York: Charles Scribner's Sons, 1971.

ERICKSON, JOHN. *The Soviet High Command: A Military-Political History, 1918–1941.* New York: Macmillan Co., 1962.

GAUCHER, ROLAND. *Opposition in the USSR 1917–67.* Translated by Charles L. Markman. New York: Funk & Wagnalls, 1969.

HANAK, HARRY. *Soviet Foreign Policy Since the Death of Stalin.* Boston: Routledge and Kegan Paul, 1972.

*HEER, NANCY WHITTIER. *Politics and History in the Soviet Union.* Cambridge, Mass.: M.I.T. Press, 1971.

HINGLEY, RONALD. *The Russian Secret Police: Muscovite, Imperial Russian, and Soviet Political Security Operations.* New York: Simon and Schuster, 1970.

HOUGH, JERRY F. *The Soviet Prefects.* Cambridge, Mass.: Harvard University Press, 1969.

HOWE, IRVING, ED. *The Basic Writings of Trotsky.* New York: Random House, Inc., 1963.

JAWORSKY, MICHAEL, ED. *Soviet Political Thought.* Baltimore: Johns Hopkins Press, 1969.

KOLKOWICZ, ROMAN. *The Soviet Military and the Communist Party.* Princeton: Princeton University Press, 1967.

KUUSINEN, OTTO, ED. *Fundamentals of Marxism-Leninism.* Moscow: Foreign Languages Publishing House, 1960.

LEDERER, IVO, ED. *Russian Foreign Policy: Essays in Historical Perspective.* New Haven: Yale University Press, 1962.

LEDERER, IVO AND VUCINICH, WAYNE, EDS. *The Soviet Union and the Middle East: The Post-World War II Era.* Stanford: Hoover Institution Press, 1974.

McNEAL, ROBERT H., ED. *International Relations Among Communists.* Englewood Cliffs, N.J.: Prentice-Hall, Inc., 1967.

*McNEAL, ROBERT H., GENERAL ED. *Resolutions and Decisions of the Communist Party of the Soviet Union.* Vol. I. Elwood, Ralph, ed. *The Russian Social Democratic Labour Party 1898–1917.* Vol. II. Gregor, Richard, ed.

The Early Soviet Period 1917–1929. Vol. III. McNeal, Robert H., ed. The Stalin Era 1929–1953. Vol. IV. Hodnett, Grey, ed. The Khrushchev Years 1953–1964. Toronto: University of Toronto Press, 1974.

MEISEL, JAMES H., AND KOZERA, EDWARD S., EDS. Materials for the Study of the Soviet System. Ann Arbor: George Wahr & Co., 1953.

NOVE, ALEX. An Economic History of the USSR. Baltimore: Penguin Books, Inc., 1972.

PETHYRIDGE, ROGER. A History of Postwar Russia. London: Allen and Unwin, 1966.

PONOMAREV, B. N., et al. History of the Communist Party of the Soviet Union. Moscow: Foreign Languages Publishing House, 1959.

POPOV, N. Outline History of the Communist Party of the Soviet Union. 2 vols. New York: International Publishers, 1934.

*RESHETAR, JOHN S., JR. A Concise History of the Communist Party of the Soviet Union. New York: Frederick A. Praeger, Inc., 1960.

*RIGBY, T. H. Communist Party Membership in the USSR 1917–1967. Princeton: Princeton University Press, 1968.

RUBINSTEIN, ALVIN Z., ED. The Foreign Policy of the Soviet Union. New York: Random House, Inc., 1960.

RUSH, MYRON. Political Succession in the USSR. New York: Columbia University Press, 1968.

*SCHAPIRO, LEONARD. The Communist Party of the Soviet Union. New York: Random House, Inc., 1971.

SKILLING, H. GORDON, AND GRIFFITHS, FRANKLYN, EDS. Interest Groups in Soviet Politics. Princeton, N.J.: Princeton University Press, 1971.

SORLIN, PIERRE. The Soviet People and Their Society. New York: Frederick A. Praeger, Inc., 1968.

TREADGOLD, DONALD W. Twentieth Century Russia. Chicago: Rand McNally & Company, 1972.

ULAM, ADAM. Expansion and Coexistence: A History of Soviet Foreign Policy 1917–1967. New York: Frederick A. Praeger, Inc., 1968.

VON LAUE, THEODORE H. Why Lenin? Why Stalin?: A Reappraisal of the Russian Revolution. Philadelphia: J. B. Lippincott Co., 1964.

WOLFE, THOMAS W. Soviet Power and Europe 1945–1970. Baltimore: Johns Hopkins Press, 1970.

WOLIN, SIMON, AND SLUSSER, ROBERT M., EDS. The Soviet Secret Police. New York: Frederick A. Praeger, Inc., 1957.

B. LENIN AND HIS TIMES

ASCHER, ABRAHAM. Pavel Axelrod and the Development of Menshevism. Cambridge, Mass.: Harvard University Press, 1972.

BARON, SAMUEL H. Plekhanov: The Father of Russian Marxism. Stanford: Stanford University Press, 1963.

BROWDER, ROBERT, AND KERENSKY, ALEXANDER, EDS. *The Russian Provisional Government 1917: Documents.* 3 Vols. Stanford: Stanford University Press, 1961.

CHAMBERLIN, WILLIAM HENRY. *The Russian Revolution 1917–1921.* Two vols. New York: Macmillan Co., 1952.

DANIELS, ROBERT VINCENT. *Red October: The Bolshevik Revolution of 1917.* New York: Charles Scribner's Sons, 1967.

DAY, RICHARD. *Leon Trotsky and the Politics of Economic Isolation.* Cambridge: Cambridge University Press, 1973.

DEUTSCHER, ISAAC. *The Prophet Armed: Trotsky: 1879–1921.* New York: Oxford University Press, 1954.

EISSENSTAT, BERNARD, ED. *Lenin and Leninism: State, Law, Society.* Lexington, Mass.: D. C. Heath and Co., 1971.

ELWOOD, RALPH CARTER. *Russian Social Democracy in the Underground: A Study of the RSDRP in the Ukraine, 1907–1914.* Assen, Holland: Van Gorcum, 1974.

FERRO, MARC. *The Russian Revolution of February 1917.* Translated by T. L. Richards. Englewood Cliffs, N.J.: Prentice-Hall, Inc., 1972.

FISHER, LOUIS. *The Life of Lenin.* New York: Harper & Row, 1964.

FRANKEL, JONATHAN. *Vladimir Akimov on the Dilemmas of Russian Marxism 1895–1903.* Cambridge: Cambridge University Press, 1969.

GETZLER, ISRAEL. *Martov: A Political Biography of a Russian Social Democrat.* Cambridge: Cambridge University Press, 1967.

GRUBER, HELMUT. *International Communism in the Era of Lenin: A Documentary History.* Ithaca: Cornell University Press, 1967.

HAIMSON, LEOPOLD H. *The Russian Marxists and the Origins of Bolshevism.* Cambridge, Mass.: Harvard University Press, 1955.

KEEP, JOHN. *The Rise of Social Democracy in Russia.* Oxford: Clarendon Press, 1963.

KINDERSLEY, RICHARD. *The First Russian Revisionists: A Study of "Legal Marxists" in Russia.* New York: Oxford University Press, 1962.

LAZITCH, BRANKO, AND DRACHKOVITCH, MILORAD. *Lenin and the Comintern.* Vol. I. Stanford: Hoover Institution Press, 1972.

LENIN, V. I. *Collected Works.* 45 vols. London: Lawrence and Wishart, 1960–1970.

LERNER, WARREN. *Karl Radek: The Last Internationalist.* Stanford: Stanford University Press, 1970.

LEWIN, MOSHE. *Lenin's Last Struggle.* Translated by A. M. Sheridan Smith. New York: Pantheon Books, 1968.

MCNEAL, ROBERT H. *Bride of the Revolution: Krupskaya and Lenin.* Ann Arbor: University of Michigan Press, 1972.

MENDELSOHN, EZRA. *Class Struggle in the Pale: The Formative Years of the Jewish Workers' Movement in Tsarist Russia.* Cambridge: Cambridge University Press, 1970.

MEYER, ALFRED G. *Leninism.* Cambridge, Mass.: Harvard University Press, 1957.

MORGAN, M. C. *Lenin.* New York: Viking Press, 1971.

PAGE, STANLEY W. *Lenin and World Revolution.* New York: New York University Press, 1959.

PIPES, RICHARD. *The Formation of the Soviet Union: Communism and Nationalism, 1917–1923.* Cambridge, Mass.: Harvard University Press, 1954.

————. *Social Democracy and the St. Petersburg Labor Movement, 1885–1897.* Cambridge, Mass.: Harvard University Press, 1963.

————, ED. *Revolutionary Russia: A Symposium.* Garden City: Doubleday and Co., 1969.

————. *Struve: Liberal on the Left.* Cambridge, Mass.: Harvard University Press, 1970.

POSSONY, STEFAN T. *Lenin: The Compulsive Revolutionary.* Chicago: Henry Regnery Co., 1964.

POSSONY, STEFAN, ED. *The Lenin Reader: The Outstanding Works of V. I. Lenin.* Chicago: Henry Regnery Co., 1966.

RABINOWITCH, ALEXANDER. *Prelude to Revolution: The Petrograd Bolsheviks and the July 1917 Uprising.* Bloomington: Indiana University Press, 1968.

SCHAPIRO, LEONARD. *The Origin of the Communist Autocracy: Political Opposition in the Soviet State, First Phase: 1917–1923.* Cambridge, Mass.: Harvard University Press, 1955.

SCHAPIRO, LEONARD, AND REDDAWAY, PETER, EDS. *Lenin: The Man, the Theorist, the Leader.* London: The Pall Mall Press, 1967.

SENN, ALFRED. *The Russian Revolution in Switzerland 1914–1917.* Madison: University of Wisconsin Press, 1971.

SHUKMAN, HAROLD. *Lenin and the Russian Revolution.* New York: Capricorn Books, 1966.

SILVERMAN, SAUL, ED. *Lenin.* Englewood Cliffs, N.J.: Prentice-Hall, Inc., 1972.

SUNY, RONALD. *The Baku Commune 1917–1918: Class and Nationality in the Russian Revolution.* Princeton, N.J.: Princeton University Press, 1972.

THEEN, ROLF. *Lenin: Genesis and Development of a Revolutionary.* Philadelphia: J. B. Lippincott Co., 1973.

TREADGOLD, DONALD W. *Lenin and His Rivals: The Struggle for Russia's Future 1898–1906.* New York: Frederick A. Praeger, Inc., 1955.

TROTSKY, LEON. *My Life: An Attempt at an Autobiography.* New York: Charles Scribner's Sons, 1930.

ULAM, ADAM. *The Bolsheviks: The Intellectual and Political History of the Triumph of Communism in Russia.* New York: The Macmillan Co., 1965.

VALENTINOV, NIKOLAY. *Encounters with Lenin.* Translated by Paul Rosta and Brian Pearce. New York: Oxford University Press, 1968.

WILDMAN, ALLAN. *The Making of a Workers' Revolution: Russian Social Democracy 1891–1903.* Chicago: University of Chicago Press, 1962.

WILSON, EDMUND. *To the Finland Station: A Study in the Writing and Acting of History.* New York: Peter Smith Publishers, 1959.

WOLFE, BERTRAM D. *The Bridge and the Abyss: The Troubled Friendship of Maxim Gorky and V. I. Lenin.* London: The Pall Mall Press, 1967.

―――. *Three Who Made A Revolution: A Biographical History.* New York: Dell Publishing Co., 1970.

C. STALIN AND HIS TIMES

ALLILUYEVA, SVETLANA. *Twenty Letters to a Friend.* Translated by Priscilla Johnson McMillan. New York: Harper and Row, 1967.

BIALER, SEWERYN, ED. *Stalin and His Generals: Soviet Military Memoirs of World War II.* New York: Pegasus Books, 1969.

BRANDT, CONRAD. *Stalin's Failure in China 1924–1927.* Cambridge, Mass.: Harvard University Press, 1948.

COHEN, STEPHEN. *Bukharin and the Bolshevik Revolution: A Political Biography 1888–1938.* New York: Alfred A. Knopf, 1973.

CONQUEST, ROBERT. *The Great Terror: Stalin's Purge of the Thirties.* New York: The Macmillan Co., 1968.

DEUTSCHER, ISAAC. *Stalin: A Political Biography.* New York: Oxford University Press, 1949.

―――. *The Prophet Unarmed: Trotsky, 1921–1929.* New York: Oxford University Press, 1959.

―――. *The Prophet Outcast: Trotsky, 1929–1940.* New York: Oxford University Press, 1963.

DJILAS, MILOVAN. *Conversations with Stalin.* Translated by Michael Petrovich. New York: Harcourt, Brace and World, 1962.

ERLICH, ALEXANDER. *The Soviet Industrialization Debate, 1924–1928.* Cambridge, Mass.: Harvard University Press, 1960.

FAINSOD, MERLE. *Smolensk Under Soviet Rule.* Cambridge, Mass.: Harvard University Press, 1958.

FRANKLIN, BRUCE, ED. *The Essential Stalin. Major Theoretical Writings 1905–1952.* Garden City: Doubleday & Co., 1972.

GITELMAN, ZVI. *Jewish Nationality and Soviet Politics: The Jewish Sections of the CPSU 1917–1930.* Princeton, N.J.: Princeton University Press, 1972.

JASNY, NAUM. *Soviet Industrialization 1928–1952.* Chicago: University of Chicago Press, 1961.

KATKOV, MICHAEL. *The Trail of Bukharin.* New York: Stein and Day, 1969.

LEVYTSKY, BORIS. *The Stalinist Terror in the Thirties: Documentation from the Soviet Press.* Stanford: Hoover Institution Press, 1974.

LEWIN, MOSHE. *Russian Peasants and Soviet Power: A Study of Collectivization.* Translated by Irene Nove. London: Allen & Unwin, 1968.

McLANE, CHARLES B. *Soviet Policy and the Chinese Communists 1931–1946.* New York: Columbia University Press, 1958.

MEDVEDEV, ROY. *Let History Judge.* New York: Alfred A. Knopf, 1971.

NIKOLAEVSKY, BORIS. *Power and the Soviet Elite.* New York: Frederick A. Praeger, Inc., 1965.

NORTH, ROBERT C. *Moscow and Chinese Communists.* Stanford: Stanford University Press, 1953.

RANDALL, FRANCIS. *Stalin's Russia: An Historical Reconsideration.* New York: The Free Press, 1965.

RIEBER, ALFRED J. *Stalin and the French Communist Party 1941–1947.* New York: Columbia University Press, 1962.

RIGBY, T. H., ED. *Stalin.* Englewood Cliffs, N.J.: Prentice-Hall, Inc., 1966.

SHULMAN, MARSHAL D. *Stalin's Foreign Policy Reappraised.* Cambridge, Mass.: Harvard University Press, 1963.

SMITH, EDWARD ELLIS. *The Young Stalin: The Early Years of an Elusive Revolutionary.* New York: Farrar, Strauss and Giroux, 1967.

SOLZHENITSYN, ALEXANDER. *The Gulag Archipelago.* Translated by Thomas P. Whitney. New York: Harper and Row, 1974.

SOUVARINE, BORIS. *Stalin: A Critical Survey of Bolshevism.* Translated by C. L. R. Jones. New York: Ziff-Davis, 1939.

STALIN, J. V. *Problems of Leninism.* Moscow: Foreign Languages Publishing House, 1953.

——. *Stalin's Correspondence with Roosevelt and Truman.* New York: E. P. Dutton, 1958.

——. *Stalin's Correspondence with Churchill and Atlee.* New York: E. P. Dutton, 1958.

——. *Works* (13 volumes, covering his career to 1934; the remainder of his life's published works are collected in Russian: Robert H. McNeal, ed., I. V. Stalin. *Sochineniia.* Vol. 1–3 (XIV–XVI). Stanford: Hoover Institution Press, 1966. Moscow: Foreign Languages Publishing House, 1952–55).

TROTSKY, LEON. *Stalin: An Appraisal of the Man and His Influence.* Translated by Charles Malamuth. New York: Harper & Brothers, 1941.

TUCKER, ROBERT. *Stalin as Revolutionary 1879–1929. A Study in History and Personality.* New York: W. W. Norton & Co., 1973.

TUCKER, ROBERT, AND COHEN, STEPHEN. *The Great Purge Trial.* New York: Grosset and Dunlap, 1965.

ULAM, ADAM. *Stalin: The Man and His Era.* New York: The Viking Press, 1973.

D. KHRUSHCHEV AND HIS TIMES

CRANKSHAW, EDWARD. *Khrushchev: A Career.* New York: The Viking Press, 1966.

DALLIN, ALEXANDER, ED. *Diversity in International Communism: A Documentary Record, 1961–1963.* New York: Columbia University Press, 1963.

FRANKLAND, MARK. *Khrushchev.* New York: Stein and Day, 1969.

GRIFFITH, WILLIAM E. *The Sino-Soviet Rift.* Cambridge, Mass.: M.I.T. Press, 1964.

JANSY, NAUM. *Khrushchev's Crop Policy.* Glasgow: G. Outram, 1965.

JOHNSON, PRISCILLA. *Khrushchev and the Arts: The Politics of Soviet Culture, 1962–1964.* Cambridge, Mass.: M.I.T. Press, 1965.

KHARMALOV, M., ED. *Face to Face with America: The Story of N. S. Khrushchev's Visit to the USA, September 15–27, 1959.* Moscow: Foreign Languages Publishing House, 1960.

KHRUSHCHEV, N. S. *Khrushchev Remembers.* Translated and edited by Strobe Talbott. Boston: Little, Brown & Co., 1970.

———. *Khrushchev Remembers: The Last Testament.* Translated and edited by Strobe Talbott. Boston: Little, Brown & Co., 1974.

LEONHARD, WOLFGANG. *The Kremlin Since Stalin.* Translated by Elizabeth Wiskemann. London: Frederick A. Praeger, Inc., 1961.

LINDEN, KARL. *Khrushchev and the Soviet Leadership, 1957–1964.* Baltimore: Johns Hopkins Press, 1966.

PALOCZI-HORVATH, GEORGE. *Khrushchev: The Making of a Dictator.* Boston: Little, Brown & Co., 1960.

PISTRAK, LAZAR. *The Grand Tactician: Khrushchev's Rise to Power.* New York: Frederick A. Praeger, Inc., 1960.

PLOSS, SIDNEY. *Conflict and Decision-Making in Soviet Russia: A Case Study of Agricultural Policy, 1953–1963.* Princeton: Princeton University Press, 1965.

ROTHBERG, ABRAHAM. *The Heirs of Stalin: Dissidence and the Soviet Regime, 1953–1970.* Ithaca: Cornell University Press, 1972.

RUSH, MYRON. *The Rise of Khrushchev.* Washington, D.C.: Public Affairs Press, 1958.

RUSSIAN INSTITUTE OF COLUMBIA UNIVERSITY, ED. *The Anti-Stalin Campaign and International Communism.* New York: Columbia University Press, 1956.

SIMMONS, GEORGE, ED. *Soviet Leaders.* New York: Thomas Y. Crowell Co., 1967.

TATU, MICHEL. *Power in the Kremlin: From Khrushchev to Kosygin.* New York: The Viking Press, 1969.

WHITNEY, THOMAS P., ED. *Khrushchev Speaks.* Ann Arbor: University of Michigan Press, 1963.

WOLFE, BERTRAM. *Khrushchev and Stalin's Ghost.* New York: Frederick A. Praeger, Inc., 1957.

ZAGORIA, DONALD S. *The Sino-Soviet Conflict 1956–1961.* Princeton: Princeton University Press, 1962.

ZINNER, PAUL E., ED. *National Communism and Popular Revolt in Eastern Europe: A Selection of Documents on Events in Poland and Hungary, February–November, 1956.* New York: Columbia University Press, 1956.

E. BREZHNEV AND HIS TIMES

AMALRIK, ANDREI. *Will the Soviet Union Survive to 1984?* New York: Harper and Row, 1970.

BROMKE, ADAM, AND RAKOWSKA-HARMSTONE, TERESA, EDS. *The Communist States in Disarray 1965–1971*. Minneapolis: University of Minnesota Press, 1972.

BRZEZINSKI, ZBIGNIEW. *Dilemmas of Change in Soviet Politics*. New York: Columbia University Press, 1969.

CONQUEST, ROBERT. *Russia after Khrushchev*. New York: Frederick A. Praeger, Inc., 1965.

DALLIN, ALEXANDER, AND LARSON, THOMAS B., EDS. *Soviet Politics Since Khrushchev*. Englewood Cliffs, N.J.: Prentice-Hall, Inc., 1968.

DORNBERG, JOHN. *Brezhnev: The Masks of Power*. New York: Basic Books, 1974.

GITTINGS, JOHN. *Survey of the Sino-Soviet Dispute: A Commentary and Extracts from the Recent Polemics 1963–1967*. New York: Oxford University Press, 1968.

HAHN, WERNER. *The Politics of Soviet Agriculture 1960–1970*. Baltimore: Johns Hopkins University Press, 1972.

KASSOF, ALLEN, ED. *The Prospects for Soviet Society*. London: The Pall Mall Press, 1968.

KATZ, ABRAHAM. *The Politics of Economic Reform in the Soviet Union*. New York: Frederick A. Praeger, Inc., 1972.

KULSKI, WLADYSLAW. *The Soviet Union in World Affairs: A Documented Analysis, 1964–1972*. Syracuse: Syracuse University Press, 1973.

LABEDZ, LEOPOLD, ED. *Solzhenitsyn: A Documentary Record*. New York: Harper and Row, 1971.

MEDVEDEV, Z. *Ten Years After Ivan Denisovich*. New York: Random House, Inc., 1974.

REDDAWAY, PETER, ED. *Uncensored Russia: Protest and Dissent in the Soviet Union. The Unofficial Journal Chronicle of Current Events*. New York: American Heritage Press, 1972.

SAKHAROV, ANDREI. *Progress, Coexistence and Intellectual Freedom*. New York: W. W. Norton, 1968.

————. *Sakharov Speaks*. New York: Alfred A. Knopf, 1974.

SALISBURY, HARRISON. *War Between China and Russia?* New York: W. W. Norton, 1969.

SOLZHENITSYN, ALEXANDER. *Letter to Soviet Leaders*. New York: Harper and Row, 1974.

STRONG, JOHN. *The Soviet Union under Brezhnev and Kosygin: The Transition Years*. New York: Van Nostrand, Reinhold, Inc., 1971.

INDEX